Rūzbihān Baqlī: Mysticism and the Rhetoric of Sainthood in Persian Sufism

CURZON SUFI SERIES

Series Editor: Ian Richard Netton

Professor of Arabic Studies, University of Leeds

The Curzon Sufi Series attempts to provide short introductions to a variety of facets of the subject, which are accessible both to the general reader and the student and scholar in the field. Each book will be either a synthesis of existing knowledge or a distinct contribution to, and extension of, knowledge of the particular topic. The two major underlying principles of the Series are sound scholarship and readability.

ABDULLAH ANSARI OF HERAT
An Early Sufi Master

A.G. Ravan Farhadi

AL-HALLAJ

Herbert W. Mason

PERSIAN SUFI POETRY
An Introduction to the Mystical Use of Classical Persian Poetry

J.T.P. de Bruijn

BEYOND FAITH AND INFIDELITY
the Sufi Poetry and Teachings of Mahmud Shabistari

Leonard Lewisohn

Rūzbihān Baqlī:

Mysticism and the Rhetoric of Sainthood in Persian Sufism

Carl W. Ernst

CURZON
PRESS

First published in 1996
by Curzon Press
St John's Studios, Church Road, Richmond
Surrey, TW9 2QA

Typeset in Baskerville by Bookman, Slough
Printed in Great Britain by
Biddles Ltd., Guildford and King's Lynn

British Library Cataloguing in Publication Data
A catalogue record for this book is available from
the British Library

Library of Congress in Publication Data
A catalog record for this book has been requested

ISBN 0-7007-0342-X

Contents

Figures

Preface

A. Rūzbihān Baqlī, a Neglected Figure in Sufi Studies

Sufism, the tradition of Islamic mysticism, is increasingly becoming known in European languages through a steady stream of translations and studies of major figures. In some cases, as with the great Persian Sufi poet Jalāl al-Dīn Rūmī (d. 1273), popular English versions of Sufi classics can be found in literally dozens of paperback editions. The vast and complex Arabic works of the prolific Sufi metaphysician of Andalusia, Ibn 'Arabī (d. 1240), are gradually becoming accessible in reliable English and French versions. In America and in Europe, Sufi orders of Arab, Iranian, Turkish, and South Asian origin have found a following. This is one area in which the encounter between Islamic civilization and Euro-America is taking place on a non-political and highly personal basis.

Yet the Sufi tradition is so immense in extent that we are still only familiar with a fraction of the major figures. Only a small portion of Sufi texts in Arabic, Persian, Turkish, and other languages have ever been printed, let alone critically edited, or translated and discussed in any European language. The most urgent tasks in Sufi studies are to produce readable and reliable translations of important texts, along with analyses of their contents which link them up with current discussions in the field of religious studies. This book, which belongs to the second of these categories, is intended to introduce one of the major figures of Persian Sufism who has only recently emerged from an undeserved obscurity.

Rūzbihān Baqlī (522/1128-606/1209) recorded in Arabic and Persian a life filled with intense visions and powerful ecstasies, interpreted in terms of a Qur'ānically based metaphysics and cast in a dense poetic style. He lived at a time when Sufism was just beginning to become a broadly based social movement after centuries of private informality.[1] As a legacy he left a series of writings that covered the entire spectrum of Sufi mysticism, from Qur'ānic commentary to Islamic law, theology, speculative metaphysics, and poetry. His descendants kept alive his teachings for several generations in Shiraz, the town where he is buried, but the Rūzbihāniyya order did not survive long as an independent institution, possibly due to anti-Sufi feeling after the Safavid dynasty made Iran a Shī'ī country after 1503. Nevertheless, a select group of readers in Central Asia, India, Ottoman Turkey, and Africa has continued to regard his writings as some of the most challenging and stimulating works in Sufi literature. If one wished to make a comparison to a figure from Western religious history, Ruzbihan could perhaps be viewed as a combination of St. Augustine (without the agonized conversion) and Hildegard of Bingen. Like Augustine, Rūzbihān had a deep impact on scriptural interpretation in his religious tradition, and both men communicated a personalized mystical theology through compelling prose; similar to Hildegard, Rūzbihān had an intensive visionary life that furnished the raw materials for expression in metaphor and metaphysics. Rūzbihān's voice is unmistakeably Islamic and Persian, however. Devotion to the Prophet Muḥammad is a constant refrain in Rūzbihān's writings. His Sufism constantly illustrates the tension between esoteric mystical knowledge and the public responsibility to divine law. His writings constitute a vast synthesis and rethinking of early Islamic religious thought from the perspective of pre-Mongol Persian Sufism. Within the Islamic tradition, the figure to whom Rūzbihān might best compared is Ibn 'Arabī, especially because both men articulated extensive visions and charted the territory of inner experience just as the Sufi orders began to take on definite shape; this potentially revealing comparison will have to be postponed, however, until the works of both Sufis are better understood in their totality.

Publication of Rūzbihān's Persian writings have led quickly to an appreciation of his style. His is an original poetic sensibility, in which the roses and nightingales are freshly stamped with the images of Persian gardens, long before those images faded into cliché in the hands of lesser writers. As Annemarie Schimmel has observed,

> What so profoundly impresses the reader in Rūzbihān's writings . . . is his style, which is at times as hard to translate as that of Ahmad Ghazzali and possesses a stronger and deeper instrumentation. It is no longer the scholastic language of the early exponents of Sufism, who tried to classify stages and

> stations, though Baqli surely knew these theories and the technical terms. It is the language refined by the poets of Iran during the eleventh and twelfth centuries, filled with roses and nightingales, pliable and colorful.[2]

In a similar manner, Muḥammad Muʿīn has pointed out, "His speech is like a rose that flutters apart once grasped in the hand, or like an alchemical substance that turns into vapor when barely heated. His language is the language of perceptions; he praises the beautiful and beauty, and loves them both."[3] These remarks hold true especially for his Persian style, but they are suggestive in a different way for Rūzbihān's Arabic writing, which at its most impassioned is lyrical and transparent despite its simplicity. But much remains to be done before we can go beyond these impressionistic remarks to evaluate Rūzbihān's literary legacy as a whole.

Despite his importance, Rūzbihān is still hardly known outside a narrow circle of specialists; his name is not even mentioned, for instance, in *The Cambridge History of Iran.* Muḥammad Muʿīn, the pioneering editor of Rūzbihān's *The Jasmine of the Lovers*, remarked about that text, that "to understand the works of mystics such as ʿAṭṭār, Rūmī, ʿIrāqī, Awḥadī-i Kirmānī, and Ḥāfiẓ, researches on this book are quite necessary."[4] I would enlarge upon this statement and say that the writings of Rūzbihān Baqlī form a vital resource for understanding the experiential basis, not simply of Persian Sufi literature, but of Sufism and indeed mysticism in general.

B. Rūzbihān Studies: A Brief Overview

Louis Massignon in 1913 was the first European scholar to draw attention to Rūzbihān, in connection with his interpretation of the Baghdadian Sufi martyr al-Ḥallāj.[5] In 1928 W. Ivanow described a manuscript of one of the biographies of Rūzbihān that he found on a trip to Shiraz, where he also rediscovered the tomb of the shaykh.[6] Massignon then contributed the first bibliographic essay on Rūzbihān in 1953.[7] Although Rūzbihān's great Qur'ān commentary was several times lithographed in India in the nineteenth century, it has only been since 1958 that the mystical writings of Rūzbihān have begun to appear in print, thanks to the pioneering efforts of Henry Corbin. Corbin edited two of Rūzbihān's Persian works, *The Jasmine of the Lovers* (with the collaboration of Muḥammad Mu'īn) and *The Commentary on Ecstatic Sayings*.[8] Corbin also wrote a lengthy essay on Rūzbihān which is still the fullest interpretation of Rūzbihān since Massignon.[9] Two biographies of Rūzbihān written by his great-grandsons, *The Spirit of the Gardens* and *The Gift of the People of Gnosis*, were published in 1969 by M. T. Dānish-Puzhūh under the title *Rūzbihān nāma* (*The Book of Rūzbihān*).[10] The Turkish scholar Nazif Hoca brought out editions of two Arabic works of Rūzbihān in the early 1970s based on manuscripts in Turkey, an abridged version of *The Unveiling of Secrets* (also published by Paul Nwyia from a Baghdad MS) and *The Spirits' Font (1001 Stations)*.[11] Javād Nūrbakhsh, present head of the Ni'matullahi Sufi order, published several new editions of Rūzbihān's Persian writings at about the same time, based on manuscripts found in the Ni'matullahi library in Tehran: these included *The Jasmine of the Lovers*, *The Treatise on Holiness*, *The Errors of Wayfarers*, and the hagiographical *The Gift to the People of Gnosis*.[12] My earlier study *Words of Ecstasy in Sufism* contained a study of Rūzbihān's interpretation of ecstatic sayings in Sufism, and in some additional articles I have addressed his use of symbolism and his teaching on love.[13] Three Iranian scholars have also published biographical studies of Rūzbihān, with special attention to his Persian poetry.[14]

Despite these promising efforts, much remains to be done before it will be possible to attempt a comprehensive analysis of Rūzbihān's Sufism. Prof. Alan Godlas of the University of Georgia has undertaken the study of Rūzbihān's immense Qur'ānic commentary, and in his Ph.D. dissertation (University of California, 1991) he edited and translated the portion of the commentary devoted to sūra 4 of the Qur'ān (constituting approximately one *juz'*, or one-thirtieth, of the entire text). His researches on the manuscript tradition will be crucial to evaluating Rūzbihān's impact on the mystical interpretation of scripture in Islam, and his ongoing work on translating the remainder of the text promises to make available one of the monuments of Islamic religious thought. Dr. Paul Ballanfat has just completed a doctoral dissertation on Rūzbihān (Sorbonne, 1994), which will include his critical edition and French translation of three important mystical treatises (*The Journey of the Spirits*, *The Commentary on Veils and Coverings*, and *The Unveiling of Secrets*) plus two shorter theological texts.

Ballanfat and I also propose to collaborate on a critical edition of the Arabic *The Language of Consciences*, which Rūzbihān himself expanded and translated into Persian as *The Commentary on Ecstatic Sayings* – the Persian text is so problematic that it will be impractical for anyone to attempt a translation of the Persian without having a sure grasp on the Arabic original. In addition, my own translation of the complete text of *The Unveiling of Secrets*, portions of which are presented here, will be published separately. From these remarks it should be evident that we are just reaching the point of having full access to all of Rūzbihān's major writings, each of which deserves full consideration in itself and in relation with the rest of his literary production. Until individual studies are carried out in detail, it will not be possible to establish with any confidence the relationships between Rūzbihān's writings, the development and maturation of his technical vocabulary, or his use of Qur'ān and *ḥadīth* texts. With the small number of researchers in this field, it may be some time before this agenda can be accomplished, but the size and stature of Rūzbihān's œuvre demands a serious effort of interpretation.

C. Aims of the Present Work

In this book I would like to present a study of the mystical life of Rūzbihān Baqlī as portrayed in three sources: his own autobiographical work *The Unveiling of Secrets*, and two hagiographies ("lives of the saints") written by his great-grandsons, *The Spirit of the Gardens* and *The Gift of the People of Gnosis*. I will not attempt to construct from these sources a single definitive narrative account of Rūzbihān's external activities, though I have briefly summarized the standard consensus; my concern is rather with his mystical experiences as viewed in these different sources, each of which needs to be understood on its own terms. In comparison to the relatively brief treatment of *The Unveiling of Secrets* by Corbin, this study covers much more of the text in detail, and it also has the advantage of drawing on the other writings of Rūzbihān that have come to light since Corbin's initial essays appeared in the late 1950s. In overall approach, this book differs from the learned and detailed intellectual biography of Ibn 'Arabī by Claude Addas, which seeks to reconstruct his spiritual itinerary and mystical experiences as described in his own writings; despite her critical attitude toward hagiographies, by taking somewhat literally Ibn

'Arabi's claims to sainthood, Addas ends by presenting her subject hagiographically.[15] I am concerned rather to articulate and describe the structure of mystical experience in Rūzbihān's writings through analysis of his rhetoric of sainthood. Although this means taking seriously Rūzbihān's vocabulary and categories of mysticism, it also requires that his claims to spiritual authority be interpreted with regard to their symbolism and significance as literary texts rather than as transparent expressions of objective spiritual status. I also take a different approach to interpreting Sufi biographical and hagiographical texts. In a previous book on Sufism in South Asia, I proposed a hermeneutical method of reading Sufi biographical texts that takes full account of the concerns of pre-modern authors, paying particular attention to the way that authors write in terms of genre, audience, patronage, and literary convention without privileging one text over another.[16] What this means in practice is that lives of the saints are not read as collections of "facts" that are to be either accepted or rejected, but that each text is a literary interpretation that needs to be elucidated on its own terms. This is not a particularly radical approach in studies of sainthood and hagiography in Christianity, but the study of the Islamic humanities continues to lag behind theoretically in dealing with the interpretation of religious texts.[17] A good example of the more theoretically sensitive approach to Islamic hagiography is the work of my colleague Prof. Vincent Cornell of Duke University; he points out that the act of interpretation is implicit in one of the standard Arabic terms used to describe hagiographies, "translation of lives of the saints" (*tarājim al-awliyā'*).

Thus I propose to examine here the "lives" of Rūzbihān, beginning with the customary summary that can be found in most of the secondary studies mentioned above. This conventional account, given in Chapter I, briefly describes the historical and political context of twelfth-century Persia, the standard reconstruction of Rūzbihān's itinerary in life, his family, his Sufi activities, and an overview of his legacy. For readers unfamiliar with the historical background of this strand of Persian Sufism, this account will provide a brief orientation that sets up the terms of the subsequent discussion. Chapter II, the longest part of the book, provides a detailed classification and analysis of the rapturous encounters with God that constitute Rūzbihān's autobiographical *The Unveiling of Secrets*, along with an introduction to the technical vocabulary that Rūzbihān uses to describe mystical experience. Some of his most distinctive visions are presented here in translation, grouped together thematically under the headings of "theophanies of majesty" and "theophanies of beauty." When the text is considered in terms of autobiography, despite giving some interesting details concerning Rūzbihān's life, it does so only in order to relate them to his inner visionary experiences. In terms of its overall style and function, *The Unveiling of Secrets* belongs to a well-established literary tradition of visionary narratives and heavenly ascensions. Chapter III moves to consider the institutionalization of the Sufi "order" that coalesced around Rūzbihān and his descendants in Shiraz. The biographical picture composed by Rūzbihān's great-grandsons differs in significant ways from the picture that he himself drew in his own writings, particularly as regards Rūzbihān's image of himself in terms of sainthood. The gap between Rūzbihān's self-portrait and that of his descendants furnishes the opportunity to locate their aims as authors, to establish the hermeneutical approach of each individual text. Finally, Chapter IV briefly reviews Rūzbihān's concept of sainthood, and how differently it can be seen in the different "lives" of Rūzbihān. Throughout this essay, extensive translations from the sources furnish examples of the extraordinary style and personal presence of Rūzbihān, something that jumps off the page of his Arabic and Persian writings. I hope that this brief study will help bring a new and larger audience to the Sufism of Rūzbihān. While this is partially aimed at those who have a special interest in Islamic studies and Sufism, I also have in mind those readers who follow the subjects of comparative mysticism and sainthood. This book is more descriptive than analytical, simply because I think it will be most useful in the first instance to present some of the most important aspects of Rūzbihān's visionary style in a way that is accessible to non-specialists.

I would like to express here my thanks to those who have contributed vital assistance to make this project possible. Dr. Leonard Lewisohn of the University of London invited me to return to the subject of Rūzbihān in connection with two memorable conferences on Persian Sufism held at the School of Oriental and African Studies, University of London, in 1990, and at George Washington University in 1992; both conferences were co-sponsored by the Ni'matullahi Sufi order. Prof. Ian Netton of the University of Exeter, a participant in those conferences and the editor of the Series on Sufism, suggested the idea for this book. Dr. Daniel Massignon and Prof. James Morris of Oberlin College both provided copies of important manuscripts and warmly supported the project; thanks also to Prof. Herbert Mason of Boston University for his timely help. My good friends Prof. Bruce Lawrence of Duke University and Prof. John Bussanich of the University of New Mexico gave much appreciated encouragement. Members of the North Carolina History of Religions Colloquium provided astute criticism to an earlier draft of Chapter II. An earlier version of Chapter III was presented at the Middle East Studies Association conference in North Carolina in 1993. Prof. Alan Godlas of the University of Georgia and Dr. Paul Ballanfat of the Sorbonne, the two most active researchers on the subject of Rūzbihān Baqlī, have shared unstintingly the unpublished fruits of their labors; without their generosity this study would not have been possible. Research for this book was supported by a Summer Research Grant from the National Endowment for the Humanities in 1993 and a study assignment from the University of North Carolina-Chapel Hill in 1994. As always, I want to thank my wife Judy Ernst and our daughters Sophie and Tess for their understanding and support.

The transliteration of Arabic and Persian follows the system of the *Encyclopaedia of Islam*, except that J is used for *jīm* and Q for *qāf*, and digraph transliterations are not underlined. Translations from Arabic and Persian are mine unless otherwise noted; these are meant to be fairly literal and generally consistent, though sometimes phrases of blessing are omitted for the sake of clarity. In discussing a text that mostly consists of visions of God, capitalization is problematic, especially since there is no capitalization in Arabic. If one follows the custom of capitalizing every term and pronoun that refers to God, the book will be so filled with capitalized words that it will resemble publications of the seventeenth century. I have followed the expedient of leaving pronouns referring to God in lower case, and capitalizing only certain crucial technical terms for transcendental realities that are not ordinarily treated as such in English (e.g., Essence, Attributes). Though admittedly inconsistent, this practice has the merit of calling the reader's attention to the importance of Rūzbihān's less familiar technical terms.

Notes

1. For an overview of recent research on early Sufism in the Iranian cultural region, see Leonard Lewisohn, "Iranian Islam and Persianate Sufism," in *The Legacy of Mediaeval Persian Sufism*, ed. Leonard Lewisohn (London: Khaniqahi Nimatullahi, 1992), pp. 11–43.
2. Schimmel, *Dimensions*, p. 298.
3. Mu'īn, introduction to *'Abhar al-'āshiqīn*, p. 100.
4. Mu'īn, Introduction to *'Abhar*, p. 84. In this respect, Mu'īn shared the view of Dr. Qāsim Ghanī, that "from the point of view of the greatness of his mystical station, and from the perspective of ecstasy and spiritual state, Shaykh Rūzbihān is on the level of Shaykh Abu'l-Ḥasan Kharaqānī and Shaykh Abū Sa'īd-i Abu'l-Khayr"; Ghanī also placed Rūzbihān prominently in his list of twenty-eight major Sufi authors. See his *Baḥth dar āthār wa afkār wa aḥwāl-i Ḥāfiẓ*, vol. 2, *Tārīkh-i taṣawwuf dar islām wa taṭawwurāt wa taḥawwulāt-i mukhtalifa-yi ān az ṣadr-i islām tā 'aṣr-i Ḥāfiẓ* (Tehran: Kitābfurūshī Zawwār, 1340/1961), p. 395, n. 2; p. 545.
5. Ḥusayn ibn Manṣūr al-Ḥallāj, *Kitāb al-ṭawāsīn*, ed. Louis Massignon (new ed., Paris: Librairie Paul Geuthner, 1913), esp. pp. 79-108. Cf. also Massignon, *La Passion de Husayn Ibn Mansûr Hallâj, martyr mystique de l'Islam exécuté à Bagdad le 26 mars 922, Étude d'histoire religieuse* (2nd ed., 4 vols., Paris: Gallimard, 1975), esp. II, 406–14, 498–501; id., *The Passion of Hallaj*, trans. Herbert Mason (4 vols., Princeton: Princeton University Press, 1982), II, 395–99, 478–83.
6. "A Biography of Rūzbihān al-Baqlī," *Journal and Proceedings of the Asiatic Society of Bengal* N.S. XXIV (1928), pp. 353-61; "More on Biography of Rūzbihān al-Baqlī," *Journal of the Bombay Branch of the Royal Asiatic Society* VII (1931), p. 1–7.
7. "La Vie et les œuvres de Ruzbehan Baqli," in *Studia orientalia Joanni Pedersen septuagenario ... a collegis discipulis amicis dicata* (Copenhagen, 1953), pp. 275–88; reprinted in Louis Massignon, *Opera Minora*, ed. Y. Moubarac (Beirut, 1963), II, 451–65.
8. *Le Jasmin des Fidèles d'amour, Kitâb-e 'Abhar al-'âshiqîn*, ed. Henry Corbin and Muḥammad Mu'īn, Bibliothéque Iranienne, 8 (Tehran: Institut Francais d'Iranologie de Téhéran, 1958; reprint ed., Tehran: Intishārāt-i Manūchihrī, 1365/1981); *Commentaire sur les paradoxes des Soufis (Sharh-e Shathîyât)*, ed. Henry Corbin, Bibliothèque Iranienne, no. 12 (Tehran: Departement d'Iranologie de l'Institut Franco-Iranien, 1966).
9. Henry Corbin, "Quiétude et Inquiétude de l'âme dans le Soufisme de Rūzbehān Baqlī de Shiraz," *Eranos-Jahrbuch 1958* (1959), pp. 51–194, reprinted in revised form in Corbin, *En Islam iranien: Aspects spirituels et philosophiques*, vol. 3, *Les Fidèles d'amour, Shî'isme et soufisme* (Paris, 1972), pp. 9–146. Corbin here discusses primarily the *Ighāna* (pp. 30–44), the *Kashf al-asrār* (pp. 45–64), and above all the *'Abhar al-'āshiqīn* (pp. 65–146). Portions of this essay have appeared in an abbreviated

form in other works by Corbin; cf. *The Man of Light in Iranian Sufism*, trans. Nancy Pearson (Boulder: Shambhala, 1978), and "The Visionary Dream in Islamic Spirituality," in *The Dream and Human Societies*, ed. G. E. von Grunebaum and Roger Caillois (Berkeley: University of California Press, 1966), pp. 381–408.

10. Muḥammad Taqī Dānish-puzhūh, ed., *Rūzbihān nāma* (Tehran, 1347/1969).
11. *Rūzbihān al-Baḳlī ve Kitāb Kaşf al-asrār'i ile Farsça bāzi Šiirleri*, ed. Nazif Hoca, Istanbul Üniversitesi Edebiyat Fakültesi Yayinları No. 1678 (Istanbul: Edebiyat Fakültesi Matbaası, 1971); *Kitāb maşrab al-arvāḥ*, ed. Nazif M. Hoca, İstanbul Üniversitesi Edebiyat Fakültesi Yayinları, no. 1876 (Istanbul: Edebiyat Fakültesi Matbaası, 1974); Paul Nwyia, "Waqā'i' al-Shaykh Rūzbihān al-Baqlī al-Shīrazī muqtaṭafāt min kitāb *Kashf al-asrār wa mukāshafat al-anwār," al-Mashriq* LXIV/4–5 (1970), pp. 385–406.
12. *'Abhar al-'āshiqīn*, ed. Javād Nūrbakhsh (Tehran, 1349/1971); *Risālat al-quds wa ghalaṭāt al-sālikīn*, ed. Javād Nūrbakhsh (Tehran: Chāp-khāna-yi Firdawsī, 1351/1972); Sharaf al-Dīn Ibrāhīm ibn Ṣadr al-Dīn Rūzbihān II, *Tuḥfat ahl al-'irfān*, ed. Javād Nūrbakhsh (Tehran, 1349/1970).
13. *Words of Ecstasy in Sufism*, SUNY Series in Islam (Albany: State University of New York Press, 1985); "The Symbolism of Birds and Flight in the Writings of Rūzbihān Baqlī," in *The Legacy of Mediæval Persian Sufism*, ed. Leonard Lewisohn (London: Khaniqahi Nimatullahi, 1992), pp. 353–66, also in *Sufi* 11 (Autumn, 1991), pp. 5–12; "The Stages of Love in Early Persian Sufism from Rābi'a to Rūzbihān," in *Classical Persian Sufism: from its Origins to Rumi*, ed. Leonard Lewisohn (London: Khaniqahi Nimatullahi, 1994), pp. 435–55, also in *Sufi* 14 (1992), pp. 16–23, Persian translation by Mojde-i Bayat as "Marāḥil-i 'ishq dar nakhustīn advār-i taṣavvuf-i Īrān, az Rābi'a ta Rūzbihān," in *Sufi* 16 (1371 [1992]), pp. 6–17; "Rūzbihān Baqlī on Love as 'Essential Desire,'" in *Gott is schön und Er liebt die Schönheit/God is Beautiful and Loves Beauty: Festschrift für Annemarie Schimmel*, ed. Alma Giese and J. Christoph Bürgel (Bern: Peter Lang, 1994), pp. 181–89.
14. Ghulāmḥusayn Nadīmī, *Rūzbihān, yā shaṭṭāḥ-i Fārs* (Shiraz: Kitābkhāna-i Aḥmadī, 1345/1966), a hagiography with some background on Pasā; Muḥammad Taqī Mīr, *Sharḥ-i ḥāl wa āthār wa ash'ār-i Shaykh Rūzbihān Baqlī* (Tehran: Dānishgāh-i Pahlavī, 1354/1975); Ghulām 'Alī Āriyā, *Sharḥ-i aḥwāl wa āthār wa majmū'a-i ash'ār ba-dast āmada-i Shaykh Shaṭṭāḥ Rūzbihān Baqlī* (Tehran: Rūzbihān, 1363/1984), a revised master's thesis primarily concerned with Rūzbihān's poetry.
15. Claude Addas, *Ibn 'Arabī ou la quête du soufre rouge*, Bibliothèque des Sciences humaines (Paris: Gallimard, 1989), esp. p. 343, where Ibn 'Arabī is presented as a universal intercessor for humanity. An English translation of this valuable study is being prepared for SUNY Press.

16. See my *Eternal Garden: Mysticism, History, and Politics at a South Asian Sufi Center*, SUNY Series in Muslim Spirituality in South Asia (Albany: State University of New York Press, 1992), esp. pp. 85–93.
17. For an overview of recent scholarship on sainthood in Islam, and a discussion of the reasons for using this Christian term in Islamic studies, see my remarks in the "Introduction" to *Manifestations of Sainthood in Islam*, ed. Grace Martin Smith and Carl W. Ernst (Istanbul: Éditions Isis, 1994).

Chart 1

The Ṭarīqa Rūzbihāniyya	Contemporary Political Figures in Fars[1]
1. Rūzbihān Baqlī Shīrāzī (522/1128–606/1209)	**Salghurid Atābegs** Muẓaffar al-Dīn Sonqur (r. 543/1148–556/1161)
Rūzbihān establishes *ribāṭ* in Shiraz in 560/1165	[Muẓaffar al-Dīn Zangī (r. 556/1161–570/1175)]
2a. Shihāb al-Dīn Muḥammad ibn Rūzbihān (d. 605/1209)	
	Saʿīd Degele (Taklā) ibn Zangī (r. 570/1175–590/1194)
2b. Fakhr al-Dīn Aḥmad ibn Rūzbihān (ca. 570/1174–645/1247)	[Toghrīl (r. 590/1194–601/1203)]
	Saʿd ibn Zangī (r. 601/1203–628/1231)
3a. Abū Bakr ibn Muḥammad ibn Rūzbihān (d. 640/1242)	Abū Bakr ibn Saʿd Qutlugh Khān (r. 628/1231–658/1260)
	[four other Atābegs]
3b. Ṣadr al-Dīn Ibrāhīm ibn Fakhr al-Dīn Aḥmad Rūzbihān Thānī (615/1218 or 603/1206–685/1286)	Jalāl al-Dīn Abū Bakr ibn Khwāja (former caliphal official?)
	Direct Mongol Rule after 668/1270
4a. Sharaf al-Dīn Ibrāhīm ibn Ṣadr al-Dīn Rūzbihān Thānī, author of *Tuḥfat ahl al-ʿirfān* (700/1300)	Amīr Bulughān (Mongol governor who converts to Islam, ca. 680/1281–681/1282)
4b. Shams al-Dīn ʿAbd al-Laṭif ibn Ṣadr al-Dīn Rūzbihān Thanī, author of *Rūḥ al-jinān* (705/1305)	
	Nuṣrat al-Dīn Aḥmad, ruler of Lur-i Buzurg (r. 696/1296–733/1333)
4c. Jalāl al-Dīn Yaḥyā ibn Ṣadr al-Dīn Rūzbihān Thānī	
5a. Ṣadr al-Dīn ibn Sharaf al-Dīn Ibrāhīm Rūzbihān Thālith	
5b. ʿIzz al-Dīn Masʿūd ibn Sharaf al-Dīn Ibrāhīm	

1. Names in brackets are not mentioned in the hagiographies dedicated to Rūzhibān and his successors

Chart 2

Rūzbihān's Initiatic Genealogy according to his Descendants

A. According to *Tuhfat ahl al-'irfān*, pp. 16–17.

1. Rūzbihān
2. Sirāj al-Dīn Khalīfa
3. Abū al-Qāsim Muḥammad ibn Aḥmad ibn 'Abd al-Karīm
4. Khaṭīb Abū Bakr ibn Muḥammad
5. Abū Isḥāq Ibrāhīm ibn Shahriyār al-Kāzarūnī
6. Ḥusayn Akkār Fīrūzābādī
7. Abū 'Abd Allāh Muḥammad ibn Khafīf al-Shīrāzī

Branch I	**Branch II**
8. Abū Ja'far Ḥaddād	8. Ruwaym
9. Abū 'Umar Iṣṭakhrī	9. Junayd
10. Abū Turāb Nakhshabī	10. Sarī al-Saqaṭī
11. Shaqīq Balkhī	11. Ma'rūf Karkhī
12. Salmān Fārsī	12. Dā'ūd Ṭā'ī
13. Mūsā ibn Zayd	13. Ḥasan Baṣrī
14. Uways Qaranī	14. 'Alī
15. 'Alī	15. Muḥammad
16. Muḥammad	

Chart 2

B. According to *Rūḥ al-jinān*, pp. 184–86.

Path I

1. Rūzbihān
2. Sirāj al-Dīn Maḥmūd ibn al-Khalīfa
3. Abū al-Qāsim Mahmūd ibn Aḥmad ibn 'Abd al-Karīm [Kāzarūnī]
4. Abū Bakr ibn [sic] Muḥammad ibn Khaṭīb Abū al-Qāsim ibn 'Abd al-Karīm
5. Abū Isḥaq Ibrāhīm ibn Shahryār al-Kāzarunī
6. Ḥusayn al-Akkār
7. Abū 'Abd Allāh ibn Khafīf

Branch I

8. Ja'far al-Ḥadhdhā'
9. Abū Turāb al-Nakhshabī
10. Ḥātim al-Aṣamm
11. Ibrāhīm ibn al-Adham
12. Dā'ūd al-Ṭā'ī
13. Ḥabīb al-'Ajamī
14. Mūsā ibn Yazīd al-Rā'ī
15. Uways al-Qaranī
16. 'Umar ibn al-Khaṭṭāb
17. 'Alī ibn Abī Ṭalib

Branch II

8. Ruwaym ibn Aḥmad
9. Abū al-Qāsim Junayd
10. Sarī al-Saqaṭī
11. Ma'rūf al-Karkhī

Sub-branch I

12. Dā'ūd al-Ṭā'ī
13. Ḥabīb al-'Ajamī
14. al-Ḥasan al-Baṣrī
15. 'Alī ibn Abī Ṭālib

Sub-branch II
(imams)

12. 'Alī ibn Mūsā al-Riḍā'
13. Mūsā ibn Ja'far
14. Ja'far al-Ṣādiq
15. Muḥammad al-Bāqir
16. Zayn al-'Ābidīn 'Ali ibn al-Ḥusayn
17. al-Ḥusayn ibn 'Alī
18. 'Alī ibn Abī Ṭālib

Chart 2

Path II

1. Rūzbihān
2. Abū al-Ṣafā' al-Wāsiṭī

Branch I

3. Muḥammad Mānkīl
4. Dā'ūd ibn Muḥammad
5. Abū al-'Abbās ibn Idrīs
6. Abū al-Qāsim Ramaḍān
7. Abū Ya'qūb al-Ṭabarī
8. Abū 'Abd Allāh ibn 'Uthmān
9. Abū Ya'qūb al-Nahrajurī
10. Abū Ya'qūb al-Sūsī
11. 'Abd al-Wāḥid ibn Zayd
12. al-Ḥasan al-Baṣrī
13. Kumayl ibn Ziyād
14. 'Alī ibn Abī Ṭālib

Branch II

3. Abū al-Maḥāsin 'Alī al-Fārmadhī
4. 'Abū al-Qāsim 'Abd Allāh ibn 'Alī al-Kharakānī
5. Abū 'Amr Muḥammad ibn Ibrāhīm
6. ibn Muḥammad al-Zujājī al-Nīsābūrī
7. Junayd

(ends abruptly)

Chart 2

C. The Initiatic Genealogy of Ṣadr al-Dīn Rūzbihān II (*Rūḥ al-jinān*, pp. 186–87)

1. Ṣadr al-Dīn Rūzbihān II

Branch I	**Branch II**
2. Fakhr al-Dīn Aḥmad	2. Sayf al-Dīn Abū ‘Ubayd Allāh Muḥammad ibn Aḥmad al-Zanjānī, in Shiraz
3. Abū Muḥammad Rūzbihān [Baqlī]	3. Jamāl al-Dīn Abū al-Maḥāsin Faḍl Allāh ibn Sarhang al-Mihrdār al-Zanjānī Bahā
etc.	4. Abū al-Maḥāsin ‘Alī al-Fārmadhī in Khurasan
	etc. [see B, Path II, Branch II above]

I

The Tradition of Rūzbihān Baqlī

A. A Sufi's Life

The conventional story of the life of Rūzbihān Baqlī has been preserved in a number of biographical reports. Here I would like simply to present a summary, noting in every case the source of our information and indicating where the shaykh's own writings bear out or conflict with the data of later writers, since these divergences will be explored later on. It will be helpful to the reader to digest this account before going on to the raptures and the inner landscapes of *The Unveiling of Secrets*, which are analyzed in the Chapter II. The contrasting literary perspectives of the later biographies will be discussed in Chapter III.

Rūzbihān's life took place in Persia during the period that Marshal Hodgson calls the "earlier middle period" of Islamic history. The 'Abbāsid caliphate in Baghdad declined precipitously after the middle of the fourth/tenth century. New waves of nomadic confederations were drawn from the steppes of Central Asia to the cultured cities of Iran and Iraq. The Seljuk Turks became Muslims and quickly were drawn to support the Sunnī caliphate and to make alliances with religious scholars and Sufis. They established domination over Iran, controlling the area where Rūzbihān would be born as early as 441/1049-50.[1] Shiraz, where Rūzbihān is buried, became the capital of the Salghurids, one of several semi-independent dynasties of Atābegs – nominal regents for Seljuk princes who seized effective power for themselves, at first as vassals for the Seljuks, then for the Khwarazmshahs, and finally for the Mongols. The Salghurids remained independent for over 120 years, from 543/1148 to 668/1270, when the Mongols finally took direct control over Fars. Political turmoil and the contest for power made it a turbulent time, though there were also periods of years of tranquillity.

Nearly all our biographers agree that Rūzbihān Baqlī was born in 522/1128 in the Persian town of Pasā (Arabicized as Fasā). The lone dissenter regarding the date is Massignon, who suggests 530/1135–6.[2] According to Rūzbihān's own testimony, which is reported in full in the next chapter, he was born in a family of Daylamite stock, and his childhood was spent among people who lacked any sense of religion. He recalls having spiritual experiences at the ages of three, seven, and fifteen, but only the last of these does he characterize as a true "unveiling" (*kashf*). That event would have taken place in 537/1142–3.[3] In one biography, his first unveiling is said rather to have taken place at age twenty-five, therefore in 547/1152–3, although that could easily have been a scribal error for fifteen.[4] In any case, he abandoned his vegetable store, cashbox, and supplies, and wandered for a year and a half (or, in a later account, six and a half years) in the desert.[5] Then around 538–9/1143–4 (or, following Massignon, in 548-9/1153-4), Rūzbihān joined the Sufis, serving them, learning their discipline, and studying and memorizing the Qur'ān. Where he stayed or how long we do not know, but he reports having an initial vision on the roof of a Sufi hospice (*ribāṭ*).[6] Massignon, following later reports, believes that Rūzbihān was associated with the *ribāṭ* of the Bānū Sālbih family in Shiraz, where he would have had access to a rich library containing the writings of Ḥallāj.[7] Rūzbihān then returned to Pasā and became a disciple of Shaykh Jamāl al-Dīn Abī al-Wafā' ibn Khalīl al-Fasā'ī, a figure about whom we know nothing aside from Rūzbihān's report.[8] Nonetheless, this Jamāl al-Dīn is the only contemporary (aside from his own son Aḥmad) that Rūzbihān names in his autobiography.

The next two decades are hard to pin down with any confidence. Rūzbihān reportedly traveled to Syria, Iraq, Kirman, and Arabia. He is said to have made the pilgrimage to Mecca twice.[9] Later biographers attempted to fill in the gap regarding Rūzbihān's teachers and masters. They suggest that Rūzbihān was for a time a disciple of a Kurdish Sufi master named Jāgīr Kurdī (d. 590/1194), who lived near Samarra in Iraq.[10] Rūzbihān's grandsons furnished him with a complete initiatic genealogy, stating that his primary teacher in Sufism was Sirāj al-Dīn Maḥmūd ibn Khalīfa (d. 562/1166–7) of the Sālbih family in Shiraz, who represented the Kāzarūnī lineage of Persian Sufism. Since Rūzbihān himself never mentions this teacher or the teaching lineage, we will return to this question later on. Other Sufi teachers he is said to have associated with include a certain Qiwām al-Dīn Suhrawardī, otherwise unknown.[11] In terms of the basic religious sciences, Rūzbihān is believed to have studied with the leading scholars of Shiraz, including Fakhr al-Dīn ibn Maryam, and Arshad al-Dīn Nayrīzī (d. 604/1208), a commentator on the great collection of prophetic *ḥadīth*, the *Maṣābīḥ*. In a fragment of one of his legal treatises, Rūzbihān himself has recorded a *ḥadīth* report from one Abū al-Ṣafā' al-Wāsiṭī on a legal point concerning ritual prayer.[13] His biographer Shams al-Dīn magnified this encounter, placing it in the context of his pilgrimage made from Pasā to the holy places of Arabia with a group of disciples. During a three-day stop in Wāsiṭ, he maintains, Rūzbihān received a Sufi cloak of initiation from Abū al-Ṣafā', and intended to make a retreat under his direction, but was told by the shaykh that he did not need this kind of discipline to become perfect.[14] Another account has it that Rūzbihān studied *ḥadīth* with the famous Sufi master Abū Najīb al-Suhrawardī in Alexandria, but it has been convincingly argued that this was a different person named Rūzbihān Miṣrī.[15] As we shall see, Rūzbihān's biographies consistently linked his name with those of other famous Sufis whom he had never met, as part of their hagiographical portrait.

The most interesting account of Rūzbihān by a near-contemporary is that of the great Andalusian master Ibn 'Arabī, who found this story still current when he visited Mecca sometime after 1201.

> The story is told of Shaykh Rūzbihān that he was afflicted with the love of a woman singer; he fell ecstatically in love with her, and he cried much in his state of ecstasy before God, confounding the pilgrims at the Ka'ba during the time he resided there. He circumambulated on the roof terraces of the sanctuary, but his state was sincere. When he was afflicted by the love of this singer, no one knew of it, but his relationship with God was transferred to her. He realized that the people would imagine that his ecstasy was for God in its origin. So he went to the Sufis and took off his cloak, throwing it before them. He told his story to the people, saying, "I do not want to lie about my spiritual state." He then became like a servant to the singer. The woman was told

> of his state and his ecstasy over her, and she learned that he was one of the great saints of God. The woman became ashamed, and repented before God for the profession she had followed, by the blessing of his sincerity. She became like a servant to him. God removed that relationship with her from his heart, and he returned to the Sufis and put on his cloak. He was not seen to have lied to God about his state.[16]

Although this story does not occur in the hagiographies of Rūzbihān, it has striking sympathies with the Rūzbihān we see in the autobiographical *The Unveiling of Secrets*, weeping in ecstasy at the beauty of God. Corbin has suggested that this incident may have served as the model for the charming dialogue at the beginning of *The Jasmine of the Lovers*, where a female interlocutor demands that Rūzbihān explain how God may be described in terms of passionate love (*'ishq*).[17]

Rūzbihān returned at last to Shiraz, where he caused a sensation when he first preached in public.[18] In the oldest version, the story goes like this:

> When the shaykh came from Pasā to Shiraz, the first day that he preached in the 'Atīq mosque, in the midst of his sermon, he said, "When I entered the mosque, in the corner of the herb sellers a woman was advising her daughter, saying, 'My dear, your mother advises you to cover your face, and don't show everyone your beauty from the window. This should not be, for by reason of your loveliness and beauty, someone may fall into temptation. Don't you hear my words and accept my advice?'"
>
> When Rūzbihān heard these words, he wanted to tell that woman, "Although you advise her and forbid her, let her show herself! She should not listen to these words of yours or accept this advice, for she is beautiful, and beauty has no rest until love becomes joined to it."
>
> When the shaykh said this, one of the travelers on the path of God was present. The arrow of these words hit the target of his heart, he cried out and gave up his spirit. The cry went up in the town that Shaykh Rūzbihān is cutting souls to bits with the sword of his words. The people of the town turned toward him and became his disciples.[19]

Later accounts add to Rūzbihān's advice to the mother the comment that "Love and beauty made a pact in pre-eternity never to be separate from one another."[20] After some time he founded his own hospice in 560/1165, according to an inscription quoted by his biographers, and there he remained occupied in supererogatory prayers and writing about the Sufi path.[21] He married several wives, who bore him two sons and three daughters.

Despite the numerous writings that Rūzbihān composed in Arabic and Persian (see Appendix A), the lack of dates and external references makes it difficult to extract from them anything like a chronology of his life and activities. It may be observed that the majority of Rūzbihān's writings were in Arabic, and unlike Jalāl al-Dīn Rūmī, Rūzbihān left little in the way of Persian poetry. Massignon has suggested that Rūzbihān was forced by hostile critics to leave Shiraz for a period of exile in Pasā; although he cites no evidence for persecution, he presumably is thinking of several passages in Rūzbihān's autobiography where critics of Sufism are castigated.[22] All that Rūzbihān tells us about this period is that he purchased an orchard in Pasā, but he could not enjoy it in the depression that he suffered on the death of a favorite wife.[23] Then Rūzbihān returned to Shiraz, completing in 570/1174 the *Commentary on Ecstatic Sayings*, which had been begun in Pasā.[24] Massignon maintains that Rūzbihān was invited to return by the newly installed Atābeg of Fars, Taklā, in 570/1175.[25] The evidence for this postulated political connection derives entirely from the hagiographies, and it will be examined in Chapter III. Of the remaining years of Rūzbihān we have only a few hints. The colophon to his treatise on spiritual states, *The Spirits' Font*, states that it was completed in 579/1184 when Rūzbihān was fifty-two, but this dating conflicts with his age as known from other sources.[26] It may be remarked in passing that this treatise, which has yet to be analyzed in detail, contains much that is helpful in understanding the experiences described in *The Unveiling of Secrets*.[27] From my analysis of *The Unveiling of Secrets* (see Chapter II), it may be suggested that Rūzbihān began writing it in 577/1181–2 at age fifty-five, and then completed it in 585/1189. The general portrait of Rūzbihān in his biographies shows him guiding disciples, praying and meditating in his *ribāṭ*, and continuing to preach in the principal mosque of Shiraz until his death. He had some followers in other regions, such as 'Imād al-Dīn Muhammad ibn Ra'īs, who became a disciple when Rūzbihān preached in Kirman; the two exchanged letters in flowery Persian in 583/1188.[28] Rūzbihān also sent *The Treatise on Holiness* with a merchant named Abū al-Faraj for the benefit of some Sufis in Central Asia. There are many stories concerning the authority of the saint; these will be examined in Chapter III. In 606/1209, Rūzbihān died in Shiraz. Two chronograms have been composed for this date: "the master of guidance and pure gnostic (*pīr-i hādī 'ārif-i pāk*)", and "the light of paradise" (*nūr-i firdaws*)."[29]

Personal descriptions of Rūzbihān are vivid though occasionally contradictory. A writer of the seventh/thirteenth century said, "I met him, and he was a master of mystical experience and absorption, continually in ecstasy, so that one's fear of him never left. He was constantly weeping, and his hours were restless, crying out, never easing his lament for an hour, passing every night in tears and lament; he feared God."[30] Rūzbihān's great-grandson Shams al-Din transmitted this description: "His face was always so beautiful that anyone who saw him was freshened and quickened in spirit, and would see the trace of sainthood on his forehead, which was the reflection of his blessed interior made external."[31] Another great-grandson, Sharaf al-Din, gave this thumbnail sketch: "The master had a fine appearance, but awe-inspiring, and most of the time he was cheerful; for him, hope was preponderant over fear."[32]

B. The "Rūzbihāniyya Order" and the Legacy of Rūzbihān

The tomb of Rūzbihān lies in the *ribāṭ* that he constructed as a hospice and residence, in the section of Shiraz then known as the New Garden. A new section was added to it by his great-great-grandson 'Izz al-Dīn Mas'ūd in the early eighth/fourteenth century, and a number of Rūzbihān's relatives and followers were buried there. At that time it was a major place of pilgrimage in Shiraz, as noticed by writers such as the traveler Ibn Baṭṭūṭa (in 725/1325) and the geographer Ḥamd Allāh Mustawfī (736/1336).[33] The popularity of Rūzbihān's shrine waned, however, and his order evidently disappeared. When the Aq-Qoyunlu crown prince Sultan Khalīl held an immense parade in Fars in 881/1476, the successors of the early Sufi masters Ibn Khafīf and Abū Isḥāq

Kāzarūnī played a prominent role, but no follower of Rūzbihān was noticed in the detailed account of this event by the philosopher and courtier Davānī.[34] By the nineteenth century the shrine (in a part of town now called Darb-i Shīkh or Bālā Kaft) had fallen into disrepair, and local people pillaged the stone for other purposes and quartered cattle there.[35] As noted above, it was Ivanow who rediscovered the tomb of Rūzbihān in Shiraz in 1928 and personally dug up the tombstone of the shaykh. It remained in a ruined state until Corbin and Mu'īn conducted an excavation of the tomb and petitioned the archeological department of the Iranian government to undertake a full restoration in 1958, comparable to what has been done in Shiraz at the tombs of the poets Sa'dī and Ḥāfiẓ. A restoration with new tile-work and inscriptions was completed in 1972.[36] It is possible that the earlier neglect of Rūzbihān's tomb was the result of anti-Sufi feeling during the Safavid period; we know, for instance, that Shah Ismā'īl in 909/1503 massacred 4000 followers of the Kāzarūnī Sufi order in Fars and desecrated many Sufi tombs in the region.[37]

Along with the tomb, Rūzbihān was memorialized by biographical writings that are best characterized as hagiographies, narrative portraits constructed around a model of holiness or sainthood. The most important of these hagiographies are two extensive monographic biographies in Persian, devoted exclusively to Rūzbihān, his life and writings, and his descendants. Both writings (analyzed in detail in Chapter III) were written by family members nearly a century after his death. Sharaf al-Dīn Ibrāhīm wrote the first of these hagiographies under the title *Tuḥfat ahl al-'irfān fī dhikr sayyid al-aqṭāb Rūzbihān* [*The Gift to the People of Gnosis, in Memory of the Chief Axis of the World Rūzbihān*] in 700/1300, while his brother Shams al-Dīn 'Abd al-Laṭīf compiled *Rūḥ al-jinān fī sīrat al-shaykh Rūzbihān* [*The Spirit of the Gardens, on the Life of the Master Rūzbihān*] five years later in 705/1305. Of secondary importance is *Shadd al-izār fī ḥaṭṭ al-awzār 'an zawwār al-mazār* [*Girding One's Loins to Lighten the Burden from Pilgrims to Shrines*], a hagiography in Arabic intended for the use of pilgrims to the tombs of the saints of Shiraz. Written late in the eighth/fourteenth century by Mu'īn al-Dīn Abū al-Qāsim Junayd (d. ca. 791/1389), it was organized into seven sections giving guided walking tours of the tombs of Shiraz, so that one might encompass them all in a week. This was then translated into Persian by the author's son 'Īsā ibn Junayd under the title *Multamas al-aḥibbā khāliṣ min al-riyā'* [*The Request of Friends Free of Hypocrisy*], but it is generally known under the title *Hazār mazār* (*A Thousand Tombs*).[38] This lengthy compendium devotes a few pages to Rūzbihān and his descendants, and it puts them into the context of a highly formalized cult of the saints. Later biographical works devoted to Sufis and poets draw entirely upon these early sources for their information about Rūzbihān.

Rūzbihān's own descendants constituted in effect a Sufi path (*ṭarīqa*) or "order," meaning a teaching lineage based on a spiritual method or practice, combined with the social and institutional supports that were gradually making Sufism a highly visible phenomenon during the sixth/twelfth and seventh/thirteenth centuries. The construction of initiatic genealogies was a device meant to ensure continuous transmission of esoteric teaching from the Prophet Muḥammad through an unbroken chain of masters and disciples. Rūzbihān's biographers furnished him with such a genealogy; although Corbin regards this as "established with certainty," we will have reason to question the value of this genealogy for Rūzbihān's own concept of sainthood.[39] Likewise, the descendants of Rūzbihān were physical embodiments of the Rūzbihāniyya for several generations. This family Sufi order seems to have ended in the fourth generation after Rūzbihān, with his great-great grandson Ṣadr al-Dīn ibn Sharaf al-Dīn Ibrāhīm Rūzbihān III (see Chart 1). The process of institutionalizing this Sufi order will be examined in Chapter III. What is of interest at this point is the legacy of Rūzbihān, and how it was transmitted.

Massignon discovered a document written by the late scholar and polymath Sayyid Murtaḍā Zabīdī (d. 1205/1791) in which a much longer extension of the Rūzbihāniyya order is described, reaching up to the author's own day.[40] This is the chain of transmission:

1. Rūzbihān Baqlī
2. Ṣadr al-Dīn Rūzbihān II (grandson of Rūzbihān) (d. 685/1286)
3. 'Abd al-Wadūd Khāluwī Farīd al-Dīn
4. 'Abd al-Qādir Ṭāwūsī
5. Ghiyāth al-Dīn Kāzarūnī
6. Nūr al-Dīn Abū al-Futūḥ Aḥmad Ṭāwūsī (d. 871/1466–7)
7. Aḥmad ibn Muḥammad Nahrawālī (d. 949/1542–3)

8. Quṭb al-Dīn Muḥammad Nahrawālī (d. 990/1582)
9. Aḥmad Bābā Sūdānī of Timbuctu (d. 1032/1624)
10. ʻAbd al-Qādir Ghassānī Fāsī (d. 1032/1624)
11. ʻAbd al-Qādir Fihrī Fāsī (d. 1091/1680)
12. Muḥammad Ṣaghīr (d. 1134/1721–2)
13. Muḥammad ibn ʻAyyūb Tilimsānī
14. Murtaḍā Zabīdī (d. 1205/1791)

The geographical spread of this transmission is remarkably extensive; nos. 6, 7, and 8 lived in India and Arabia, and the remainder up to Zabīdī are from North Africa (Timbuctu, Fez, Tlemcen). Not too much weight should be placed on this chain as evidence of a functioning Sufi order, however. The first few steps seem shaky, as Ṣadr al-Dīn Rūzbihān II is made to transmit from his grandfather, who died when he was at most three years old. It may be, too, that this represents no more than the transmission of a single *dhikr* chant rather than a full-fledged Sufi teaching. Zabīdī was known to be something of a collector of such affiliations in all the religious sciences, and he boasted of having studied with over 300 teachers of all sorts.[41] Those figures from this lineage for whom biographies are available are known primarily as members of a particular *ḥadīth* transmission who also participated in Sufi lineages, but the Rūzbihāniyya was evidently not visible enough to receive mention in their biographies alongside functional institutional orders like the Suhrawardiyya and the Naqshbandiyya.[42] Still, it is possible that some aspect of his teaching was kept alive in this fashion, although Godlas has found indications of mistakes in identification in this lineage.

What is perhaps of greater significance is the likelihood that Rūzbihān's Sufism served as a source for the great Persian poet of Shiraz, Ḥāfiẓ (d. 791/1389). Corbin has traced out the contours of a relationship between Rūzbihān and Ḥāfiẓ, beginning with the anonymous commentary on Rūzbihān's *The Jasmine of the Lovers* that uses a number of verses by Ḥāfiẓ to explain the subtleties of Rūzbihān's doctrine of love. More explicitly, the Turkish commentator Sūdī (d. ca. 1591) has quoted an unidentified biography of Ḥāfiẓ that describes him as a member of a branch of the Rūzbihāniyya order. The sequence is: Rūzbihān Baqlī, Fakhr al-Dīn Aḥmad ibn Rūzbihān, ʻAbd al-Salām, Maḥmūd (or Muḥammad) ʻAṭṭār "Pīr-i Gul-rang" ("the rose-colored master"),

Ḥāfiẓ. Corbin argues that it is precisely the adoration of beauty and the religion of love that forms the common thread between Rūzbihān and Ḥāfiẓ. In Rūzbihān's mystical theology, theophanies of beauty require embodiment in forms and symbols that are intelligible to those initiated into the esoteric vision, and this is arguably one of the primary lines of interpretation of the ambiguous verses of Ḥafiẓ. Corbin also finds a link between the shaykh and the poet in the concept of self-blame (*malāma*), a form of early Sufi piety that required perfect obedience to the law in private and outrageous behavior designed to incur censure in public.[43] Although some have expressed caution about accepting the connection between Rūzbihān and Ḥāfiẓ, it remains an intriguing juxtaposition of these two outstanding writers from Shiraz.[44]

The writings of Rūzbihān had a particularly wide circulation among a select group of readers in Iran, India, Central Asia, Ottoman Turkey, and Africa. Without pretending to be exhaustive, we can list a number of these readers simply to give an idea of the circulation of his writings (see also the manuscripts of Rūzbihān's works listed in Appendix A). All these later figures testified to the difficulty of Rūzbihān's style, which at times is admittedly convoluted and obscure. Jāmī of Herat (d. 898/1492) remarked that "he has sayings that have poured forth from him in the state of overpowering and ecstasy, which not everyone can understand."[45] The Mughal prince Dārā Shikūh (d. 1069/1659) found his style "fatiguing."[46] Nonetheless, Rūzbihān's reputation was widely known, particularly in South Asia. In eighth/fourteenth-century India, Sufis of the Chishti order knew Rūzbihān as an advocate of listening to music.[47] His Qur'ān commentary, *The Brides of Explanation*, was imitated by Ashraf Jahāngīr Simnānī (d. 829/1425), a member of the Chishtī order who also commented on Rūzbihān's *The Jasmine of the Lovers*.[48] Another Sufi of Shiraz, Shāh Dā'ī (d. 870/1465–6), composed several poems in praise of Rūzbihān.[49] In pre-Safavid Iran the philosopher Jalāl al-Dīn Davānī (d. 908/1502–3) quoted with approval *The Jasmine of the Lovers*, calling Rūzbihān "the emperor of the people of love and gnosis."[50] An Anatolian Naqshbandī Sufi named 'Abd Allāh Ilāhī Sīmābī (d. 892/1487), who had visited Jāmī in Herat, wrote a commentary on Rūzbihān's *The Treatise on Holiness*.[51] Another Naqshbandī, Khwājagī Ahmad

Kāshānī (d. 949/1542), was interested in Rūzbihān's visions of God in the form of a beautiful Turk.[52] The Chishtī scholar Shaykh 'Azīz Allāh (d. 975/1567–68), who used to attend musical sessions at the tomb of Niẓām al-Dīn Awliyā' in Delhi, taught his students *The Brides of Explanation* along with other Sufi classics.[53] Rūzbihān's metaphysical views are quoted in a work on political philosophy written 984/1576, dedicated to Rāja 'Alī Khān Fārūqī, ruler of the small Deccan kingdom of Khandesh.[54] Rūzbihān's Qur'ān commentary inspired a commentary on the "light verse" of the Qur'ān written by the Indian Qādirī Sufi scholar 'Abd al-Ḥaqq Muḥaddith Dihlawī (d. 1052/1642).[55] In 1047/1637-8, the Mughal prince Dārā Shikūh commissioned a Persian translation of Rūzbihān's Qur'ān commentary from Badr al-Dīn Sirhindī, a biographer of the Naqshbandī master Aḥmad Sirhindī, and at least a fourth of the whole commentary was completed.[56] Dārā himself also wrote a summary and extension of Rūzbihān's *Commentary on Ecstatic Sayings*.[57] Within the last century, the great Chishtī master of the Punjab, Khwāja Ghulām Farīd, lectured to his disciples on difficult passages from Rūzbihān's Qur'ān commentary.[58] The impact of Rūzbihān on North and West Africa remains to be elucidated, but Alan Godlas has found materials indicating that major excerpts from Rūzbihān's Qur'ān commentary are quoted in Sufi writings from those regions, up through the nineteenth century. It is also worth noting as evidence of Rūzbihān's importance in Iran the recent work of Dr. Javād Nūrbakhsh, head of the Ni'matullahi Sufi order, who has edited a number of important works by Rūzbihān and continues to cite them in his own writings on Sufism.

Notes

1. Nadīmī, p. 9.
2. Massignon, p. 452, argues that Rūzbihān was fifty-five years when he wrote the *Kashf al-asrār*, and that it was completed in 585/1189, thus indicating a birth date of 530/1135–6. This view does not square with the dating of *Mashrab al-arwāḥ*, and it does not take account of the possibility that the *Kashf al-asrār* was completed eight years after its commencement, as suggested below (Chapter II). Corbin (introduction to *'Abhar al-'āshiqīn*, p. 52, n. 90) points out that the date of 530 is impossible if one accepts the report that Rūzbihān studied with Abū Bakr ibn Muḥammad Barkar (d. 540/1145–6). It also seems unlikely that Rūzbihān's descendants would be mistaken

about so basic a piece of information as the shaykh's age at death (eighty-four lunar years).

3. So *Kashf al-asrār*, §7, §10.
4. *Tuhfat ahl al-'irfān*, p. 13.
5. Massignon (p. 452) says Rūzbihān wandered for six and a half years (545-551), evidently accepting the birth date of 530 and referring to the report in *Tuhfat ahl al-'irfān* (p. 13), that he spent seven years on Bamūy mountain north of Shiraz, with only a single cloak, performing lustration and ablution in summer and winter, never removing the cloak. The date of 545–551 is repeated by Mu'īn (p. 8).
6. *Kashf al-asrār*, §12.
7. Massignon, p. 456. This conclusion is based on the initiatic genealogy of Rūzbihān supplied by his great-grandsons, stating that Rūzbihān received the Sufi cloak (*khirqa*) from Sirāj al-Dīn Mahmūd ibn Khalīfa of the Sālbih family. Rūzbihān states, however, "I did not have a master at that time" (*Kashf al-asrār*, 13).
8. *Kashf al-asrār*, §13. *Tuhfat ahl al-'irfān*, p. 169, states that his first vision took place in a *ribāṭ* in Pasā, and it fails to mention the name of Jamāl al-Dīn at all. Massignon, p. 542, adds that Rūzbihān found "a first *ribāṭ*" in Pasā, that of Abū Muhammad al-Jawzak, but this seems to have been only an overnight stay during a pilgrimage tour in Fars (*Kashf al-asrār*, §41).
9. *Tuhfat ahl al-'irfān*, p. 113.
10. Rūzbihān appears to mention him once by name (*Sharḥ-i shaṭḥiyyāt*, p. 455), as the source of information about the burning of Ḥallāj's books, though in Corbin's edition the name is given as "the *quṭb*, Jākūs Kurdī." From the mention of his name here and not in the corresponding place in the Arabic original (*Manṭiq al-asrār*, fol. 42b, where this source is referred to simply as "one of the masters"), Massignon (*Passion*, II, 509, etc.) deduces that the Persian text was completed after the death of Jāgīr, on the grounds that Rūzbihān would have respected his master too much to mention his name while he still lived.
11. *Hazār mazār*, p. 291.
12. See Mu'īn, pp. 18-20; Corbin, introduction to *'Abhar al-'āshiqīn*, p. 51.
13. *Rūḥ al-jinān*, p. 318, quoting Rūzbihān's *al-Muwashshaḥ fī 'ilm al-fiqh*.
14. *Tuhfat ahl al-'irfān*, p. 177.
15. Corbin, introduction to *'Abhar al-'āshiqīn*, pp. 24–25, 52; Mu'īn, p. 11.
16. Muḥyī al-Dīn ibn 'Arabī, *al-Futūḥāt al-Makkiyya* (Beirut: Dār Ṣādir, n.d.), chapter 177, II, 315–16; Persian translation in Jāmī, *Nafaḥāt*, p. 257.
17. Corbin, *En Islam iranien*, III, 68–71.
18. Nadīmī, p. 10, suggests that this return to Shiraz took place as early as 543/1148–9 or 545/1150–1.
19. *Tuhfat ahl al-'irfān*, pp. 110–111. Another version (*Rūḥ al-jinān*, p. 224) omits the story of the woman and her daughter, but relates that the

consternation aroused by this sermon caused the local scholars to seek his expulsion from the town; the Atābeg Sonqur was exposed to Rūzbihān's spiritual powers, and so invited him instead to preach weekly in both major mosques.

20. Jāmī, *Nafaḥāt*, p. 256, following *Hazār mazār*, p. 291.
21. *Rūḥ al-jinān*, pp. 178–79. On the date of the *ribāṭ*, Dānish-Puzhūh, Introduction, p. 14, reads *sitta* rather than *sana*, giving a date of 566/1171, but the Arabic inscription on the *ribāṭ* as quoted in *Rūḥ al-jinān* is clearly Ramaḍān 560/July-August 1165.
22. Massignon, *Passion*, II, 407.
23. *Kashf al-asrār*, 109; cf. 131.
24. Corbin, introduction to *Sharḥ-i shaṭḥiyyāt*, pp. 20–23; the date is given on p. 635 of the text. Massignon ("La Vie," p. 453) suggests that this date refers to the completion of the Arabic original, and that the Persian translation and expansion was made after the death of Jāgīr Kurdī in 591/1194–5; since the vision of Ḥallāj that inspired the *Sharḥ-i shaṭḥiyyāt* does not occur in *Manṭiq al-asrār*, Massignon concludes that the *Sharḥ-i shaṭḥiyyāt* was written later. He also speculates (*Passion*, II, 407, 498) that the writing of this work took place at the *ribāṭ* of Abū Muḥammad Jawzak, though it is mentioned by Rūzbihān (above, n. 8) only as the site of a brief stopover.
25. Massignon gives the date 571 for Taklā's accession, but this is incorrect, and would in any case be after the completion of *Sharḥ-i shaṭḥiyyāt*; cf. Clifford Edmund Bosworth, *The Islamic Dynasties: A Chronological and genealogical Handbook*, Islamic Surveys, 5 (Edinburgh: at the University Press, 1967), p. 125.
26. *Mashrab al-arwāḥ*, p. 320. The text gives the date of early morning Wednesday 16 Dhū al-Qa'da 579/1 March 1184, saying that Rūzbihān was fifty-two years old at the time of writing, whereas with a birth year of 522 he would have been fifty-seven in 579/1184. There is the further discrepancy that 1 March 1184 was a Thursday, making it appear that the editor's reading may be in error. If we wish to consider emending the text, the year could be read as 574, making the equivalent date 25 April 1179, a Wednesday. This copyist's error (*tis'a* for *arbi'a*) would be visually more likely than than mistaking fifty-two (*ithnayn wa khamsīn*) for fifty-seven (*sab'a wa khamsīn*).
27. Some of the experiences detailed in *Kashf al-asrār* are identical with stations presented in *Mashrab al-arwāḥ*. From these examples it is also clear that the formula of definition at the end of most of the entries on the stations ("the gnostic said," *qāla al-'ārif*) is the statement of Rūzbihān and not of any of his masters.
28. *Rūḥ al-jinān*, pp. 206–7. The correspondence is given in *Tuḥfat ahl al-'irfān*, pp. 117–21, repeated with some variation in *Rūḥ al-jinān*, pp. 319–24.
29. Mu'īn, p. 15, citing *Rayḥānat al-adab*, II, 399, and Muḥammad Fāḍil ibn Sayyid Ḥasan Ḥusaynī Tirmidhī Akbarābādī, *Mukhbir al-wāṣilīn*, ed. Muslim Aḥmad Niẓāmī (Delhi: Kutub Khāna Nadhīriyya, 1358/1939–40), pp. 51–52 (composed 1060/1650).

30. Faqīh Ṣā'in al-Dīn Ḥusayn (d. 664/1265–6), in *Hazār mazār*, p. 289. On this scholar, whose lost hagiography is a major source for *Hazār mazār*, see ibid., p. 201, n. 85.
31. *Tuḥfat ahl al-'irfān*, p. 15.
32. *Rūḥ al-jinān*, p. 179.
33. Corbin, introduction to *'Abhar al-'āshiqīn*, p. 72; Hamd Allāh ibn Abī Bakr ibn Muḥammad ibn Naṣr Mustawfī Qazvīnī, *Nuzhat al-qulūb*, ed. Muḥammad Dabīrsiyāqī, Zabān u Farhang-i Īrān, 21 (Tehran: Kitābkhāna-i Ṭuḥūrī, 1336/1958), pp. 138–39.
34. Vladimir Minorsky, "'Arḍ-nāma-i Davānī," *Puzhūhishi dar bāra-i umūr-i niẓāmī wa ghayr niẓāmī-i fārs*, trans. Ḥasan Javādī, *Bar-rasī-hā-yi Tārikhī* 3/6 (n.d.), p. 203.
35. Mu'īn, pp. 15–16.
36. Mīr, *Sharḥ-i ḥāl*, pp. 19–20, with photographs following.
37. Said Arjomand, *The Shadow of God and the Hidden Imām: Religion, Political Order, and Societal Change in Shi'ite Iran from the Beginning to 1890* (Chicago: University of Chicago Press, 1984), p. 112. Corbin, Introduction to *'Abhar al-'āshiqīn*, p. 73, also suggests the possibility of Shī'ī hostility to Rūzbihān Baqlī due to a confusion of names with an anti-Shī'ī polemicist named Faḍl ibn Rūzbihān.
38. 'Īsā ibn Junayd al-Shīrāzī, *Hazār mazār*, Persian trans. from the Arabic *Shadd al-izār*, ed. Nūrānī Wiṣāl (Shiraz: Kitābkhāna-i Aḥmadī, 1364/1985), pp. 285–98; I have consulted this edition, which has detailed notes on textual divergences from the Arabic original. Cf. Storey, *Persian Literature*, p. 1123.
39. Corbin, introduction to *'Abhar al-'āshiqīn*, p. 53.
40. Massignon, "La Vie," pp. 455–56, citing Abū al-Fayḍ Muḥammad Murtaḍā Ḥusaynī Wāsiṭī Zabīdī Bilgrāmī, *'Iqd al-jawhar al-thamīn fil-dhikr wa ṭuruq al-albās wal-talqīn*, 53.
41. 'Abd al-Ḥayy ibn Fakhr al-Dīn al-Ḥasanī, *Nuzhat al-khawāṭir wa bahjat al-masāmi' wa al-nawāẓir* (9 vols., 2nd ed., Hyderabad: Dā'irat al-ma'ārif al-'Uthmāniyya, 1382/1962–1396/1976), VII, 489.
42. Nūr al-Dīn Abū al-Futūḥ Aḥmad Ṭawūsī was initiated into Suhrawardī, Kubrawī, Ṭāwūsī, Mayhanī, Ni'matullāhī, and Naqshbandī lineages, and he transmitted *ḥadīth* to Aḥmad ibn Muḥammad Nahrawālī in Gujarat (ibid., III, 23–27). The latter (b. 870/1466–7, d. 949/1542–3 according to ibid., IV, 25–26) and his son Quṭb al-Dīn Muḥammad Nahrawālī (b. 927/1521, d. 990/1582, ibid., IV, 285–90; Brockelman, GAL II, 381, GALS II, 514) were known primarily as *ḥadīth* scholars in a lineage famous for Methuselah-like longevity, although Quṭb al-Dīn had a Naqshbandī initiation.
43. Corbin, introduction to *'Abhar al-'ashiqīn*, pp. 56–62.
44. R. M. Rehder, "*Le Jasmin des fideles d'amour*: Review Article," *Muslim World* 53 (1963), pp. 319–20, is skeptical about the Ḥāfiẓ connection. Alan Godlas has discovered some new material in support of this thesis which will be published in a forthcoming study.

45. Jāmī, *Nafaḥāt*, p. 255, a comment based on *Hazār mazār*, p. 289 ("he has sayings that most listeners cannot understand").
46. Dārā Shikūh, *Ḥasanāt al-ʿārifīn*, ed. Makhdūm Rạhīn (Tehran, 1352/1973), p. 3.
47. Somehow a saying that Rūzbihān quoted from the early Egyptian Sufi Dhū al-Nūn became known as a quotation from Rūzbihān's own *Kashf al-asrār*; see my "Rūzbihān Baqlī on Love" for details.
48. On Simnānī's interpretation of Rūzbihān, see *Words of Ecstasy*, p. 22 with n. 43, and "Rūzbihān Baqlī on Love as 'Essential Desire.'"
49. Mīr, *Sharḥ-i ḥāl*, pp. 44–46.
50. Jalāl al-Dīn Davānī, *Akhlāq-i Jalālī* (Lahore: Tāj Book Depot, n.d.), p. 174, citing *ʿAbhar al-ʿāshiqīn*, pp. 6–7.
51. This commentary, entitled *Manāzil al-qulūb*, is printed in *Rūzbihān nāma*, pp. 387–420, from a MS from Yugoslavia. 2 other MSS of this text are in Egypt, and another is reported to be in Manisa, Turkey; cf. *Mashrab al-arwāḥ*, introduction, p. 1.
52. Hellmut Ritter, *Das Meer der Seele: Mensch, Welt und Gott in den Geschichten des Farīduddīn ʿAṭṭār* (2nd ed., Leiden: E. J. Brill, 1978), p. 448. This citation is close to *Kashf al-asrār*, 97, but it has been translated into Persian and adapted to the topos of "the cap awry" (cf. Schimmel, *Dimensions*, p. 290).
53. ʿAbdu-'l-Qādir ibn-i-Mulūkshāh al-Badāonī, *Muntakhabu-'t-tāwarīkh*, trans. Wolseley Haig, Bibliotheca Indica, 97 (Calcutta: The Asiatic Society of Bengal), III, 17.
54. ʿAbd al-Laṭif Munshī Nazīl al-Haramayn, *Nafāʾis al-kalām wa-ʿarāʾis al-aqlām* (MS no. 948, H.L. 946, Khuda Bakhsh Library, Patna), fol. 15a, a passage in Persian on absolute existence.
55. Muhammad Zuber Qureshi, "The Library of Hazrat Pir Muhammad Shah at Ahmedabad," in *Islam in India: Studies and Commentaries*, vol. 2, *Religion and Religious Education*, ed. Christian W. Troll (New Delhi: Vikas Publishing House Pvt Ltd, 1985), p. 291; there is another copy in the British Library (Rieu, II, 843A).
56. Aḥmad Sirhindī, *Ḥaḍarāt al-quds*, comp. Badr al-Din Sirhindī (Lahore: Maḥkama-i Awqāf, 1971), pp. 6, 159. This work is not extant.
57. See *Words of Ecstasy*, pp. 23–24.
58. Khwāja Ghulām Farīd, *Maqābīs al-majālis*, Urdu trans. from Persian by Wāhid Bakhsh Siyāl (Lahore: Islamic Book Foundation, 1399/1979), pp. 401, 409–11 (discussion taking place in 1314/1896).

II

The Inner Structure of Sainthood

A. The Unveiling of Secrets: Structure and Contents

The Unveiling of Secrets is an unusual document in terms of Sufi literature. Paul Nwyia has described this text as "unique in the field of Islamic mysticism, rather in world mystical literature," and Corbin held the same view.[1] We have very few texts in pre-modern Islamicate literature that could be called autobiographies in the modern sense of the term.[2] al-Ghazālī's (d. 505/1111) *Deliverance from Error* has often been compared to Augustine's *Confessions* as a conversion narrative, but al-Ghazālī's work is much less revelatory of a self, concealing crucial inner events behind a veil of esotericism and a programmatic presentation of the options available to Muslim intellectuals in his day.[3] In *The Unveiling of Secrets*, Rūzbihān offers far less in terms of a description of his exterior life than al-Ghazālī, but far more detail of his inner experiences. As Rūzbihān tells us, "Not a day or night has gone by me, by God, during all the time extending up to now, when I am fifty-five years old, without an unveiling of the hidden world" (§56). It is precisely these unveilings that constitute the subject of this text. Although there are rich traditions of biographical and hagiographical writing in Islamic literature, these do not seem to have served as models for Rūzbihān's self-disclosure. We shall return later to the problem of classifying the literary genre of this text.

The title of the work contains two terms that are crucial to understanding Rūzbihān's mysticism. Commonly used throughout Sufi discourse, unveiling (*kashf*) means literally removing a veil, and with its derivatives it often stands as a general term for insight, which can apply to intellect, the prophetic faculty, or to a kind of vision most fully realized in the afterlife.[4] The Qur'ān makes a strong link between unveiling and vision: "We have unveiled you, and today your eye is sharp" (50:22). Early Sufis like Qushayrī treated unveiling (in the form *mukāshafa*) as a transitional stage between being situated in the presence of God and having a full vision of the divine reality, though other authors such as Hujwīrī and Sarrāj consider unveiling and vision to be one and the same. Often the momentary character of unveiling is signaled by comparing it to a lightning flash.[5] For Rūzbihān, it has a precise technical meaning that he has defined in his lexicon of mystical terminology, indicating a form of transcendent vision that "sees" the qualities of God: "Unveiling is clarifying the veiled to the understanding, as though one sees with the eye. Its reality is the manifestation of the kingdom, the dominion, and the eternal glory of might to the eye of the gnostics. To their eye the radiance of their own glory is veiled, so that they may see with it the beauty of God's face. Then they look upon his hidden kingdom, and in gnosis they obtain an understanding of every Attribute."[6] The most frequent expression in *The Unveiling of Secrets* is "I saw him" (*ra'aytuhu*). It is no exaggeration to say that vision (*ru'ya*) is the most important general category for mystical experience in Rūzbihān's vocabulary.[7] We shall return later to the metaphysical terms cited in this passage as well as the symbolism of veiling, but for the moment it suffices to say that unveiling is the mystical perception that is the characteristic of the saints. For Rūzbihān this perception is not abstract or philosophical knowledge, but a vision clothed in form, especially human form; it is cognitive but apparitional, revealing knowledge through divine light.

The other term of the title is ambiguous; although *sirr* can be rendered as "secret" as the title is translated above, *sirr* has both an objective and a subjective meaning. It can be a secret or mystery that is hidden from general knowledge, but in Sufi psychology it is also a faculty of the inner self that is subtler than the spirit (*rūḥ*) or the heart (*qalb*). It may often be translated as "conscience," implying both an inner consciousness and the shared knowledge that constitutes a secret.[8] Rūzbihān says, "The secret/conscience is a hidden thing between non-existence and existence. The reality of the secret/conscience is that which the tongue of knowledge does not utter. The gnostic knows [it] from himself immediately, but he cannot reveal it. These are hidden unveilings of the kingdom and the angelic world."[9] A number of other Sufi books have carried the same title *Kashf al-asrār*, for instance the great Persian Qur'ān commentary by Maybudī, based on the teachings of 'Abd Allāh Anṣārī of Herat. Some modern polemical works in Persian (including one by Ayatollah Khomeini) have used the same title, but in the sense of "exposé." For Rūzbihān, *The Unveiling of Secrets* conveys the meaning of the perception of the secrets of his inner conscience through the narration of the mysteries that were unveiled to him.

The Arabic text as we have it is still in manuscript, though a critical edition and a French translation are being prepared by Paul Ballanfat. For the time being, I have relied on the two known manuscripts, which were partially edited by Henry Corbin, though he unfortunately did not complete this project.[10] Some comparison has also been possible with an abridged recension (about one-fourth of the text), separately edited by Paul Nwyia and Nazif Hoca. There are no divisions and no apparent structure or headings, but it has been possible to divide it into paragraphs (cited here by §) where the narrative suggests breaks between visions, usually introduced by the phrase, "And then I saw him with the aspect of majesty and beauty ... " Up to now the most extensive discussion of the text has been that of Corbin, who has analyzed and translated sections amounting to about one-seventh of the entire treatise.[11] Although Corbin has pointed out a number of important themes, he did not study the text closely enough to grasp the full details of its structure. He remarked, for example, that "after the episodes of first youth, these visions and revelations related throughout this *Diarium* are not arranged in chronological order."[12]

A closer study suggests that text may be divided into two parts. The first part, up to §56, is a retrospective autobiography written in 577/1181–2 at the age of fifty-five, as he states in two places (§7, 56). Taking up about one-fourth of the entire work, it may be divided as follows: childhood and youth (§7–13), earliest visions (§14–24), miscellaneous early visions (§25–40), pilgrimages in Fars (§41–44), an initiatic vision (§47–49), visions of Mecca (§50–53), other visions (§54–55). At this point Rūzbihān stops to reflect on what has been written, and the second part of the text begins to shift from the retrospective mode into a diary form. "I have not recalled this previously, nor what happened to me in days past ... Now I will write, with God's aid, what happens to me of affairs of unveiling and mysteries of witnessing ... " (§56). Phrases such as "last night" (§71) indicate that the text now reflects Rūzbihān's ongoing experiences.

It is not clear when or how often he returned to this diary to record his current visions, but there are several lengthy sequences that reflect powerful experiences: the descent of God (§72–74), visions of Rūzbihān's family in paradise (§80–84), and two visions where Rūzbihān's status in the Sufi tradition is proclaimed (§136–39, 161–62). Nonetheless, a clear temporal sequence indicates that a large section (§128-59) was composed all at once during the month of Ramaḍān, when Rūzbihān evidently had the leisure to record the fruits of his meditations during the traditionally contemplative month of fasting. Although we do not know in which year this Ramaḍān section occurred, a final dating is apparent in the final pages of the document (§200–09), when Rūzbihān records a plague in Shiraz during Rajab and Sha'bān of 585/August–October 1189. Thus I would suggest that the second part of *The Unveiling of Secrets* (§57–210) is something like an occasional diary, intermittently recorded over a period of eight years, and completed when Rūzbihān was sixty-three years old. In the analysis that follows, a preliminary section summarizes the beginning of the book up to the end of Rūzbihān's youth. Subsequent sections in this chapter discuss his visions in terms of their subject matter and literary genre.

B. The Prologue and Early Years

The text begins as is customary with a benediction and praises of God and the Prophet Muḥammad. This is followed by a brief prologue on the nature of sainthood, which will be examined below. Rūzbihān then explains the purpose of the book, in a passage consisting of a litany of the technical terms of Islamic mysticism as they had developed by the sixth/twelfth century:

> A lover, one of the sincere ones who depart from the existent things and temporality with the character of isolation seeking gnosis and unity, asked me with a perfect love to tell him of the events of unveilings and the secrets of witnessings that occur to me, of the brides of the angelic realm and the wonders of the lights of might that are unveiled to me, of the particularities of manifestation and descent in the station of clothing with divinity, of the pure unveiling of the sublimities of the Essence, in my ecstasies, my intoxication, and my

> sobriety, by day and by night, and the unknown sciences that God the transcendent opened to me from his presence; thus it would be for him the proclamation of his path and his intimate companion in his heart and spirit in the hidden world (§4).

This announcement makes no attempt to cater to anyone outside the elite circle of Sufi adepts. It scarcely resembles the program for an autobiography as understood today. The unnamed person who asked Rūzbihān to describe his experiences is referred to as a lover, one of the "sincere ones" (*ṣiddīqūn*), a group that he usually connects with the prophets. As one of those who seeks the divine unity, which Junayd defined as "the isolation of the eternal from the temporal," Rūzbihān's interlocutor is interested in unveilings, secrets, manifestations, and divine promptings, which can serve in some sense as a guide for his own inner spiritual life. While Rūzbihān is to a certain extent acting as a spiritual master for his Sufi friend, he does so in an informal manner, occasionally making side remarks to him (e.g., §105, 112, 162, 193). Rūzbihān regularly asks God to assist both him and his friend (§158, 175, 185, 193), but he regards spiritual states and ecstasy as a grace, not as the result of striving, as we see from a passage at the end of the first part:

> Not a day or night has gone by me, by God, during all the time extending up to now, when I am fifty-five years old, without an unveiling of the hidden world. I saw great witnessings, eternal attributes, and exemplary ascensions time and again, and that is from the grace of God Most High toward me. "Grace is from the hand of God, and He gives it to whom he wishes" (Qur'ān 3:73). He chooses for His mercy whom he wishes. Praise be to God who ennobles by these stations his saints and his prophets without cause or reason, not because of striving or discipline, not as the philosophers say – may God purify the earth of them! (§56)

The experiences that Rūzbihān is about to describe constitute a map only insofar as they reveal where he has been. Although he is willing to confide these experiences to an intimate friend, he is not prescribing a method of meditation.

Rūzbihān goes on to describe his own reaction to his friend's request, reflecting that it is very difficult to provide accounts of spiritual experience to the uninitiated, who fail to see the close relationship between the Sufi saints and the prophets:

> This was difficult for me, because there is a great hardship in presenting these stages when the people of conventional knowledge do not comprehend them. So they criticize us and censure that, and they fall into the ocean of affliction. I fear that the people of Muḥammad will fall into denial and opposition, and they will be destroyed, for one who does not believe in the unveilings of the sincere ones disbelieves in the miracles of the prophets and messengers. For the oceans of sainthood and prophethood interpenetrate each other . . . (§5).

So in a sense the need to express the events of his inner life cannot be denied; the proofs of sainthood should be displayed, by implication. As a consequence, Rūzbihān will find it necessary to say something about his own life and circumstances, something that does not prove easy at first.

> My friend, I have delayed your demand for these exemplary stations and these noble states. For I was in my youth, and in the days of my intoxication, extravagance, and effervescence. Unveilings of the angelic world and the manifestation of the wonders of power took place in my heart, spirit, conscience, and intellect. I swam in the primordial and ultimate oceans, in eternity and subsistence, and I discovered the unveiling of Attributes and the Essence, which deaf stones and lofty mountains cannot endure. If I wrote down all that happened to me from the beginning of my life to now, it would be heavy loads of books and pages (§6).

But once Rūzbihān picks up his pen, the revelations begin to flow. Slowly at first, he relates his spiritual experiences and life circumstances from his earliest memories up to the age of fifteen, when he left his profession of selling vegetables and joined the Sufis. Ironically, it is from this brief youthful period as a greengrocer (*baqlī*) that the surname derives, by which Rūzbihān the Sufi is distinguished from several lesser-known religious scholars of the same name who lived in Persia during that time. Nonetheless, it is preferable to refer to him as Rūzbihān, as indeed God does when he calls the saint by name.

Just as he begins the narrative proper, Rūzbihān lets fall another piece of information. "I was fifteen years old when the beginning of these secrets befell my heart," he notes, "and now I am fifty-five years old." So this memoir has been written in the fullness of forty lunar years of a spiritual life, around 577/1181–2. Still, Rūzbihān is somewhat hesitant to begin. "How shall I explain to you the secrets of my unveilings, and my subtle witnessings, things that have escaped you? But I shall explain some things that were unveiled to me in days past, and I shall mention to you what happened to me after that, God willing" (§7).

The overtly chronological memoir forms a relatively small part of the text, and it is worth examining in detail. Rūzbihān's earliest recollections date from the age of three, when he recalls asking other children about the nature of God, a question that caused him to experience an incipient ecstasy.

> Know (may God bless your understanding!) that I was born among ignorant drunkards who had gone astray, and raised by common people of the market, "as though they were asses taking fright, fleeing from a lion" (Qur'ān 74:50-51), up to the age of three. The question occurred to my heart, "Where is your God and the God of the people?" We had a mosque at the gate of my house. I saw some children and asked them, "Do you know your God?" They said, "It is said that he has no hands or feet." For they had heard from their parents that God Most High transcends limbs and members. But when I asked that, I was filled with joy and ran, and something happened to me similar to what happens with the lights of recollection (*dhikr*) and the visitations of meditation, but I did not know the reality of what happened (§8).

Rūzbihān's caustic remarks about his irreligious upbringing are characteristically framed by a scriptural reference. His recollection of this early theological inquiry and response reads back into it the standard Islamic theological position that describes God as beyond physical attributes. From his retrospective position, Rūzbihān analyzes his subsequent spiritual experience as similar to the results of Sufi meditative exercises, though he was incapable of recognizing this at the time.

The next milestone occurred at age seven, where even more Rūzbihān sees the signs of his later dedication to the Sufi life. This is described as a spontaneous mood of recollection (*dhikr*) and obedience of God, followed by a spectacular outburst of passionate love (*'ishq*) leading to ecstasies described in all the vivid metaphors that characterize his later visions.

> I reached the age of seven, and in my heart there occurred a love of recollection (*dhikr*) and obeying Him. I sought my conscience (*sirr*), and I knew it. Then passionate love occurred in my heart, and my heart melted in passionate love. I was then mad with love, and my heart was then a diver in the ocean of eternal recollection and in the scent of the perfumes of sanctity. Then visitations of ecstasies without grief appeared to me, and they agitated my heart with kindness and my eyes with tears. I did not know what it could be except the recollection (*dhikr*) of God Most High. And at that time I was seeing all of existence as though it were beautiful faces, and during this period I grew fond of seclusions, prayers, devotions, and pilgrimage to the great shaykhs (§9).

Here Rūzbihān sees his vocation coming into focus, attributing this precocity to his spontaneous recollection of God, emulating the meditative recollection of divine names in Sufi *dhikr* practice. The experience that follows is typical of the tone of his later visions of creation as a theophany of beauty. Rūzbihān maintains that he then became drawn into the meditative and ritual practices of Sufism, including the desire to visit the tomb-shrines of the great Sufi masters.

All these premonitions and adumbrations of his future life as a Sufi came to a head in an extraordinary moment when Rūzbihān was fifteen.

> When I reached fifteen years, it was as though I was addressed from the hidden world, and it was said to me, "You are a prophet." I said in my conscience, "I have heard from my parents that 'There is no prophet after Muḥammad,' so how can I be a prophet, when I eat and drink, answer the call of nature, and have private parts?" I thought that the prophets do not have these defects. Time passed, and I was lost in passionate love. I arose from my shop after dinner, and I went out into the desert seeking water for ablutions. I heard

> a beautiful voice, and my conscience and my longing were agitated. I said, "You who speak! Stay with me!" I climbed upon a hill near me, and I saw a beautiful person in the form of the shaykhs, but I was unable to speak. He said something concerning the divine unity (*tawḥīd*), but I knew nothing of that. A ravishing and a bewilderment befell me (§10).

This sudden voice that calls out to Rūzbihān announces that he is a prophet, challenging the received wisdom of standard Islamic theology regarding the finality of Muḥammad's prophecy. This passage forms a parallel with his earlier quest to find God at the age of three. There too standard wisdom would have drawn a line beyond which humanity cannot go, but this was refuted by a spontaneous ecstasy. Curiously, Rūzbihān's biographers found this passage controversial, and they suppressed it in their summary of his early life.[13] He himself in retrospect saw nothing problematic about this announcement. Then when a Sufi master appeared speaking enigmatically about the divine unity, Rūzbihān described his reaction using terms that indicate advanced stages of love, "ravishing" (*walah*) and "bewilderment" (*hayamān*).[14] In *The Spirits' Font*, Rūzbihān has referred to being called a prophet as a normal experience.

> The station of God calling out to his friend/saint, calling him to himself with the name of the prophets. This is the station of kindness and the appearance of benevolence, pre-eternal election, and the precedence of post-eternal grace. Sainthood and prophethood are twins, in gnosis. The gnostic says (may God sanctify his conscience), "There is no harm [in that]. He, the transcendent, called him [the saint] by his own eternal name in the moments of union." [The Prophet] (peace be upon him), said, "The scholars of my community are like the prophets of the Israelites."[15]

This goes even further than Rūzbihān's earlier observation that "the oceans of sainthood and prophethood interpenetrate each other" (§5); now they are twins. Rūzbihān's argument here seems to be that if God calls one a prophet or even a divine name, there is no objection, because this is said in the heat of union. From this it might also be concluded that Rūzbihān felt that it was God who addressed him as a prophet. This whole passage, it must be confessed, goes much farther toward erasing the distinction between prophet and saint than most Sufi authorities would allow.

The next stage in this vision led to a dramatic crisis, what may be considered to some extent a conversion scene.

> I was afraid, and people were walking around. I was out in a ruin,[16] and remained there till night fell. Then I left and returned to my shop, and remained there until dawn in ecstasy, grief, sighs, and tears. I was astonished and bewildered. On my tongue without volition came the words, "Your forgiveness! Your forgiveness!" My tongue was stilled, and it was as though I was there for hours and days together. I sat there for another hour. Then ecstasy overwhelmed me, and I threw into the road the money box and whatever was kept in the shop for time of scarcity. I tore my clothes and headed to the desert. I remained in that state a year and a half, ravished and astonished, weeping and ecstatic. Great ecstasies and hidden visitations happened every day. In those ecstasies I saw the heavens, the earth, mountains, deserts, and trees as though all of that were light. Then I settled down from that disturbance (§11).[17]

The emotional consequences of this enigmatic encounter would be typical of Rūzbihān's later experiences – ecstasy, grief, tears, and sighs. He is impelled into dialogue with God, repeating a phrase, "[give us] your forgiveness" (*ghufrānaka*), that in the Qur'ān (2:285) is recited by the faithful who follow and obey the prophets – this evidently does not indicate any unusual amount of sin, but the heightened consciousness of human imperfection found in prophet and saint alike. Finally the moment comes of turning away decisively from the world, typically considered the beginning of the Sufi path. Rūzbihān hurls his possessions into the street and heads to the desert, where he is overwhelmed by ecstasy. Here we see no anguish over conversion as with Augustine, but an ecstatic response to a personal visitation in the form of a Sufi master, though it is not clear whether it was a human, an angel, or God who spoke. His long study and discipline with the Sufis will later give Rūzbihān a vocabulary with which to analyze and describe these early experiences.

Rūzbihān relates his first encounters with the Sufis with scant detail, indicating only that he was shaved in a ceremony signifying his initiation, and that he undertook the customary personal service, devotional exercises, and study of the Qur'ān.

> I recovered from that veiling, and I longed for the service of the Sufis. So I shaved my head, though I had fine and beautiful hair. I entered among the Sufis, and worked in their service, and undertook strivings and exercises. I studied the Qur'ān and memorized it. Most of my time was spent among the Sufis, in ecstasy and spiritual states. But nothing in the way of hidden unveilings happened to me until one day I was on the roof of the *ribāṭ*, meditating on the hidden world. And I saw the Prophet Muḥammad, with Abū Bakr, 'Umar, 'Uthmān, and 'Alī in front of him, and this was my first unveiling (§12).

It is remarkable that Rūzbihān considers ecstasy and spiritual states to be his normal condition during this time. But at this point his first "unveiling" takes place, a vision of the Prophet Muḥammad and his first four successors (*khalīfas*), the Caliphs, who are the forerunners of the Sufi saints in initiatic genealogies. This vision appears to signal at once Rūzbihān's connection to the Prophet Muḥammad and his proximity to those who are his closest heirs.

Up to now Rūzbihān has not found it necessary to mention the names of any of the Sufis with whom he studied or the places where he went. Yet he attained spiritual experiences of a high order, evidently without the benefit of direct guidance of any master, as he next makes clear:

> I did not have a master at that time, and I returned to my home [Pasā] seeking a master and guide who was one of the saved. Then God Most High guided me to Shaykh Jamāl al-Dīn Abī al-Wafā' ibn Khalīl al-Fasā'ī (may God have mercy on him), and he too was a beginner. And God Most High in his company opened to me the doors of dominion and uninterrupted unveilings, and in his company the spiritual states were gushing with hidden sciences and religious mysteries, until innumerable ecstasies and unveilings took place (§13).

We know nothing about Rūzbihān's compatriot and first master, Jamāl al-Dīn, aside from this brief reference. Yet it is striking that Rūzbihān refers to him as also being a beginner (*wa-kāna huwa ayḍan fī badw al-amr*), especially since it is in his company that an astonishing series of revelations begins to take place. Rūzbihān's biographers were apparently uncomfortable with this unknown Sufi colleague, who acted as a guide without being certified by any position of authority or by any known lineage. Shams al-Dīn in fact suppressed the name of Jamāl al-Dīn, when he translated the opening sections of *The Unveiling of Secrets* into Persian while recounting the life of Rūzbihān; according to Shams al-Dīn's edited version in *The Spirits of the Gardens*, Rūzbihān's "innumerable ecstasies and unveilings" were simply a continuation of his vision of the Prophet and the Caliphs, which is now moved to a *ribāṭ* in Pasā.[18] This censorship indicates that the presence of Jamāl al-Dīn, like the heavenly voice that had called Rūzbihān a prophet, was in conflict with the model of sainthood that the hagiographer wished to convey. Instead, the hagiography substitutes a fully detailed initiatic genealogy to guarantee the legitimacy of Rūzbihān's Sufism.

C. Theology, Cosmology, Psychology

Before proceeding further into the exploration of the visions that constitute the bulk of *The Unveiling of Secrets*, it will be helpful to consider them from the viewpoint of the principal Islamic theological terms that form his basic references throughout. The summary that follows is based on well-known materials in the history of Islamic religious thought, highlighting terms and concepts that are defined in the writings of Rūzbihān, to help make intelligible the passages analyzed subsequently. In general terms, there was a fairly widespread consensus of Sufis in the Seljuk period that the theology of al-Ash'arī (d. 324/935) offered an acceptable doctrinal description of the nature of God and humanity. In this position Rūzbihān followed the example of his great predecessor in Shiraz Ibn al-Khafīf (d. 371/981) as well as the Khurasanian Sufi Abū al-Qāsim al-Qushayrī (d. 465/1072). The theological position of Ash'arism was an "orthodox" adaptation of the rationalist theology of the Mu'tazilīs, whose position was generally viewed by Sufis as too intellectual to allow for mystical experience or the omnipotence of God; some Sufis went further in their distrust of rationalism and adopted the pietistic faith of Aḥmad ibn Ḥanbal.[19] To be sure, the Ash'arī position was not without controversy; Qushayrī in particular testifies to violent persecution of Ash'arism in Khurasan at the hands of political figures of a Mu'tazilī persuasion.[20] Polemical remarks in Rūzbihān's theological writings indicate that Mu'tazilism was still a force to be reckoned with in Shiraz in his own day. Nonetheless, the theological categories of Ash'arism had become increasingly common in Sufi circles, because their emphasis on the omnipotence of God and the limitations of reason fit well with the experiential basis of Sufism.

Without attempting to describe the full complexity of Islamic religious thought in the Seljuk period, we can see how Rūzbihān in another text presented a kind of Islamic catechism on basic religious beliefs. This text, *The Paths of Unity*, is a commentary on four principles of faith: the Essence, Attributes, and Actions of God, and the afterlife. The first three of these terms in particular appear over and over in Rūzbihān's descriptions of his visions, so it will be helpful to begin from a basic understanding of the nature of God as Rūzbihān (who, after all, was also a preacher) explained it to for the benefit of his community.

The basic position of Ash'arism on the Essence (*dhāt*) of God is that it is utterly transcendent and unknowable in itself. Beyond that one can only say that God's Essence is one and that it is real existence. As Rūzbihān summarizes:

> He exists eternally without beginning or end. He is really existent, not like the existence of things that depend on something else; his existence depends on itself, without body, substance, or accident, for substance is the locus of accidents. . . . The Essence of him who is exalted does not enter things or depart from them, nor is it a state inhering in something or imposed on it. Rather, he transcends any relation with temporality, for he is one in every respect.[21]

The unknowable Essence of God is, however, knowable only through the divine Attributes (*ṣifāt*), which are commonly considered to be the names of God as mentioned in the Qur'ān:

> He is knowing, powerful, hearing, seeing, speaking, living, willing. These Attributes are eternal without beginning or end in his Essence. It is likewise with all the names and qualities by which he has described himself [in scripture]. He speaks by his speech, knows by his knowledge, wills by his

volition, lives by his life. These Attributes are an augmentation to the Essence, though not in the sense of division, joining, or separation.[22]

What is common to all the divine Attributes is that they are modes through which the Essence can interact with the temporal world. The Attributes of God can be divided into two types: Attributes of majesty that mediate the power and wrath of God, and Attributes of beauty that convey the grace and mercy of God.

On a slightly lower level, everything created may be called a result of the Actions (*af'āl*) of God.

Understand that [everything] from the throne to the earth is the creation of God Most High; everything but his existence is his Action. He brought them into existence from pure non-being. So it is with whatever is originated in his kingdom for eternity without end. The actions of creatures are also the creation of God Most High, although they are acquired by creatures.[23]

Within these parameters adopted from Ash'arism, the Essence, Attributes, and Actions of God are the primary categories for understanding the divine reality and its relation to the world.

Parallel with these categories of the divine nature are several cosmological terms that play an important role in metaphysics. Chief among these are the two terms "throne" (*'arsh*) and "footstool" (*kursī*), ancient symbols drawn from the vocabulary of divine kingship.[24] These are of course the throne and footstool of God, as mentioned in the Qur'ān. The religious imagination has created luxuriant depictions of these entities, as for instance the theory that both throne and footstool are made out of immense jewels, or that the throne is guarded by a winged serpent.[25] These fantasies are usually qualified by the admonition that God does not have spatial attributes, so that throne and footstool should be understood symbolically as referring to God's absolute authority. In any case, the throne is the loftiest thing in the created universe; visually conceived, it is the apex of the cosmos, the point through which the divine nature manifests to creation. It floats upon the waters of the highest firmament, and it radiates lights that attract the spirits of the saints to their divine source.[26]

Rūzbihān frequently uses the phrase "from the throne to the

earth" to indicate all of creation. Other important terms, also Qur'ānic in origin, designate the different worlds or levels of reality in creation. "Kingdom" (*mulk*) usually means the visible world. Opposed to it are two terms, roughly synonymous: "angelic realm" (*malakūt*) and "the hidden world" (*'ālam al-ghayb*).[27] The opposition between the visible world and the hidden world has an eschatological sense in the Qur'ān, as the hidden means the future and especially the afterlife. Sufi references to the hidden world still preserve something of this eschatological meaning, but it now means also the realm of internal consciousness revealed through meditation.[28] Although Neoplatonic philosophers use the term *malakūt* as an equivalent for the realm of intellect, Rūzbihān sees this and the hidden world as the locus for his visionary encounters with angels, prophets, and God, so "angelic realm" is the translation adopted here.[29] He describes it as follows: "The angelic realm of the gnostic is his heart, in which is the world of God, the wonders of God, the rarities of his secrets, the graces of his lights, the manifestation of his Essence and Attributes, and the forms of his Actions. When one's heart takes on this character, it becomes a mirror for the angelic realm of God. He sees in his heart all that is in the angelic realm, either with the [external] eye or as an [internal] witness."[30] As we shall see, Rūzbihān's visions give abundant testimony to the possibility of seeing apparitions from the angelic realm with the physical eye. In between the kingdom and the angelic realm is the world of "might" (*jabarūt*), which philosophers identify as the intermediate realm of Platonic ideas, the world of the imaginal.[31] Rūzbihān sees this more as the locus for experiencing the wrathful and powerful manifestations of the Attributes of majesty.[32]

Another aspect of the divine-human relation is expressed in the relation of eternity to time. The Sufi vocabulary is exceptionally rich in terms describing various shades of emphasis in the concept of timelessness. "Pre-eternity" (*azal*) is eternity conceived as without beginning, deriving from the perception of divine power as pre-existent. "Post-eternity" (*abad*) is eternity without end, an extension of the personal sense of duration in time. Another term, "eternity" (*qidam*) without qualification, is a more general term for timelessness. Rūzbihān reflects on these as follows:

"Pre-eternity" is like "eternity," but eternity is a special

> characteristic and pre-eternity is a special characteristic. Each of them has a taste, a quality, and a name that is closer to one of them than the other. "Pre-eternality" is the appearance of the majesty of primordiality to the spirits, clothing them in the lights of power... . "Post-eternity" is the name of "subsistence," but it is a special characteristic with a special manifestation and a special training. Seeing it necessitates endless passionate love, eternal longing without end, and joy and intimacy with the divine unity.[33]

Using a typical rhetorical device for reinforcing the sense of transcendence, Rūzbihān often doubles these terms, referring to "the pre-eternity of pre-eternities" and "the post-eternity of eternities." The contrasting term is "temporality" (*ḥadath*), which basically means things created in time. "Temporality is the name of something that [at one time] did not exist and then existed. Its reality is that a causal existence based on the knowledge of eternity brings it into existence from non-being."[34]

In terms of mystical psychology, Rūzbihān inherited a highly developed technical terminology relating to the states (*aḥwāl*) and stations (*maqāmāt*) as articulated by earlier Sufis. Since these features of Sufi teaching have been often discussed, this summary will be limited to terms that are characteristic of Rūzbihān.[35] The states are typically looked on as experiences sent by God as graces unasked for, while the stations are the result of the effort and striving of the aspirant. The states are the particular subject of *The Unveiling of Secrets*, as Rūzbihān chronicles the "events of unveilings and the secrets of witnessings" (§4) that have occurred to him. Rūzbihān records these as taking place in a variety of modes. One characteristic mode is the emotional polarity between expansiveness (*basṭ*) and constriction (*qabḍ*), which are responses to the Attributes of majesty and beauty.

> These are two noble states for gnostics. He gives them constriction with the wrath of unity, the veils of authority, the accumulated lights of greatness, and the mounting of magnificence in their hearts, so that they are removed from the qualities of humanity. When he gives them expansiveness, with the beauty and loveliness of the Attributes and the delight of speech [with him], he gives them intoxication and purification with the state of ecstasy, so that they dance and

> listen to music, speaking and giving. The principle of constriction is the annihilation of the conscience in eternity, while the principle of expansiveness is the subsistence of the conscience in the witnessing of post-eternity.[36]

Constriction, as described in *The Unveiling of Secrets*, sometimes resembles a negative spiritual state, a "dry spell," or a dark night of the soul. Rūzbihān does not see this as a fall from grace, however, but as an experience of the divine aspect of wrath; it is just as important as the intoxication of expansiveness.

Other terms of mystical psychology are defined in different writings by Rūzbihān. Particularly useful in this connection is the lexicon of Sufi terminology that forms an appendix to the *Commentary on Ecstatic Sayings*; some of these terms are particularly revealing about the modalities of spiritual states. Also helpful is *The Spirits' Font*, which in its 1001 stations includes many of the idiosyncratic experiences of Rūzbihān. Here I will simply present a number of these definitions as an indication of the phenomenology of spiritual experience as Rūzbihān classified it. Parallel to the state and the station are terms that signify less developed experiences circumscribed by minute qualitive differences. "Moment" (*waqt*) is "the portion of time in meditation (*murāqaba*) between past and future. Its reality is the graces of the hidden that appear in the heart."[37] "Apparition" (*bādī*) is "that light of witnessing which appears in the heart in the moment of meditation, in the form of speech."[38] "Visitation" (*wārid*) is "that which enters the heart and settles in the heart, encountering the conscience. It is unlike the apparition, which appears and disappears. The basis of visitation is the unveiling of the goal of the gnostic, which enters spontaneously, increasing his longing."[39]

Some terms by their very names convey the ability of these experiences to shock and overload the normal faculties of the mind. "Onslaught" (*hujūm*) is "the accumulation of spiritual states and their existence in consciences, and the entry of the spirits into the angelic realm in the form of boldness among the lights."[40] "Overwhelmings" (*ghalabāt*) are "the flight of the spirit in the angelic realm, the journey of the conscience in might, and the assault of attraction in the manifestation of divinity and the essence of pre-eternality, in the form of the quaking of spirits and bodies."[41] "Astonishment" (*ḥayra*) is "something that suddenly enters the heart of the gnostic by the path of meditation, which then astonishes him. He falls into the storm of unknowings and gnosis, so that he knows nothing any more. The basis of astonishment is the relaxation of the conscience from abandoning the search to comprehend the substance of eternity, and entering into the knowledge of fate in the form of total ecstasy."[42] "Ecstasy" (*wajd*) is "the heart's comprehension of the sweetness of encountering the light of pre-eternality, the purity of witnessing, and the delight of speech."[43] All these terms indicate the prevalence of experiences of the numinous power of God.

Certain key terms relate to the domain of sight and inner vision. "Witnessing" (*mushāhada*) is "seeing God with the eye of the spirit, so that one sees his beauty on the level of presence."[44] "Vision of the heart" (*ru'yat al-qalb*) is "gazing at the legacies of the Hidden with the eye of certainty and the realities of faith. Its reality is the encounter of the eye of the spirit with the beauty of might and the angelic realm."[45] This kind of vision is to be distinguished from the veridical dream (*ru'yā ṣāliḥa*), a form of communication traditionally recognized as equivalent to one forty-sixth part of prophecy. While Rūzbihān acknowledges the validity of the veridical dream, and of the inspiration that occurs between waking and dreaming, it is above all the waking vision with which he is concerned.[46] There is a fundamentally visual basis for the common term "manifestation" (*tajallī*), from its root meaning of brilliance and clarity; Rūzbihān defines it as "the dawning of the light of God's care for the hearts of those who care for him."[47] While these visual terms suggest the passivity of mystical experience, other categories emphasize its reciprocal nature, as a process of internal dialogue with God. "Interlocution" (*muḥādatha*) is "the speech of God with the gnostic in the place of stability, in the form of divulging secrets." Much like prayer, "intimate conversation" (*munājāt*) is "the speech of consciences, during the purification of recollection, with the Graceful Forgiver, in the form of indigence."[49]

In any case, Rūzbihān describes mystical experience as oscillating between annihilation and subsistence, two poles that reflect the negation of created qualities and the affirmation of divine ones. "Annihilation" (*fanā'*) is "the departure of knowledge in the witnessing of nearness, the annihilation of the conscience in the light of the Kingdom, the annihilation of existence in the essence of unity, the annihilation of creaturehood in lordship, and the annihilation of humanity in taking on the qualities of God."[50] Its counterpart, "subsistence" (*baqāʾ*), is "the subsistence of the spirit in witnessing without disturbance, the subsistence of the conscience in unity, and the subsistence of creaturehood by the departure of the animal soul."[51]

D. Unveiling and Clothing: The Fundamental Metaphor of Mystical Experience

Throughout the writings of Rūzbihān, and particularly in *The Unveiling of Secrets*, the metaphor of unveiling and clothing runs as a continuous theme. Unveiling, as mentioned above, is a kind of transcendental perception of the divine nature, which by its name still retains the sense of someone ripping off a veil. In a society where veils are associated with the veiling of women, the action of unveiling has the connotation of breaking the barrier of seclusion, of sudden admittance to intimacy. Likewise clothing has many associations of a ceremonial and ritual kind, some of which relate to the investiture ceremonies of the caliphal court and the parallel use of initiatic robes in Sufism. For Rūzbihān, these social connotations are also symbolic of the dynamics of the divine-human relationship. Knowledge of God is a process of unveiling in which the veils of created nature are successively ripped away until, in theory at least, the divine Essence stands revealed. Yet divine manifestation takes place through visual theophanies of the Attributes and Actions, and when God bestows these qualities on a human being, this manifestation bestows on humanity a clothing with divinity (*iltibās*). These two movements of unveiling and clothing create a paradox, however, because any form of manifestation, no matter how exalted, places a barrier between God and humanity; every manifestation is inevitably a veil.

From Rūzbihān's other writings, particularly the *Commentary on Ecstatic Sayings*, it is clear that veiling is not merely an obstacle to vision, but is a symbolism revealing creation as a theophany. Returning to the term "clothing with divinity" (*iltibās*), we find that Rūzbihān links it to two Prophetic sayings that refer to "form" (*ṣūrat*) as the link between God and humanity.[52] First is the well-known saying (recalling Genesis 1:27), "God created Adam in his own form."[53] This asserts that the qualities of God have been made part of human nature at the time of creation (*khalq*). The other *ḥadīth* relates a visionary experience of Muḥammad, which he recalls saying, "I saw my Lord in the most beautiful of forms."[54] Connecting the vision of God's form to the moment of creation is the goal of the Sufi's meditation, in order to follow the injunction of another *ḥadīth*, "take on the qualities of God."[55] "Clothing with divinity" thus means theophany both as the divine mode of creation and as the revelation of beauty in visionary form to the gnostic.[56]

The phenomenology of veiling and unveiling is so important a subject that Rūzbihān has elsewhere devoted an entire treatise to it, the *Commentary on Veils and Coverings*.[57] That text takes the form of a commentary on the Prophetic saying on the 70,000 veils (*ḥujub, astār*) that separate God from creation. Here I would like to examine this pervasive symbolism in *The Unveiling of Secrets*, contrasting unveiling as transcendence with "clothing with divinity" as manifestation. When seen together, these two terms help explain Rūzbihān's visionary encounters with God as an endless game of hide and seek. A typical example of the dialectic between veiling and clothing with divinity is the following passage:

> The wonders of unity appeared to me, but the effects of the world of Actions remained with me. I said, "My God, let me reach you with the quality of isolating unity." Then the world of creation appeared to me as the moon of fourteen days, when it rises like a full moon from the mountain peak, or like the sparks of smokeless flame. God made me enter that world. I shed the skin of external accidents, but I could not get completely rid of them, for that station is the station of sanctity, transcendence, and annihilation. He explained to me there the realities of reality, and my conscience was burned. It was said to me, "This is the world of unicity," and what I read in my book was, "There is nothing like him" (Qur'ān 42:11) (§66).

Here Rūzbihān begins with a revelation that is still linked to the manifestation of divine Attributes, so that he asks God to let him approach through the isolation (*tajrīd*) of unity (*tawḥīd*), that is, through unity stripped bare of any multiple aspect. God shows him a vision of creation transfigured into the world of unicity (*waḥdāniyya*), and Rūzbihān attempts to transcend his limitations by shedding his creaturely qualities as a snake sheds its skin.[58] His effort fails, however, and when God explains reality to him he is consumed. This all constitutes a visionary commentary on a famous Qur'ānic text on God's incomparable transcendent nature. In this example, the actual metaphor of unveiling is barely alluded to in the image of a snake shedding its skin, reinforced by the image of burning away impurities. Still, the problem of transcending created qualities is ambiguously juxtaposed with the manifestation of divine qualities.

Rūzbihān reflects more generally on the problem of representing the divine transcendence in an extended vision that also comments on a Qur'ānic text on God's uniqueness.

> I saw him after midnight as though he appeared in a thousand kinds of beauty, among which I saw a glory of lofty likeness, "and he has the loftiest likeness [in the heavens and the earth,] and he is the mighty, the commanding" (Qur'ān 30:27). It was as though it were like the glory of the red rose, and this is a likeness. But God forbid that he have a likeness – "There is no likeness unto him" (Qur'ān 42:11). Yet I cannot describe except by an expression, and this description is from the perspective of my weakness and incapacity and my lack of comprehension of the qualities of eternity. In the river bed of pre-eternity there are deserts and wastelands in which dwell the snakes of wrath. If one of then opened its mouth, none of creation or temporality would escape. Beware one who describes the pre-eternal dominator, for in the oceans of his unicity all spirits and consciences are drowned, and they vanish in the sublimities of his greatness and might (§87).

Rūzbihān struggles to conceptualize his overwhelming vision of the divine beauty in the theophany of the red rose. Although there are scriptural supports for conceiving God through a likeness, they are opposed to another trend that powerfully insists on the incomparability of the divine nature. Rūzbihān confesses that this is the fundamental problem of the inadequacy of symbolism, but to convey this he ironically resorts to more dramatic symbols of divine wrath (snakes, oceans) to indicate how likenesses are consumed in infinity.

The oscillation between divine manifestation and concealment is vividly conveyed in a dramatic passage from the diary that recounts in nuanced detail the experiences of the Sufi's questing soul, portrayed as a bird in flight, as it ascends but is thwarted by its own limitations.

> I saw God from one of the windows of the angelic realm in a form that would have melted all creation from sweetness and pleasure. He spoke to me and was kind to me repeatedly. I remained thus until the time of the call to prayer. The doors of the hidden opened, and my bird flew away in the form of thought and temporality, seeking the beauty of the merciful, who is exalted and sanctified. But it was not able to traverse existence, because it reached the crossing point of temporality by knowledge, not by witnessing, and beyond that it saw nothing but blindness and imagination. It did not perceive anything of the lights of sanctity, and it suffered, returned, and hesitated for a long time. God manifested in the form of beauty, and he put me in his vision with perfect longing for his nearness and union. Then he hid and I was idle. He manifested in the form of majesty, and made me bewildered and passionate with his countenance. Then he abandoned me and hid, and the sweetness of witnessing him remained in my heart. The scents of the breezes of holiness dried up in the station of intimacy, and the light of awe filled my heart, as though God were next to me in the form of greatness, suddenly. My thoughts and heart were confused, and my spirit flew, and my intellect fled, and my secrets cooled off, and my ecstatic moment was joyful. He displayed to me the light of his glory (§160).

What is striking about this account is the sense of movement and encounter, a back and forth between the soul and God that is never resolved. The ascent of the soul is blocked, God manifests and hides, but there is no finality; this alternation between manifesting and hiding occurs in dozens of passages. The problem is insoluble through knowledge, for that leads only to blindness and (as Rūzbihān says elsewhere) unknowing; for Rūzbihān, only mystical modes of experience such as witnessing serve as a medium for encountering God.

At times Rūzbihān was frustrated with the limitations of vision, and demanded that God take him beyond to the divine Essence.

> I saw God in the form of majesty and beauty, force and

> greatness; I saw by intimations of clothing with divinity, and I said, "My God, my friend, and my lord, how long will you make me see the chosen vision within the limits of clothing with divinity? Show me pure eternity and subsistence!" And he said, "Moses and Jesus perish in this station." And God revealed himself in an atom of the light of his eternal essence, and my spirit nearly vanished. Because of that I feared death and the end of my life in that interval, in my condition at that hour (§45).

Even a hint of the revelation of the Essence is almost enough to destroy the visionary. Yet he must continue to ask for vision and more than vision, like a beggar.

> God unveiled to me the veils of greatness, and I saw beyond the veils a majesty, force, power, and might, and oceans and lights, which are impossible to show to creation. I was at the door of greatness like a bewildered beggar. He spoke to me from the pavilions of greatness, saying, "Beggar! How did you get here?" I felt expansive toward him and said, "My God, my friend, and my lord! From your favor, generosity, and munificence" (§55).

The tension between absolute transcendence and the necessity of manifestation is never abolished. Rūzbihān insists on both, and it is the movement between the two that creates the dynamism of his experience.

In order to express the transcendence of God, Rūzbihān occasionally resorts to conventional theological language, particular the formula "without [asking] how" (*bi-lā kayf*); pietist groups such as the Ḥanbalīs and Ash'arīs used this phrase to insist on the literal truth of seemingly anthropomorphic scriptural passages without engaging in intellectual speculation about their modality.

> He transcends change in his singleness and cannot be encompassed by his creation. I was watching God, awaiting the unveiling of Attributes and the lights of the Essence, and God manifested his eternal face "without how" to my heart; it was as though I was looking at him with the external eye, and the hidden world shone from the appearance of his glory. Then he appeared and hid, repeatedly (§92).

For Rūzbihān this phrase "without how" indicates more than an abstract fideist creed; it describes a vision that cannot be described. In another example, we see Rūzbihān rejecting the forms that appear to his eyes, seeking a transcendental vision, but despite this God manifests to him in a human likeness.

> Whenever wonders of the hidden appeared to me as shapes, I rejected them, until I saw God "without how," with the quality of majesty and beauty. . . . Then I was astonished in the primordiality of God, and I saw him in the most beautiful of forms. I thought in my heart, "How did you fall from the world of unity to the station of symbols?" He came near and took my prayer carpet, saying, "Stand! What are these thoughts? You doubt me, so I made a likeness of my beauty in your eye, so you would be familiar with me and love me." There were lights of majesty and beauty upon him the number of which I could not count. Then I saw him at every moment in the beauty of another [form] (§117).

Although the manifestation of God in form is in tension with his transcendence, both modes are inherent in the divine nature as seen from the human perspective.

When Rūzbihān meditates on divine transcendence, he sometimes appears almost to be trying to convince himself that visions are really not to be relied upon. He asserts standard formulas about how God is above all created things, neither similar to creation through anthropomorphism (*tashbīh*), nor cut off from it by abstraction (*ta'ṭīl*). But suddenly he is taken off guard by a divine manifestation, and God appears to him in a beautiful form.

> God transcends space and time. I said to myself, "If anything like these existents and temporality existed now as [real] existence, then the like of that would exist forever, above and below, to the right and left, before and behind. This is God, who transcends all of that [creation] and [any] incarnation in it. How will one seek God, and who will see him, if God does not want to manifest his essence to him? He subsists in his essence in pre-eternity and post-eternity." I was astonished by seeking, and when I saw him in the form of majesty and beauty in my house "in the most beautiful of forms," I was ravished, in love, and in longing, and my love and affection increased. In

> my ecstasy and spiritual state my heart did not remember the story of anthropomorphism and abstraction, for in seeing him, the traces of intellects and sciences are erased (§157).

Theological formulas vanish before visions.

Rūzbihān occasionally uses a rhetorical device of doubling his terms to indicate divine transcendence. In this way he can apply a defined descriptive term to God, but at the same time he indicates that God is beyond the limitations of the term: "That is the state of the nearness of nearness, the proximity of proximity, the union of union. That remained until he annihilated everything except for him from my thought and my conscience. I remained in that, in the essence of the essence, and the reality of reality (§126)." This rhetorical doubling of terms signifies the transcendence of the limitations of the term while preserving its modality.

Rūzbihān does defend the legitimacy of visions, however. After recounting a vision in which the angels and the prophets weep at hearing Rūzbihān's words, and God murmurs his approval, he addresses his reader as follows:

> My son, whoever has suspicions about these unveilings does so with the suspicion of anthropomorphism; he will not attain union nor achieve results, though he scent the fragrances of sanctity and intimacy. These are the experiences of the holy, the intentions of the sublime, and the stations of the transcendentals[59] among the perfect ones. The people of religion recognize that they are lordly commands, appearances of the lights of eternity, and qualities of the Attributes by means of the Actions (§84).

Visions are not the results of an anthropomorphic theory, but the products of divine favor. Those who reduce unveilings to the status of abstract doctrine are, in Rūzbihān's view, incapable of experiencing them.

Visionary experience is not, however, just any kind of bizarre internal occurrence. Rūzbihān displays a keen sense of differentiating kinds of internal experience that are to be rejected because their source can be traced to lower psychological faculties.[60] This discrimination still leads him to a positive evaluation of visions and likenesses of God, since knowing God as manifest through these veils is necessary before one can know God as hidden.

> One night I was confronted with psychic imaginations, trivial imaginations, and spiritual imaginations. I tore their veils and saw their graces, and I thought about some of their shapes, from the sight of which my heart fled. My breast was constricted by the vision of some of them, and I was astonished at my [low] degree, until the beauty of God appeared to me suddenly, and there was such loveliness and beauty that I cannot describe it. I said, "My God! What are these likeness in which I have been veiled before witnessing?" He said, "This is for one who seeks me in the first unveilings of my majesty, until he knows me through these veils, and this is the station of gnosis; one who does know me through them is not a [true] knower of me. This is the station of striving of the people of witnessing." Then he made me enter the veils of the hidden, and showed me his attributes with most of the clothing of majesty and beauty. Then he hid, and I abased myself before him, because I found the sweetness of union and the pleasure of longing for beauty (§180).

Once again, veiling is inseparable from divine manifestation, as transcendence is inseparable from the hidden.

The appearance of God in visionary forms extended even to Rūzbihān's experience of other people, and indeed of the whole world. In a characteristic meditation invoking the romance of Joseph and Zulaykhā (as told in sura 12 of the Qur'ān), Rūzbihān is immersed in a theophany of divine beauty.

> Then his beauty appeared to me in different kinds of people, all being kind to me due to my subsistence after annihilation in the qualities of pre-eternity. He wined me with the wine of intimacy and nearness. Then he left and I saw him as the mirror of creation wherever I faced, and that was his saying, "Wheresoever you turn, there is the face of God" (2:109). Then he spoke to me after increasing my longing for him, and that was after I had a thought, and said to myself, "I want to see his beauty without interruption." He said, "Remember the condition of Zulaykhā and Joseph, for Zulaykhā depicted her form to Joseph in all six directions, so that Joseph did not see in any direction without seeing her form there. This is your condition in the abode of my majesty." I saw God from every atom, though he transcends

> incarnation and anthropomorphism. But he is a secret known only to those drowned in the oceans of unity and to the knower of the secret of the actions of eternity in the station of passionate love (§191).

When Rūzbihān warns the reader against interpreting this vision in terms of the heresies of incarnation and anthropomorphism, he indicates that this is instead a vision of divine beauty that inspires love.

Within the overall context of unveiling and clothing with divinity, Rūzbihān interprets mystical experience as exclusively a product of divine grace. No amount of theorizing about divine Attributes or operations can bring about vision.

> This is a spiritual state, and its secret is not made possible by the articulation of these lordly secrets, the production of the Attribute, the appearance of graces, sufficing mercy, or restful blessing. He arouses affection in his servants who are gnostics and lovers, and were it not for his favor, how would they comprehend the lights of the sublimities of his face, from keeping company with the accidents of temporality? If he appeared with the perfection of his power, all of creation would be consumed. Do not be concerned, my friend; the like of these unveilings have descended upon most prophets and the sincere ones, but they have not reported it except by the utterance of "clothing with divinity." He transcends anyone conceiving his Essence and Attributes by the attributes of individuals (§112).

The reports about God from prophets and saints are not deceptive, because they are based on genuine unveiling, transmitted again through the forms of prophetic and saintly reports that are theophanic "clothings with divinity," though these reports are admittedly limited and will not by themselves recreate the unveiling for anyone.

So markedly did unveiling dominate Rūzbihān's inner life that he evidently abandoned at a fairly early stage in his life the specific meditative exercises that the Sufis call "discipline" (*riyāḍa*) and "striving" (*mujāhida*), and even the *dhikr* chanting or recollection of the names of God. In a highly unusual passage, he recalls having abandoned these practices for over twenty years, suggesting that this abrupt departure from standard Sufi exercises took place when Rūzbihān was thirty-five.

> I recalled the days of discipleship, and the requirements of striving that overwhelmed me, and their falling away from my heart for a space of twenty years. I remained without discipline or striving, and the chants (*adhkār*) of the masters and their many preceding disciplinary exercises fell away from my heart, as though I did not approve of them in the court of gnosis. For gnosis with me makes use of grace and things besides them [i.e., besides discipline and striving], for that is the gnosis of the common people. But I rejected my thought in that, and was concerned whenever a thought occurred to my heart. A visitation of the hidden befell me and God was unveiled to me twice. The first time was in the form of beauty, and the second time in the form of greatness. I looked at the beauty of his face with the eye of the heart, and he said to me, "How can they reach me by strivings and disciplines, if my noble face remains veiled to them? These are the elite among my lovers and the near ones among the gnostics; there is no way to me except through me, and by the unveiling of my beauty." After the ecstasies, the spiritual states, and the visitation, I returned to the creed of unity and the election of his favor through what he wishes, to whom he wishes, as he wishes: "Grace is in the hands of God, he gives it to whom he wills" (57:29). And the sweetness of that remained until I slept (§164).

Even as Rūzbihān recalled his unusual departure from Sufi practice, he found this thought to be a distraction from his quest from vision, and indeed in the subsequent experience God spoke directly to the problem of grace in relation to effort and discipline. The answer is unambiguous: grace, as experienced through the ensemble of mystical experiences, is the only avenue to the fullest experience of God.

E. Theophanies of Majesty

The manifestations of the divine Attributes are divided into two basic categories, majesty (*jalāl*) and beauty (*jamāl*). This standard Islamic division of divine aspects can also be described in terms of wrath (*qahr*) and grace (*lutf*).[61] Though dualistic in appearance, this is a way of portraying God's activity in relation to the world in terms of polarity. This classification of divine Attributes into majesty and beauty is well known among Sufis, and was probably developed initially in Sufi circles because of the experiential results of meditating on the divine names. Hujwīrī links majesty with the experience of awe (*haybat*) and beauty with the experience of intimacy (*uns*). He states that "those whose witness in gnosis is the beauty of God continually long for vision (*ru'yat*), while those whose witness is the majesty of God continually reject their own qualities, and their hearts are in the state of awe."[62] Beginning with the theophanies of majesty, I include under this heading several kinds of unveilings: all the visions having to do with authority, including the initiatic visions revealing the status of Rūzbihān; visions that describe the relationship between saints and prophets as spiritual authorities; and pure theophanies of divine power.

It may seem odd at first glance to devote so much time to visions about the status of Rūzbihān and other saints, since they apparently concern human beings rather than the divine Attributes of majesty. After all, the witnessing of the Attributes of majesty is supposed to engender an abhorrence of flawed human characteristics. In placing Rūzbihān's initiatic visions under the heading of theophanies of majesty, I suggest that the key to his rhetoric of sainthood rests on experiences that take on the divine qualities of authority. Far from being fanciful products of cosmically inflated egotism, these visions partake of the awe-inspiring majesty of God's own authority. Sufi tradition has incorporated into its earliest dialogical pronouncements the rhetorical features of the pre-Islamic Arabs' boasting contest (*mufākhara*).[63] Statements regarding one's spiritual authority partook of the ritual form of the boasting contest, even as they served as evidence of one's spiritual state. This well-established interpretive principle was basic to the understanding of ecstatic utterances in general, as when Ḥallāj's dictum "I am the Real (the Truth, God)" was understood as evidence of the annihilation of his ego. For Rūzbihān's visionary mode of experience, there can be no knowledge of the transcendent divine Essence without vision; consequently, there can be no knowledge of God without visionaries. His is a mystical universe; it should not be surprising that mystics play the most crucial role within it. As with Ibn 'Arabī, the creation – and above all the saint – is essential to the manifestation of God.

Initiatic Visions

Rūzbihān's visions record his spiritual authority in varied forms. One of the most striking visionary sequences draws on the ancient cosmic symbolism of the world-axis, or pole (*quṭb*), which in Sufi thought is the title of the highest office in the invisible hierarchy of 360 saints; Rūzbihān has himself elaborated on the nature of the hierarchy in several of his other writings.[64] In this early vision, two mysterious figures dressed like Sufi masters, but looking just like Rūzbihān, prepare for him a meal consisting of pure white bread buttered with the oil of the Little Bear. This pronouncement is not so enigmatic as it first appears; the constellation of the Little Bear (Ursa Minor) happens to be the constellation closest to the celestial north pole (also called *quṭb* in Arabic), around which the heavens revolve.[65] The idea of "the oil of the Little Bear" is apparently that of a spiritual oil reduced as an essence from the milk of the Little Bear. Here is the text, recording a vision seen on the roof of Rūzbihān's house:

> I saw two handsome shaykhs in Sufi dress, who looked like me. I saw a kettle suspended in the air, and the sticks of the two shaykhs burned with a subtle burning, without smoke. I saw a tablecloth hanging from their tent. I greeted them, and they smiled, facing me; they were good-looking shaykhs. One of them took his tablecloth and opened it up, and in the tablecloth was a lovely bowl and some loaves of pure white bread. He broke some of the loaves in the bowl and over the bowl he upended the [contents of the] kettle, which was like a pale oil, weightless but with a subtle spiritual substance. He gestured to me, indicating that I should eat, so I ate it. They ate a little with me, until I ate it all. One of them said, "Don't you know what was in the kettle?" I said, "I don't know." He said, "This is the oil of the Little Bear; we got it for you." When I got up, I thought about it, but it was some time later that I realized that this was an allusion to the seven poles (*quṭbs*) in the angelic realm. God Most High chose me for the pure essence of their stations, and that is the rank of the seven

> who are on the face of the earth. Then I turned toward [the stars of] the Little Bear, and I saw that they were seven windows, from all of which God manifested to me. I said, "My God! What is this?" God, who transcends every imagination, said, "These are the seven windows of the throne" (§19).

In this vision, the symbolism only became clear to Rūzbihān after some thought. The entire incident shows him absorbing the spiritual essence of the seven stars that indicate the seven *quṭb*s or poles of the world. In the sequence following this vision (§20–21, with polar language echoed again in §85–86 and §185), Rūzbihān keeps vigil on these stars as "windows" to heaven, and God manifests to him from the Little Bear and causes him to undergo untold transformations, until he announces, "I have chosen you in your time for this station over all creatures." The initiation that began with the heavenly meal, administered by figures symbolizing Rūzbihān's inner self, culminates with the affirmation of his status as the unique spiritual figure of the age. The archaic cosmic substratum to the vision reinforces the importance of the visual world as the locus of spiritual manifestation.

The initiatic visions of Rūzbihān actually begin from the very first unveiling. Immediately after recounting his sojourn in Pasā with Shaykh Jamāl al-Dīn, Rūzbihān records a direct revelation of his own spiritual authority.

> I saw God on the roof of my house, with the qualities of might, majesty, and eternity. I saw as it were the world entire, a resplendent light, manifold and great. And he called me from the midst of the light, in the Persian tongue, seventy times: "Rūzbihān, I have chosen you for sainthood (*wilāya*) and selected you for love. You are my friend (*walī*) and lover. Fear not nor sorrow, for I am your God, and I keep watch over you in your every aim." I was kneeling, and I kneeled repeatedly. Then oceans of ecstasies seized me, I was overwhelmed by sobbing and increasing cries; I received much blessing from that (§14).

As Chodkiewicz points out, the injunction neither to fear nor sorrow is an allusion to the Qur'ānic passage (10:62) most frequently quoted in reference to sainthood: "The friends of God have no fear over them, neither do they sorrow."[66] From the beginning of his spiritual career, Rūzbihān is certified as a "friend of God" (*walī*) or saint.

Rūzbihān's visions frequently allude to his status as the unique saint of his age. Nowhere is this more dramatically affirmed than in an extended sequence (§47–49) that culminates in the identification of Rūzbihān as the vicegerent (*khalīfa*) of God on earth. It is important to realize that this office is to be distinguished from *khalīfa* as vicegerent or successor to the Prophet, i.e., caliph. Being vicegerent of God is a role that the Qur'ān assigns explicitly to Adam (2:30), so Rūzbihān is here singled out for a particularly cosmic role.[67] This vision begins with revelations of God's beauty in a scene of great intimacy; after tender conversations, Rūzbihān recalls, "he gave me to drink wines from his presence, wines that I am unable to describe" (§47). At this point Rūzbihān inquires about the prophets, and God informs him that they have been annihilated in divinity. Nonetheless, they appear, along with the first four caliphs and all the angels, and God showers everyone with roses and pearls. After Rūzbihān receives a kiss from all the prophets, angels, and caliphs, God announces to them all:

> I have chosen my servant Rūzbihān for eternal happiness, sainthood (*wilāya*), and bounty, and I have placed in him the receptacles of my knowledge and my secret; the affairs of separation will not befall[68] him after that. I have preserved him from disobeying me after that, and I have made him one of the people of stability and rectitude. He is my vicegerent (*khalīfa*) in this world and all worlds; I love whosoever loves him, and I hate whosoever hates him. None disobeys my judgements, and none rejects my order, for I am "one who acts when he wishes" (Qur'ān 107:11) (§49).

This breathtaking display of divine authority before the supreme leaders of heaven and earth serves to indicate only one thing: Rūzbihān is appointed as God's deputy over creation. Having received the divine knowledge and secret, Rūzbihān is also (in language reminiscent of the attributes of the Shī'ī imams) "protected" (*'aṣamtuhu*, related to *ma'ṣūm*) from sin or disobedience to God.

On one other occasion Rūzbihān returns to this same statement of his selection as vicegerent over creation. In this case the announcement is couched in associations that even more forcefully assert the divine authority, using some of the trappings of Persian royal symbolism that will be discussed in further detail below. As the vision commences, Rūzbihān sees God playing the lute at the door of the *ribāṭ*, causing happiness in all creation. From this light moment the vision shifts into the category of majesty:

> I saw him frequently before that, above every above, playing on drums (*ṭabūl*). By that he indicates that he does this to display my authority (*salṭanatī*). He selected me in my time for authority and vicegerency (*khilāfa*) over the world. This and similar things are examples of the display of election, acceptance, being chosen, and true union. He transcends what the hearts of cherubs and spirituals think, and what the hearts of mortals think. These are the manners of his favor to the saints, and there are many similar things in hadith. How is this related to the saying of the leader of the messengers, prophets, and saints? Anyone who thinks that I am dubious, after the display of these unveilings, is a fool who has not scented a single fragrance of the ecstasies of the saints and the raptures of the Sufis, by which they understand the symbolic hadith. He [the Prophet] said, "God Most High will show the form of his Essence in the way that he wishes" (§114).

The drums are the ritual court accessories of Persian kingship, a jealously guarded privilege.[69] They are a sign of Rūzbihān's authority (*salṭana*), a term related to *sulṭān*, "emperor." His selection as vicegerent is part of God's grace to the saints, and the proof is supplied by unveilings that only idiots would deny.

On numerous other occasions, Rūzbihān is confirmed in his special status as the object of God's love; he is the beloved of God. God has come repeatedly on pilgrimage to Rūzbihān's home town, long before the saint was created. "He said, '70 times I came to seek you from the wombs of the hidden before I created you, and I visited your places for you, though between me and that region and the hidden were deserts and oceans, a journey of more than 70,000 years.' Then he approached me until he drew near, and drew near, until I was hidden and annihilated" (§111, recalled again at §163). God announces to the inhabitants of heaven, "People of paradise! I come every day 70,000 times to this window from the world of eternity, and I look upon paradise with longing for the meeting with Rūzbihān" (§96).[70] On many occasions God caressingly or thunderingly calls Rūzbihān by name (§52, 94, 104, 133, 135, 204). Rūzbihān joins the prophets and angels in flight like a falcon, returning to the wrist of God to receive his endearments (§194). God sits with him and weeps like a lover, assuring him that he helps him and watches over him while he sleeps (§198). "Here I was the beloved of God, and he loved me and was kind to me with a kindness that none of God's creatures could bear to hear of if I told them, except what God wills" (§148).

Rūzbihān's authority is further confirmed by the Prophet Muḥammad, who appears in many visions. On several occasions, the Prophet (followed by other prophets and saints), kisses Rūzbihān in scenes with strong initiatic associations, sometimes also giving him a date to eat and a turban (§29, 49, 201). One lengthy encounter takes place in the deserts of eternity:

> I was seeking God in the deserts of the hidden. I saw Muḥammad on the paths of those deserts; his stature is like Adam's, and he was wearing a white shirt and a pure white turban; his face was like a red rose. The Attributes announce him, smiling, as his face advances upon the world of eternity in search of God. When he saw me, he drew near me; we were like two strangers in the desert with the same destination and purpose. He was kind to me and said, "I am a stranger, and so are you; come with me in these deserts so that you may seek God." So we went on the path for 70,000 years, sitting at certain places to eat and drink. He fed me and treated me kindly, like a stranger dealing compassionately with another stranger. When we approached the curtain of eternity and the pavilions of pre-eternity, we stopped for a long time, and did not see God. We were concerned about his absence. Then God appeared to Muḥammad, and I saw him; perhaps he left him alone, but I was looking at God and how he dealt with his beloved. Time passed, and secrets occurred between them of which I was unaware. I thought in my heart that I saw them both, and they both have accepted me (§120).

This vision is more ambiguous; Rūzbihān is present primarily as a witness and follower of the Prophet in an enigmatic itinerary in search of God, but the end result is that he is accepted by both God and the Prophet.

Rūzbihān's initiatic scenarios include other prophets besides Muḥammad. In a vision that recalls the vision of Ezekiel in the Hebrew Bible (Ezekiel 3:1-3), Rūzbihān receives the holy books of the major prophets and eats the scriptures, signifying his complete internalization of their inspiration:

> I saw in the hidden world a world illuminated from a shining light. I saw God in the clothing of majesty, beauty, and glory; he poured me a drink from the ocean of affection, and he honored me with the station of intimacy. He showed me the world of holiness, and when I passed through the atmosphere of eternity, I stopped at the door of power. I saw all the prophets present there; I saw Moses with the Torah in his hand, Jesus with the Gospel in his hand, David with the Psalms in his hand, and Muḥammad with the Qur'ān in his hand. Moses gave me the Torah to eat, Jesus gave me the Gospel to eat, David gave me the Psalms to eat, and Muḥammad gave me the Qur'ān to eat. Adam gave me the most beautiful names [of God] and the Greatest Name to drink. I learned what I learned of the elect divine sciences for which God singles out his prophets and saints (§32).

The kinds of knowledge bestowed upon Rūzbihān were by no means to be a degree inferior to the knowledge of the prophets. He saw God manifest to him as God manifested to Adam in paradise, and to Muḥammad at "the lotus of the boundary" (Qur'ān 53:14) (§102). Replicating these prophetic experiences is implied by Rūzbihān's statement that "the oceans of sainthood and prophethood interpenetrate each other . . . ." (§5). This principle receives form in visions showing the prophets and the angels dressed as venerable Sufi masters, in the company of great historical Sufis, before all of whom Rūzbihān performs as a lute player or an intoxicated dancer (§130, 188).

Rūzbihān even goes to the extent of characterizing his unveiling by the term "revelation" (*waḥy*), a term usually reserved for the experience of the prophets as distinct from the "inspiration" (*ilhām*) of the saints. In a rare allusion to his poetry, Rūzbihān characterizes it as a byproduct of this revelation. He goes on to cite a Qur'ānic passage that refers to God's loving oversight of the abandoned infant Moses, implicitly comparing his revelation with that of the Israelite prophet.

> He agitated me so that I would compose poetry, and applaud, and weep, and he made me pass away. May God endow us and you with abundant great miracles and exemplary gifts! The source of this unveiling is the encounter with special revelation (*waḥy*), after I awoke but before I arose from my bed. He said, "I endowed you with a love from me, so that you would be nourished in my sight" (Qur'ān 20:39). I knew that he would come with gifts of secrets and sparks of light (§185).

The vision concludes with God summoning Rūzbihān to the celestial pole again, another allusion to his spiritual status. Elsewhere (§187) Rūzbihān consoles himself for his suffering (the death of a favorite wife) with a Qur'ānic passage (68:1–4) addressed to Muḥammad, reassuring himself of divine favor. None of these passages goes to the extent of the strange announcement at the beginning of Rūzbihān's career, that identified him as a prophet. Still, that unsettling comparison reverberates at a distance in these visions where Rūzbihān adopts prophetic qualities. The relation between prophecy and sainthood will be taken up in more detail later on.

A further set of initiatic visions show Rūzbihān in relation to the great Sufi saints of the past and to figures such as 'Alī and Khiḍr who play special initiatic roles in Sufism. There is even a brief appearance by the founders of the four Sunnī legal schools (al-Shāfi'ī, Abū Ḥanīfa, Mālik, and Aḥmad ibn Ḥanbal), all with shaven heads like Sufi novices, to congratulate Rūzbihān (§199). One initiatic vision portrays Rūzbihān swimming across an ocean of knowledge that had previously only been crossed by 'Alī (§17); as we shall see below (p. 123), this vision was reinterpreted by Rūzbihān's descendents in the direction of 'Alid pietism, to become an instance of the grace of 'Alī rather than the attainment of Rūzbihān. Similar is another early vision in which the immortal spiritual guide Khiḍr offers Rūzbihān the literal fruit of gnosis:

> At that time I was ignorant of the sciences of realities. I saw Khiḍr (peace be upon him), and he gave me an apple, and I

> ate a piece of it. Then he said, "[Eat] all of it, for that is how much of it I ate." I saw as it were an ocean from the throne to the earth, and I saw nothing but this. It was like the radiance of the sun, and my mouth opened involuntarily, and all of it entered into my mouth. Not a drop remained but I drank it (§16).

Here, as Ballanfat points out, the image of the apple recalls the fruit of Paradise eaten by Adam, but for Rūzbihān it is a necessity for attaining gnosis of divine truths rather than a forbidden fruit.[71] In both these visions, the initiation presided over by the esoteric teacher signifies the transmission of a knowledge that is truly oceanic in character.[72]

Not all of the initiatic visions are clear assertions of Rūzbihān's authority, or at least we should stipulate that the role he is to play was not always clear. This is the case in a disturbing vision that links Rūzbihān with the figures from the invisible hierarchy of saints known as the Substitutes (*abdāl*), next in importance to the Pole. Here is how Rūzbihān saw himself in relation to them:

> I plunged at the crack of eternal dawn into the blood of the Substitutes, and he manifested that to me, and I was dyed in the blood of the Substitutes. I said to myself, "Who am I among them? Perhaps I am one of them." I saw a dye more delicate than that dye, above their dye, and he indicated that that was my blood. I went into ecstasy from joy, and cried out repeatedly (§158).

This certainty did not remain, for on reflection Rūzbihān wondered if this vision might be related to an earlier experience in which he saw himself slaughtered by God, so that his blood filled ditches and the angels anointed themselves in it (§28); it was possible that the new vision was a portent of disaster, as the previous one had turned out to be. But he asked God's help and quickly lost himself in the stations of intimacy. This identification of Rūzbihān with the rank of the Substitutes does not seem to have been of great importance, given his other visions relating to the Pole and other positions, but he later briefly records seeing the Substitutes in the company of Khiḍr and Ilyās and the Sufi saints, performing curious actions (§173, 181).

As discussed above, Rūzbihān makes scarcely any mention of

living Sufis, but from an early age he had been drawn to perform pilgrimage to the shrines of the saints of old. At the concluding part of his reminiscences of youth, we find Rūzbihān relating a series of pilgrimages to Sufi tombs in the region of Fars (§41–44). These were not exactly well-organized tourist trips, as he and his companions sometimes lacked transport animals, and at other times got lost at night in frightening places like "the pass of the jinn." During this journey, Rūzbihān and his companions were once saved by an apparition of a tenth-century Sufi named Shaykh Fāris Abū Muslim of Pasā, and when they reached Pasā they went to the shaykh's tomb to ask pardon for some unspecified transgression. There Rūzbihān had a vision of "the masters of Abū Yazīd," evidently the masters of the great early Sufi Abū Yazīd Bistāmī, among the descendants of the shaykh buried there. This led to a further series of visions in which Rūzbihān saw himself identified as the "camel of God" of Qur'ān 7:73, a point confirmed in a vision of Shaykh Fāris and the most famous saint of Shiraz, Shaykh Abū 'Abd Allāh ibn Khafīf. Although the content of this unveiling is elusive, it is significant that famous Sufis of earlier centuries come forth to affirm the status of Rūzbihān.

The role of the local saints of Fars was extremely important in the certification of Rūzbihān's position, but the initiatic visions reporting these affirmations pertain only to saints of the past. In one instance Rūzbihān reports,

> I saw myself as though I were in Shiraz, and the doors of heaven opened, until I saw the throne and the footstool. I saw the master Abū 'Abd Allāh ibn Khafīf and all the masters separating and gathering, as if they were anticipating that God would summon me there. God manifested to them and they were sighing and moaning in that moment, and all of that was from their longing for me (§103).

This general appreciation of Rūzbihān by the saints of Shiraz had a particular significance when he was living in Pasā, and was thinking about moving to Shiraz. At that time a confirmatory vision involving the saints of both places testified to good auguries for the move. Rūzbihān saw himself in a graveyard in Pasā, and saw a saint leave his tomb wearing red clothes, with a red hat on his head. When he stood, all the masters of Pasā stood with him. Then they came with him to Shiraz, and when they drew near

Shiraz, all the masters of Shiraz arose from their tombs to welcome them, until they reached the town (§136).

Beyond the circle of local saints, Rūzbihān relates striking visions that show his relationship to the most famous of early Sufis. These visions partake of the rhetoric of boasting to a remarkable degree; the assertions made here by Rūzbihān are so extravagant that they deserve a full scrutiny, so that all the nuances may come out. Here is one:

> Then I saw Shaykh Abū ʻAbd Allāh ibn Khafīf, Abū Isḥāq Shahryār, Junayd, Ruwaym, Bāyazīd al-Bisṭāmī, and all the masters go on horseback together to God. They were standing before God, and Junayd and Abū Yazīd and several great masters saluted me, wishing to come nearer to God than I was. They all longed for him, and they shouted, turned away, and agitated, so that the world trembled from them. I saw God on a holy mountain, and he made me approach. The mountain was high, and God had me sit near him, and repeatedly poured me the wines of intimacy. He graced me in a form that I cannot tell to any of God's creatures, and he was unveiled and there manifested from him the lights of his beautiful attributes. The Sufis were on the foothill of that mountain, unable to ascend the mountain, and God called that mountain Mt. Greatness. The lights of the world of unicity were joined to that mountain. I was intoxicated there, in such a state that the people of the world would melt from the extreme beauty. God clothed me with the sublimities of his description, and he was scattering red roses on my face and tresses. A rose fell from my face in the midst of the Sufis, and they shouted at that and began to dance (§161–62).

The names of the Sufis mentioned in this vision belong to the inner circle of early Sufi masters. The picture of them riding around on horses, vainly asking to approach as close to God as Rūzbihān, is faintly ridiculous. The culmination comes when God, as in many visions, showers Rūzbihān with red roses; when a single one of these falls among the Sufis they are overcome with ecstasy. As will be seen later, this particular vision caused some controversy, which in one case was settled by a dream in which Bayazid confirmed the truth of the account (below, p. 95).

An even more bizarre account of the jealousy of the Sufi saints toward Rūzbihān occurs in a sequence that shows them actively attacking him until God intervenes.

> I saw myself as though I were in refreshing states in the desert. There the masters stood with their jeweled crowns and their couches, and in the hand of each was a frying pan, with which they threw stones at me continuously, as though they threw stones from a catapult. Our master and leader Abū Yazīd (may God sanctify his spirit) was the most active in inciting this. But my momentary state constricted there, and I sought God's help. God manifested and cast great stones at them, and they all stopped and threw away their frying pans. They approached me and were kind to me, and at that moment I reached the pavilions of greatness (§171).

As the scene unfolds, it turns out that the prophets also begin pushing and shoving from their jealousy of Rūzbihān.

> I saw all the prophets, messengers, angels, and saints. The one farthest along to God in the presence and the closest of them to God was our Prophet. Then came the senior prophets, such as Adam, Idrīs, Noah, Abraham, Moses, and their equals among the prophets. They pushed me, as though they wished to overwhelm me. God approached me from the lef[t], and he was like a column of red gold. He turned to me and his face was light. God manifested, and God magnified me there. When they saw me in the form in which God the transcendent had clothed me, by the doors of power, every prophet and sincere one took his drink from the wine of the presence, showing me which of them would drink for me and for the love of me. Then I saw God with his drink, and he showed them that he took that for my sake and for love of me, and this was the perfection of his grace to his servant. I awoke in the night with delight and happiness, singing spontaneous sounds like the buzzing of bees (§171).

Divine favor causes all to abandon opposition and drink to the sainthood of Rūzbihān. The closing reference to bees recalls the Qur'ānic reference to bees as recipients of revelation (16:28, in the sūra called "The Bees").

The initiatic visions of saintly authority are complemented by a class of visions that illustrate Rūzbihān's authority with images based on kingship. This first appears in an early vision, in which God bestows this rank on Rūzbihān spontaneously.

> In the days of youth, I used to keep vigil in the middle of the night. I prayed one night, and God passed me by in the most beautiful of forms. He laughed in my face and threw me a bag of musk. I said, "Give me something greater than that." He said, "Both of them are kings, but you are the king of Persia" (§22).[73]

The imagery of kingship as applied to the spiritual authority of the Sufis was by no means unprecedented. As early as 374/984, an important Arabic treatise on Sufism by an anonymous author used the title *The Manners of Kings, in Explanation of the Realities of Sufism*; in it, the author argued that "The Sufis have renounced all the paraphernalia of the world and became kings . . . How should they not deserve the name of kingship, when they have no aspiration other than God?"[74] The invisible hierarchy of saints were the real rulers, under the guidance of God; in the centuries following the decline of the Sunni caliphate, many Sufis used titles like *shāh* and *sulṭān* with their names.

Rūzbihān's visions of royal and saintly authority have a characteristically Persian flavor (he sometimes even uses the Persian word for king, *shāh*, rather than the Arabic equivalent *malik*). One extended passage shows him approaching the court of God, which is guarded by angels and prophets, "standing like princes at the door of the angelic realm" (§133). Rūzbihān sees the famous jurist al-Shāfiʿī in the back rows, like a beggar, but he proceeds within the door and through the rosy veils that surround the inner sanctum of the court.

> Then God called to me in the world of the cosmos, saying, "My beloveds! No one loves him." Then he arose and called out, and named me by my name, so I loved him. Then he showed me the special nearness that he had singled me out for, among all humanity on the face of the earth. And during those hours I was to the saints like a king (*shāh*) among princes, and like a red rose in spring among all the fragrant herbs, all in rows, in ecstasy, reddened and drowned in tears, that entered the deserts of the hidden (§133).

In this particular vision, the identification of Rūzbihān as a king among princes shows his status in relation to the other saints. More explicitly, God also tells him, "I congratulate you, for you are one of the emperors of my saints and one of those elected for my love and gnosis" (§183). Other visions use the imagery of kingship for its sheer esthetic power; like the visions of angels to be explored below, the image of the king combines warlike power and authority with a feminine ideal of beauty.

> I experienced a moment of witnessing from intoxication and sobriety, wearing the clothes of brides, with tresses on my head like the tresses of women with unveiled head and breast, like a beautiful king (*shāh*) emerging from the bridal bower among his boon companions (§141).

The king has not only a feminine retinue but also official boon companions (*nadīm*, pl. *nudamā'*) as part of the court ritual that was traced back to Cyrus and Xerxes. It should not be forgotten that this court ritual regularly involved wine, so that the frequent scenes in which God pours wine for Rūzbihān should be seen as in part recalling that royal motif. The use of royal symbolism tells us little, however, about Rūzbihān's actual relations with the court of the Salghurid Atābegs in Shiraz. The only reference he makes to earthly politics in *The Unveiling of Secrets* comes, curiously, as the very final remark in the book, in the form of a prayer uttered after mention of the plague that devastated the city in 585/1189:

> Then I asked God that he free me from entering the courts of princes. After dawn, one of God's orders came down, and he freed me from seeing them or associating with them at that time. God is transcendent, I have hope from him, and by his grace he makes me independent of any other than he. I seek his aid, and he is sufficient for me (§209).

This is doubtless formulaic in terms of the saintly ideal, so the discussion of Rūzbihān's political relationships must be postponed until his biographies are examined, below.

Sainthood and Prophethood

Enough questions have been raised about the relationship between sainthood and prophethood to make a more detailed examination of this topic worthwhile. The descriptions of the Prophet

Muḥammad show him as the highest of authorities, the intercessor for humanity, the cosmic light that is the closest thing to divinity, and the model of the ecstatic Sufi master. One example shows the Prophet Muḥammad surrounded by the saints like a king with his entourage.

> The Prophet was in the midst of the prophets and messengers, and his companions stood in front of him, and in front of the prophets were the Sufi masters. I saw among them al-Sarī al-Saqaṭī, and he was the greatest among them, like a chamberlain, and he wore the robe of princes, with an outer garment of blue silk, and upon his head was a patched hat, and in his hand was a bow with an arrow in it to drive people away from in front of the prophets. He was the chamberlain of our Prophet, and they came all together, and the Prophet stood beneath these rooms with all the people and raised his hand as though interceding with God (§86).

Despite the presence of the early Sufi saint al-Sarī al-Saqaṭī (d.253/867) in the role of chamberlain, the Prophet Muḥammad retains his unique role as intercessor for his people; in another vision (§179), it is Muḥammad who performs the role of chamberlain in relation to God. Prophethood and the Prophet Muḥammad in particular remain central in Rūzbihān's experience.

Although he appears briefly in many of the visions, Muḥammad is the special focus of several, which elaborate on aspects of his prophetic function. One of these is the light of Muḥammad, the well-known doctrine of his cosmic aspect as the first light created by God.[75] Rūzbihān describes it thus:

> I saw a great light from the direction of Medina. A quarter of the sky and the earth was seized and joined to that light, and when I saw that I knew that that light was the light of Muḥammad. It was in the midst of a divine light. I could not look at it from its overpowering majesty and awe (§93).

The special status of Muḥammad is indicated by his light being surrounded by the light of God, which is the primordial light. Other comments on the nature of Muḥammad's prophethood turn on the interpretation of Qur'ānic passages that relate to the Prophet. One such crucial text is Qur'ān 17:79, where in the context of recommending supererogatory prayer and vigil by night, mention is made of a "praised station" (*maqām maḥmūd*) that God may grant. Rūzbihān links this concept with the light of Muḥammad in an extended visionary sequence:

> It often came to mind in the past: What is the meaning of "the praised station" (17:79)? And one night I saw a mighty ocean in the divine presence without any shore, and I saw all the prophets by themselves in the ocean, and also the saints and the angels. I saw a thick veil hanging over the ocean, and I saw Adam in the ocean, and the ocean was up to his chest; the person nearest to God was nearer than that veil. Adam and the great ones among the messengers were in front of the veil. So I went close to the veil, since I wanted to learn what was beyond the veil, and I went to the end of the veil. When I reached it, I saw from beyond the veil a great light, and I saw a person like the moon from head to foot. His face was like the face of the moon, and he was greater than the heavens in their entirety. That person had taken all the divine presence so that no place as big as the head of a pin remained, but that it was filled with it. There was upon his face a light continuous with the divine presence and uninterrupted. I wanted to go in beyond the veil but was unable to do so. So I said to myself, "What place is this? And who is this person?" And a call came in my conscience, "This is the praised station, and that is Muḥammad, and that which you see on his face is the light of manifestation. If you had been able to enter, you would have seen God Most High without a veil." And it was said to me, "This station is exclusively Muḥammad's, and no one else has access to this station" (§31).

One imagines here a great veil suspended like a curtain, separating all the prophets and angels in the ocean of the spirit from the divine presence. Only Muḥammad is beyond the veil, so that he alone can see God without a veil; his proximity to the divine presence is emphasized by the outpouring of light from him. Elsewhere (§179) Rūzbihān relates "the praised station" to Muḥammad's function as intercessor for humanity.

Muḥammad's special status as a prophet is indicated particularly in accounts of his ascension, in which he sees all the angels and the prophets who are stationed in each heaven. Rūzbihān frequently alludes to ascension as the mode by which he, in imitation of the Prophet, journeys to see God (§18, 20, 56, 135, 152). In one place he relates a vision of the Prophet in the angelic realm, where he heard the Prophet give this report of his ascension:

> I saw the saints and masters, and I saw Gabriel and Michael, and the poles of the cherubs. Then I reached the greatest angelic realm and saw the throne and the footstool; I saw a world of white pearls, and God welcomed me in the form of majesty and beauty, facing me with the brightness[76] of the Attributes, and in the form of satisfaction. The veiled ones of majesty and beauty appeared, and he showered pearls and jewels from the lights of his power. I never saw anything whiter than those jewels, from the throne to the earth (§199).

The rhetoric and descriptions in this account, to be sure, are closer to Rūzbihān's style than to the classical *ḥadīth* reports on the Prophet's ascension. Still, this passage points to the importance of the model of the Prophet for the interior ascension of the Sufi.

On a more personal level, Rūzbihān's visions of Muḥammad illustrate the role that the Prophet performs as the master initiator of the Sufis. This is revealed in visions that show Muḥammad as the leader of ecstatic rituals, performing symbolic actions as the celestial winebearer.

> I saw one night a great ocean, and the sea was of red wine. I saw the Prophet sitting cross-legged in the midst of the deep ocean, drunk, and in his hand a cup of wine from that ocean, which he drank. When he saw me, he ladled out a cup of wine and gave it to me to drink. After that something was revealed to me, and I knew he was above all the rest of creation, since they die thirsty and he is drunk in the midst of the ocean of beauty (§30).

This takes the imagery of wine-drinking to the limit. Wine as the symbol of the forbidden had been transferred from the realm of profane poetry to the mystical by standardized allegorical treatment. Rūzbihān explicitly glosses the "drunkenness" of the Prophet as the appropriate response to the divine beauty, preserving the Prophet's unique status and thus absolving a statement otherwise construable as blasphemy. A similar scene (§52) shows the Prophet and the chief angels turning in an ecstatic dance around the Ka'ba in Mecca, inviting Rūzbihān to join them as if the Prophet were an ecstatic Sufi master.

Of all the other prophets besides Muḥammad, it is Moses who plays the role of most significance for the Sufis.[77] Moses, known as "the speaker with God" (*kalīm allāh*), is a paradigmatic mystical figure because of his dramatic confrontation with God on Mt. Sinai. In other contexts, Moses can be the stock figure of the person taken in by appearances, as in a story that Rūzbihān relates in a moralistic fashion (§147), oddly falling into the mode of the Friday preacher for a moment in the midst of his unveilings. More typical, however, is the following meditation, when Rūzbihān asks God why he cannot have the perfections of Moses.

> My mind recalled the story of Moses, up to his proximity to God, his vision of him, certain lofty stations and noble miracles, as is handed down in traditions. My thoughts vanished, and I said, "God, you transcend relationship with creatures. You gave to Moses these miracles and these stations, and you chose him for perfection. What is the relationship between you and him, in terms of nearness? I too am from the sons of Adam; What have you given to me?" And he manifested to me in the form of majesty and beauty, and said to me, "Moses came to me, but I came to you 70,000 times between the time you lay down and the time you woke up. Each time I unveiled the covering from your face while you were sleeping, and I awaited your awaking." When I heard that, I was seized by clashing waves of the ocean of unity (§152).

God's response to this demand does not directly respond to the question of the Sufi's relation to this prophet; it is instead an overwhelming statement of intimate concern for Rūzbihān, reasserting his special status by God's constant visitation of him.

Moses also has an appealing human weakness, evident in his swoon when he sees a mountain disintegrate from the manifestation of God. From this perspective, Moses becomes the type of the intoxicated Sufi.

> I sought God at dawn on this night, and he spoke to me as he spoke to Moses there [at Sinai], and several mountains split open. I saw in Mt. Sinai a window in the mountain itself from

> the east side. God manifested to me from the window, and said, "Thus I manifested myself to Moses." I saw Moses as though he saw God, and he fell from the mountain, intoxicated, to the foot of the mountain. I saw a witnessing of grace more beautiful that this witnessing (§145).

Rūzbihān's variation on the story of Moses has Moses actually see God, something that never happened in the Qur'ānic account of this prophet. In another vision, he sees himself in a landscape of infinite deserts, rolling naked in the dust before God as a sign of complete annihilation, following the example of Moses.

> I saw him in the deserts of the hidden, and I saw myself rolling in the dust before him in these deserts, and I rolled before him from the first desert to the last desert, more than a thousand times. God was looking at me with the eye of might and majesty. Then he said, "Thus did Moses, rolling in the dust with no clothes on, every Thursday, humbling himself before God and submitting to his might" (§157).

The final nature of Moses' experience remains as ambiguous, however, as the annihilation of the ego. If the ego of Moses was annihilated, then who descended from Mt. Sinai?

> I also saw God (Glory be to Him) descend from Mount Sinai in the dress of a great shaykh, and the mountain melted under the blows of the power of his wrath. Then he disappeared, then he appeared, then he disappeared, then he appeared, repeatedly. Then he said, "Thus I have done to Moses" (§35).

The intermittent manifestation and withdrawal of God in one's consciousness (whether prophet or saint, for the two are continuous) makes a final distinction of identity impossible.

The Power of Wrath

The theophanies of majesty include manifestations of divine wrath, which can be a violent force unleashed against the persecutors of the saints, or a sheer revelation of creative power that consumes even the saints and prophets. Rūzbihān had a keen sense of the fragility of the spiritual life, and his lengthy litany of the persecutions of the Sufi martyrs in his *Commentary on Ecstatic Sayings* furnishes a good example of this sensitivity.[78] Certain of his visions set forth scenarios of divine retribution for these crimes against the saints.

> God appeared on the steed of pre-eternity, with a Turk's bow in his hand, and he was angry at people who persisted in hunting his servants. I saw 'Alī ibn Abī Ṭālib come out from a mountain enraged at those people, and he attacked them, for some of the oppressors were his descendants. Before this chastisement they had oppressed the devotees, but the rights of their houses were not abrogated (§134).

It is particularly striking that 'Alī, prince of the martyrs, comes out to avenge those of his descendants who have persecuted the Sufi saints. This suggests that Rūzbihān is referring to offences against Sufis committed under Shī'ī authority, possibly during the period of Būyid rule over Fars (932–1062).

It is in reflecting on the persecution of Sufis such as Ḥallāj (d. 309/922) that Rūzbihān becomes most indignant. The affair of Ḥallāj, which involved lengthy trials and entailed considerable political maneuvering, was the most sensational and controversial of the persecutions of Sufis.[79] Obviously alluding to this, Rūzbihān struggles to forgive the persecutors. He then sees in a vision a yellow dog that punishes the slanderers.

> One day I encountered the story of some of the Qur'ān reciters and officials in the case of the ecstatics and realizers of truth among the gnostics, the unitarians among the unveilers, and the sincere ones among the witnessers. They attacked the claim of the masters and their spiritual stations. I regretted that and asked God to forgive them for what I heard from his saying, "Compensation for calumny is to ask forgiveness from those who are offended." Then I prayed the evening prayer, and I saw a yellow dog in the deserts. I saw all the slanderers with their mouths open, and the dog with his tongue was pulling the tongue of every one out of his mouth, and he ate all their tongues in less than an instant. I finished with that, and it was the night before the 20th of Ramaḍān. Someone was saying, "This dog is one of the dogs of hell; every day its food is the tongues of slanderers. The

> fasting of anyone whose tongue is eaten by this dog is unacceptable to God" (§146).

Despite Rūzbihān's wish to forgive, he still sees the persecutors of the Sufis receiving their deserved punishment.

The embodiment of divine vengeance in the yellow dog has a powerful mystical parallel in a vision of a lion, to which Rūzbihān provides the interpretation.

> In a certain revelation I saw a tawny lion of mighty form, clothed with mighty power, walking on top of Mount Qaf. He ate up the prophets, the messengers, and the saints, and their flesh remained in his mouth, and the blood dripped from it. I thought, "If I were there, would he eat me as he ate them?" And I found myself in his mouth, and he ate me. This is an allusion to the wrath of the confession of unity and its authority over the confessors of unity. God manifests from the qualities of eternal greatness in the form of the lion. The significance of its realities is that the gnostic is a morsel for the wrath of unknowing in the station of annihilation (§57).

This consuming lion serves as a vivid visual metaphor for the overwhelming divine power that annihilates created limitations. In *The Spirits' Font*, Rūzbihān categorizes this vision as follows:

> The vision of the lights of the Attributes of might and greatness in the clothing of the lion, on top of Mt. Qaf, when it eats all the prophets and the saints. By seeing this station, from the eye of the elect conscience, the great successors and sincere ones are broken, and the spirits of the unitarians vanish. The gnostic says, "I saw that lion when it ate me, and I became more powerful than the world from joy at that."[80]

In a slightly different vision (§181), Rūzbihān sees a lion "clothed in the greatness of God," before which all the prophets and saints flee; Rūzbihān remains standing, however, and the lion attacks him and leaves him for dead. He regards these manifestations of power as part of God's testing (*imtiḥān*) of the saints and prophets (§188).

F. Theophanies of Beauty

The manifestations of divine power, wrath, might, and greatness would be incomplete without the theophanies of divine beauty, and the concomitant qualities of grace, kindness, and generosity. God's beauty appears to Rūzbihān above all in visual forms of lush and intense richness, with showers of roses and pearls providing a suitable side effect. God appears, moreover, in beautiful human forms of prophets like Adam and Joseph, as well as more obscure individuals. Given the predominant anti-anthropomorphic emphasis of Islamic theology, it is at first sight surprising that Rūzbihān can include such visions within the limits of what is acceptable. Rūzbihān takes us to visionary landscapes of endless mountains, deserts, and oceans, to meet angels who embody at once feminine beauty and the warlike qualities of Turkish soldiers. The visual manifestation of God in these forms of beauty underlies the continuity between human and divine love.

"The red rose is of the glory of God."

The rose has been a symbol of great importance in the Persian literary tradition for centuries, so much so that the primordial tale of the nightingale's hopeless love for the rose has been turned into a cliché by countless second-rate poets. I have argued elsewhere that the most powerful source for understanding metaphors like the rose or the bird in this tradition lies in the writings of Sufis like Rūzbihān.[81] The experiential directness of the metaphor is still fresh, not yet the hackneyed convention it would later become.

> In the middle of last night, after sitting on the carpet of devotion in search of the manifestation of hidden brides, when my conscience soared in the regions of the angelic realm, I saw the majesty of God in the station of clothing with divinity, in the shape of loveliness, repeatedly. It did not satisfy my heart, until from it came a revelation of the perpetual majesty that consumes the consciousness and thoughts. I saw a face vaster than all of heaven and earth, and the throne and the footstool, scattering the lights of glory, and it transcended analogies and similitudes. I saw his glory with the color of the red rose, but it was world upon world, as if he were scattering red roses, and I saw no limit to it. My

> heart remembered the saying of the Prophet, "The red rose is of the glory of God." And that was the extent of my heart's comprehension (§71).[82]

The connection between the divine beauty and the beauty of the rose, as an emblem of creation, is unmistakeable. This is couched as a visionary commentary on a Prophetic saying, which in his Qur'ān commentary Rūzbihān relates via the early Sufi al-Wāsiṭī (d. 320/932).[83]

The many visions of God surrounded by roses, red or white, underline the celestial significance of the rose. Outpourings of divine grace are experienced as showers of roses, as we see in this vision of an epiphany in Shiraz.

> I saw myself as if I were on the roof of my *ribāṭ* in Shiraz. I looked up and saw God in our market in the form of majesty and beauty. By God, if the throne saw him in that form, it would melt from the pleasure of his beauty. I entered the oceans of ecstasy, spiritual states, and gladdening visitations weighed with longing, love, and passion. Then I saw myself sitting on the patio of the *ribāṭ*, and God came in that form with even more of his beauty, and with him were how many red and white roses! He cast them in front of me, and I was in the station of intimacy and happiness, and the spirit was in a place such that I melted. When the beauties of his attributes and admirable qualities were unveiled to me, then he hid from me (§143).

As a variation on this theophany of beauty, God sometimes appears showering pearls, or even "white roses with pearl brocade" (§58). Pearls, like roses, have an ancient history as a symbol of divine qualities, in this case a beauty that is rendered more precious by its inaccessibility in shells under the ocean. "Then I saw above me an atmosphere of white light, from which came showers of white pearls. That is from God's beauty, and he was scattering them on me. It is beyond expression, nor can intellects comprehend it" (§76). Prophets like Adam and Muḥammad partake of the divine beauty and are themselves dressed in clothes of white pearl (§201).

The Body of Revelation

Rūzbihān faces a particularly delicate problem when he attempts to describe visions in which God appears in human form. In what we know as the mainstream of Islamic theology, the severest criticism is reserved for those who assert that God has the form of a created physical being. There have always been tensions, however, between the iconoclastic impulse and the desire to accomodate the apparently anthropomorphic descriptions of God in the Qur'ān. How does one understand references to God's face, hand, sitting on the throne, etc., without anthropomorphism? While some theologians have elaborated positions that treat these descriptions as metaphors, and others hold to an unquestioning literalism, it is less well known that during the early Islamic centuries, there were many enthusiastic religious thinkers who asserted that God has a human form.[84] While some of these may have been theoretical positions, Rūzbihān's diary is filled with visions in which he sees the face of God, the hand of God, and God explains to him the meaning of sitting on the throne. As mentioned above (p. 35) in connection with the doctrine of "clothing with divinity," statements regarding the theomorphic nature of humanity can be found in the principal *ḥadīth* collections, especially the saying, "God created Adam in his form." In the passage that follows, Rūzbihān reflects on a particularly powerful vision of God, linking the theomorphic nature of humanity with the scene in the Qur'ān where the prophet Joseph's brothers recognize him and fall down prostrate before him.

> I wanted to describe some of his attributes that I saw, for my disciples and sincere ones, but I could not, because he appeared in the form of the garment in which they concealed Adam. He displayed it to the cherubs and spiritual beings, and "They fell prostrate before him [Joseph]" (Qur'ān 12:100) involuntarily. Thus the Prophet said, "God created Adam in his own form." Understand, were it not for fear of the ignoramuses who accuse us of making likenesses of the created, I would have indicated something of what I have seen of God: the light of his glory, the brilliance of his holiness, his great majesty, and his gracious beauty, and the qualities with which he clothed Adam, Moses, Joseph, Abraham, John, and Muḥammad. By these qualities, of

> which they inherited the most luminous, they stand above the world and its creatures. When the glory of the lightning of his Attributes manifests in something, all creation and temporality submits before it (§128–29).

Rūzbihān reveals here (as at §39) his reticence to describe fully what he has seen, for fear of the accusations of heresy that may be made against him (one pauses to wonder what he considers to be exhibitionism). Yet he feels that the power and truth of the investitures of the prophets is indicated with certainty by the universal recognition of their authority.

Rūzbihān sees God manifest in the form of Adam (§89, 166), recapitulating the primeval manifestation of beauty in human form. These visions constitute a likeness (*mathal*) to God, which in one place the Qur'ān rejects: "There is no likeness unto him" (42:11). Rūzbihān sees here, however, a clear connection between Qur'ānic references to God's "highest likeness" (30:27) and the "signs" (*āyāt*) which God shows the faithful within the world. Continuing the metaphor of "clothing," the form of Adam becomes the "garment" of God.

> I saw him in the form of Adam facing the world of eternity, and he was in the form of greatness and beauty. . . . God [manifested] with the light of the beauty of pre-eternity, and with it he filled creation and temporality. A light crossed the regions of the heavens and earth and shone upon the likeness, "for his is the highest likeness" (Qur'ān 30:27), like the radiance of the red rose and red gold . . . Everything overwhelmed me, and I said, "What is this?" It was said to me, "This is the manifestation of the garment (*ridā'*) of God." Then he cast into my mind his saying, "We shall show them our signs on the horizons and in themselves," up to his saying, "truly he witnesses everything" (Qur'ān 41:53) (§166).

It is in the human forms of the prophets that God's beauty is most fully displayed. There are times when Rūzbihān reacts against the image; repeatedly his visions are followed by disavowals, and by the insistence that God transcends all form. In this connection he returns to the question of God's "highest likeness."

> I saw him after midnight as though he appeared in a

> thousand kinds of beauty, among which I saw a glory of high likeness, "for his is the highest likeness [in the heavens and the earth,] and he is the mighty, the commanding" (Qur'ān 30:27). It was as though he were like the glory of the red rose, and this is a likeness. But God forbid that he have a likeness – "There is no likeness unto him" (42:11). Yet I cannot describe except by an expression, and this description is from the perspective of my weakness and incapacity and my lack of comprehension of the qualities of eternity (§87).

There is no easy way to reconcile the need for vision and expression with the utter transcendence of God. Invoking again the prophet Joseph, the pinnacle of human beauty, Rūzbihān recalls wondering how created things are related to attributes of majesty (§151). In answer, God recites from the Qur'ān (12:31) the words of Zulaykhā telling Joseph to go out before the women of Egypt at her banquet, whereupon they cut their hands in astonishment at his beauty. Thus God's relation to the creation is a theophany of beauty, just like the prophet Joseph parading before the adoring women.

God does not only appear in the form of the prophets, though. The emphasis on beautiful faces as the manifestation of God intersects with another saying of the Prophet, "I saw my Lord in the most beautiful of forms," which Rūzbihān cites frequently; in most versions, this *ḥadīth* describes God as appearing in the form of a handsome young man of Mecca. Rūzbihān's visions include celestial encounters with God in the form of a handsome Turk, parallel to some of the visions of angels discussed below.

> I saw in the desert of the hidden that God arose in the form of beauty in the shape of the Turks, and in his hand was a lute that he brought near. He played that lute, and it agitated me, increasing my passion and longing. I became restless from the ecstatic pleasure of beauty and the loveliness of union (§176; cf. §36).

Since the time of Sultan Maḥmūd of Ghazna (d. 421/1030), the Turk, particularly the male Turkish military slave, had become the principal idol in the religion of beauty celebrated in Persian lyrical poetry.[85] As Muḥammad Mu'īn has pointed out, Rūzbihān's use of the imagery of Turks (both in prose and in verse) is fully in tune with the poetic tradition from Farrukhī up to Ḥāfiẓ.[86] What is surprising here is Rūzbihān's explicit identification of this image as a concrete mystical experience. The image of the Turk, like the rose, doubtless was first used in lyrical and secular poetic contexts. Rūzbihān demonstrates how fully these images were taken over and interiorized in Sufi circles, to serve as the refractive lenses of visionary experience.

These reflections on the divine beauty manifesting in human form inevitably raise the question of the relation between human and divine love. We can only briefly allude to this here, since it forms a major topic primarily in other works by Rūzbihān, notably *The Jasmine of the Lovers*. Certainly the anecdote concerning Rūzbihān's first sermon in Shiraz, when he protested a young woman's veiling of her face, suggests the fundamental tenor of Rūzbihān's adoration of beauty. In *The Unveiling of Secrets*, on several occasions he uses the imagery of bridal mysticism to convey his intimacy with God.

> I saw him surrounded by all his curtained canopies and veils. I saw the assemblies of intimacy within these curtained canopies.[87] I sat on every carpet, and he displayed himself to me with the most beautiful quality. He poured me the wines of proximity; it was as though I was in that place like a bride in the presence of God. What took place after that cannot enter into expressions (§91).

The continuity between human and divine love includes not only the lover and beloved relationship, but also the love of parent and child; these relationships can even shift into one another as part of the kaleidoscopic movement of the visionary experience: "I was like a child in the room of his mother. He caressed me with the caress of the beloved for a lover" (§95). Rūzbihān's depiction of angels as brides (discussed below) should stand as a reminder that the bridal metaphor is one of the fundamental expressions for mystical experience as unveiling. When referring to the practice of meditation, Rūzbihān describes himself as "sitting on the carpet of devotion in search of the manifestation of hidden brides" (§71). And his mystical commentary on the Qur'ān, *The Brides of Explanation*, by its title invokes the unveiling of the bride in a loving encounter as the model for initiation into the esoteric knowledge of God.

The visions of God taking human form juxtapose the finiteness and limitation of a human being with the infinity and transcendence of God. It may be paradoxical, but to Rūzbihān it remains an experience. Here is an example where he sees God in the form of a former teacher, an intoxicated Sufi who was a "self-blamer" (*malāmatī*), deliberately acting in an outrageous fashion to attract the blame of others.

> In my youth I had a master, a gnostic master who was intoxicated all the time, and he was a self-blaming master whose appearance was unknown. One night I saw one of the deserts of the hidden world, and I saw God Most High in the form of that master sitting at the edge of the desert. I went down to him, and he indicated to me another desert. I went to that desert, and I saw a master like him, and that master was God. He indicated to me another desert, so that 70,000 deserts were unveiled to me, and at the edge of each desert I saw the like of what I had seen in the first (§34).[88]

The endless reflection of this divinized master in the deserts of annihilation leads Rūzbihān to reflect on God's transcendence, and he realizes that these manifestations allude to the unlimited Attributes of God. Although at times Rūzbihān doubts the ultimacy of his visions, he sees that theophany in human form is a necessity if humans are to comprehend anything of God.

> Then I was astonished in the primordiality of God, and I saw him in "the most beautiful of forms." I thought in my heart, "How did you fall from the world of unity to the station of symbols?" He came near and took my prayer carpet, saying, "Stand! What are these thoughts? You doubt me, so I displayed an image of myself in your eye, so you would become intimate with me and love me." There were lights of majesty and beauty upon him, the number of which I could not count. Then I saw him at every moment in the beauty of another [person] (§117).

This is a wonderful example of vision justifying itself, on the grounds that human nature is incapable of seeing the divine Essence. The language of this passage is rich with associations. The "fall from the world of unity to the station of symbols (*mutashābihāt*)" uses the Qur'ānic term for the "ambiguous" or "allegorical" verses that contain anthropomorphic language and other difficulties requiring interpretation. God's announcement, "I displayed an image of myself (*tamaththaltu*) in your eye," recalls Qur'ān 19:17, where, in the annunciation to Mary, the angel Gabriel "was displayed in the image (*tamaththala*) of an upright man." When God tells Rūzbihān to "become intimate (*tasta'nasa*) with me and love me," he invokes the famous saying of Dhū al-Nūn on intimacy with God as the cause of the love of all beautiful things.[89] The result is a continuous revelation of the divine beauty in a succession of different human forms.

The theophanies of beauty finally include manifestations that take place not through visual form but in words. The Sufi tradition from a very early date has employed poetry, including poetry derived from secular literature, as a medium for the expression of mystical insights. Rūzbihān relates an example of paying a visit to a session for listening to musical recitation of poetry (*samāʿ*), where some strange verses in the style of the ʿAbbāsid poet Abū Nuwās were recited, on the subject of hangover, verses which were undoubtedly intended to be humorous in their original secular context. Rūzbihān was intensely affected by the poetry, but in a one-sided and subjective fashion, and upon reflection he realized that he had missed the presence of God entirely during this assembly.

> One day it happened that someone invited me the day before, after the last evening prayer, to an occasion that included listening to music (*samāʿ*), and the singer recited:
>
> > Does one appear in the morning with bloodshot eyes, but the wineskins' nostrils had not bled?
> > Winebearer, relieve those souls who have risen up with their worries to their collarbones [i.e., pour a glass for those who have nearly expired from their hangover].[90]
>
> Ecstasies, kindnesses, communications, and speeches from the station of expansiveness overwhelmed me, but there was nothing there except the visitation, the ecstasy, and certain gleams and illuminations. The moments of encounter were made happy by that interior discourse. When I became collected and departed, I passed the night until the next day. I recalled[91] these states until night came again, and I performed prayer between the two evening prayers, saying to

> myself, "What was going on? The hidden wonders were not revealed in the music last night." And I suddenly saw God at the windows of the angelic realm, dawning on me with the qualities of beauty and majesty. I said with expansiveness, "Where were you when you hid during the music?" (§64–65).

In the subsequent conversation, God reveals to Rūzbihān that he was in fact present throughout, and with this realization new revelations follow, until Rūzbihān finally "gets the joke" and sees God manifest from "the station of laughter." The appearance of apparently profane verses in these Sufi musical seances shows how even the grossest poetry could be interpreted in an allegorical sense; in addition to the usual Sufi exegesis of wine as divine love, Rūzbihān understands the crude humor of the verse as a manifestation of the divine quality of laughter, so it becomes a theophany.

A Transcendental Landscape

The visions presented so far have taken place in many "locations," though Rūzbihān might agree that their true place is in what he calls the angelic realm. While some of these (to be discussed below) concern visions of the gardens of paradise, and others occur right in the home and hospice of Rūzbihān, the majority take place in landscapes far removed from humanity and its urban environment. Oceans of unlimited extent, filled with surging waves, indicate the powerful psychic forces unleashed in visions. A good example is the following:

> I was seeking God in the hidden world, but when I sought him, he avoided creation and certain imaginations. I sought God's help in that, and he made me comprehend his grace and expelled my consciousness from the regions of existence, so that I reached the ocean of love. It was wider than the world, but I crossed it until I reached the ocean of gnosis. I crossed that and then reached the ocean of unity. I crossed that until I reached the ocean of unknowing and might. I crossed that until I reached the ocean of Attributes. Then I reached the ocean of the Essence. I was astonished at the absence of the reality of God; I remained still for hours. God appeared to me in the form of majesty and beauty, and

> everything I saw in comparison with his majesty was like a drop in the ocean (§79).

Here the ocean serves as the best available metaphor for transcending space. Sometimes he sees himself swimming and diving into the ocean's depths to retrieve divine knowledge, but at other times he is overwhelmed by the waves, drowning in their power.

> He hid from me and put me in oceans like the air, having no dimensions. The might of God encompassed me. I saw myself in these oceans like a drop, with no left or right, no before or behind, no up or down. I saw nothing but glory upon glory, power upon power, majesty upon majesty, might upon might, greatness upon greatness, eternity upon eternity, post-eternity upon post-eternity. Then he said, "From the wombs of the hidden, this is endless eternity and perpetual subsistence" (§110).

Initiatic visions show Rūzbihān drinking an ocean, or receiving a glass from an ocean of wine. Altogether the ocean signifies the vast reservoir of spirit that reveals itself in waves of ecstasies.

The oceans in turn are ringed by vast mountains, among which must be counted Mt. Sinai, the source of revelation, and Mt. Qaf, the Olympus of Persian mythology. It is from the mountain that God, or Moses, or a Sufi master, or a combination of all three, descends, bringing revelation. The mountain is the region of divine inaccessibility; sometimes Rūzbihān is the only one to be invited there.

> I saw God on a holy mountain, and he made me approach. The mountain was high, and God had me sit near him, and repeatedly wined me with the wines of intimacy. He graced me in a form that I cannot tell to any of God's creatures, and he was unveiled and there manifested from him the lights of his beautiful attributes. The Sufis were on the foothill of that mountain, unable to ascend the mountain, and God called that mountain Mt. Greatness (§162).

The mountains are the greatest and most enduring of earthly things; when God manifests his power to them, they shatter and melt away.

Beyond the oceans and the mountains Rūzbihān finds endless deserts, which signify the emptiness of annihilation. This symbolism was common in the writings of al-Ḥallāj, who spoke of "the desert (*mafāza*) of the knowledge of reality."[92] The desert likewise serves in the symbolic recitals of the Illuminationist philosopher Suhrawardī as the location for the movement of the soul towards transcendence.[93] The desert near Pasā was the scene of Rūzbihān's earliest unveilings. He seeks God in "the hidden deserts above the seven heavens" (§15), because the desert is where God may be found. Rūzbihān emphasizes the psychological nature of this landscape. "He manifested to me in the deserts of the heart, and he indicated himself, saying, 'I am your lord'" (§77). There are no distractions in the desert. All is empty, leaving only the possibility of encounter with the one that is sought. When Rūzbihān speaks of meditation, he describes it as follows: "The nets of concentration were extended over the deserts of the hidden to trap the birds of the lights of might and the angelic realm" (§169). If the desert is not the site of a rendezvous with God, it will be the place of annihilation of the soul. "In the river bed of pre-eternity there are deserts and wastelands in which dwell the snakes of wrath. If one of then opened its mouth, none of creation or temporality would escape" (§87).

Angelic Encounters

Rūzbihān frequently sees the angels appearing to him in the celestial pleroma. Often the angels simply accompany the prophets and the saints in whatever they are doing, an indication of the continuity of spiritual authority in creation; just as the prophets are dressed as Sufi shaykhs, so the angels can be seen wearing patched robes like Sufis (§188). An early vision that briefly describes an ascension to heaven gives a fairly conventional account of the activities of the angels, as gathered in hosts around the throne, praising God.

> I passed with my conscience through the regions of the created, and my spirit ascended to the heavens. I saw in every heaven the angels of God most high, but I passed them by until I reached the presence. I saw that his creations, the angels, were greater than his creatures on earth; they were

> performing prayer, witnessing the nearness of God, with voices thundering his praise (§20).

The angels can also be present to the vision of the mystic during ritual prayer, as in this scene where Rūzbihān sees God at his *ribāṭ* in Shiraz, leading the prayers:

> I saw God on the roof of the *ribāṭ*, facing the direction of prayer and giving the call to prayer. I heard God say, "I testify that Muḥammad is the messenger of God." The earth was filled with angels, and when the angels heard God's call to prayer, they wept and sighed and could not keep themselves from coming nearer to God, on account of his tremendousness and greatness. In my conscience the saying of God was recited, "They fear their lord from above them and they do what they are ordered" (16:50) (§113).

In these visions the angels appear primarily as celestial beings who continually worship God.

For both angels and humans, words are an appropriate response to the presence of God. These words can be formulaic, ecstatic, or intimate and conversational.

> When he approached them, they were overwhelmed by intoxication and ravishing, and intoxicated words ran over their tongues, such as boasting (*laghz*), ecstatic expression (*shaṭḥ*), and unknown expressions such as I say in ecstasies of intimacy. So I knew the meaning of his saying, "those who recite a recollection" (Qur'ān 37:3). That is the station of awe in intimacy, and happiness in love, and longing in sweet union (§107).

In the Qur'ānic phrase quoted, the term "those who recite" (*tāliyāt*) employs the same root used for the recitation (*tilāwa*) of the Qur'ān, and "recollection" (*dhikr*) has of course a technical meaning in Sufism, to designate the recollection of God by systematic repetition (silent or spoken) of divine names and other sacred phrases. Rūzbihān here assimilates both these ritual forms of speech with the ecstatic speech that he and the angels employ with God. For him, the transition from ritual language to ecstatic speech is one of emphasis only.

Often, however, the angels are of soldierly appearance, as he discovers when meditating on the fuller Qur'ānic context concerning them.

> My heart heard the criers of the hidden recite his saying, "By those who are set in ranks, and who drive away with reproof, and who recite a recollection (*dhikr*)" (Qur'ān 37:1–3). [I considered] its meaning, but I did not know what God intended by this saying. I saw the presence filled with angels as though they were made of hyacinth and ruby, standing in rows like Turks before sultans. Thus I understood the meaning of "by those who are set in ranks" (§107).

The reference to Turks makes it clear that the angels are like Turkish military slaves attached to the courts, though in this case they have the luminous jewel-like appearance that indicates their heavenly origin. The resemblance of angels to Turkish soldiers includes their performing military music as well, as we see from a vision of the descent of the angels during the "night of power" in Ramaḍān that commemorates the descent of the Qur'ānic revelation mentioned in sūra 97.

> I saw the regions of the heavens opened as far as the utmost 'Illiyyīn [the highest heaven]. I saw in it the cherubs and spiritual beings, as though they were sighing from their descent into a world. I saw the clamor in the gardens; [the angel] Riḍwān ordered the houris of the garden, and he saw them stain their hands and feet like brides. I saw some of the angels holding drums and bugles and military [band] instruments. I saw at the door of the presence Turkish drums, and they were about to beat them (§145).

The soldierly appearance of the angels, and their function as court attendants, makes them to this extent manifestations of divine authority and power. But this militant and authoritarian aspect of the angels is always mitigated in Rūzbihān's visions by their qualities of feminine beauty; the angels are also attractive beauties, adorned like brides. This feminine depiction of angels should not be surprising; it recalls the long-haired angels in the sumptuous Timurid manuscripts illustrating the Prophet Muḥammad's ascension to heaven. These paintings have a Central Asian flavor, but they reflect a long tradition of portraiture with Iranian roots. As Marie-Rose Séguy points out,

"The angels, who look like young women, have round faces, large dark eyes and arched eyebrows; their hair falls to their shoulders, except for two braids arranged in loops on top of the head in the Turfan fashion. The manner of their portrayal goes back to Iranian pictorial tradition as exemplified by the Abbasid school."[94] With their combination of warlike and beautiful aspects, the angels combine the qualities of grace and wrath in a way that leaves them intensely ambiguous.

In whatever form the angels appear, they are especially prominent in the "night of power" visions from the Ramaḍān sequence. As the Qur'ān mentions, "on it [the night of power] the angels and the spirit descend, with the permission of their lord, with every command" (97:4). For Rūzbihān, the annual arrival of the night of power was a special occasion for contact with these emissaries of God, but the channel of communication to paradise is a two-way street; the ascending mystic can then see the angels in their heavenly habit.

> Not a year passed without God Most High unveiling to me the night of power, showing me all of the angels in the semblance of a man, laughing, greeting one another. Gabriel was among them there, the most beautiful of the angels. They have tresses like the tresses of women, and their faces are like red roses, and some have veils of light on their heads or jeweled hats, or garments of pearls. I frequently saw them in the form of Turks. I saw Riḍwān and the garden, and I entered it. I saw the houris and heavenly youths just as God described them [in the Qur'ān]. I entered the castles and drank from streams; I ate the fruits of the garden, and I ate melons in the garden (§24).

The principal message that the angels bring to Rūzbihān is one of beauty, love, and longing. This is true of the archangels like Gabriel as well as minor figures like the interrogators of the dead, Munkir and Nakīr (§37), and the recording angels who observe every deed of humanity.

> I saw before me the two noble recording angels, as though they loved me and longed for me, like two lovely youths, in the semblance of drunkards, acting wary and afraid. I saw Gabriel seated before them like a bridegroom, like the moon

among the planets; he had two tresses, long like the tresses of women, and he was dressed in red clothing adorned with green silk. He wept for my sake and longed for me. In the same way, all the angels were happy to see me, as though they longed for me and rejoiced at my state (§68).

Whether as handsome warlike Turks or long-haired maidens, the angels act as one more channel for the theophanies of beauty.

G. *The Unveiling of Secrets* as a Literary Text

Autobiographical Aspects of Rūzbihān's Self-Presentation

Can *The Unveiling of Secrets* be called autobiographical? To be sure, the term "autobiography" is relatively recent, and as a literary genre it is most fully applicable to modern memoirs of the past two centuries. Though first-person narratives can be traced back over several millennia, it was only in the nineteenth century that autobiography became widely accepted as a source for biographical and historical information, as a mode of representing the self, and as a form of literature.[95] The initial and easy answer is that sixth/twelfth-century Iran shared few of the historiographical, psychological, or literary concerns of nineteenth-century Europe. Rūzbihān was not attempting to draw a portrait of his times, or to reveal the kind of self that would be recognizable in modern Western culture. Despite a vast biographical literature in Islamicate countries, until recently there has not been a recognized genre of first-person narrative in Arabic literature, apart from the more concrete literary category of the travel and pilgrimage narrative. First-person narratives do occur in a variety of other literary contexts, but they have not acquired sufficient gravity in themselves to cohere as an independent type of text.[96]

As mentioned above, there are only a few examples of first-person narratives in the Sufi tradition with which Rūzbihān's *The Unveiling of Secrets* can be compared. One possible precursor of Rūzbihān in the self-disclosing narrative is the early Sufi al-Ḥakīm al-Tirmidhī (d. ca. 932), whose *Beginning of the Affair* (*Buduww al-sha'n*) discusses his spiritual life. This differs considerably from Rūzbihān's writing, in that Tirmidhī reports few if any of his own visions or dreams. The bulk of this short work consists of reports of the dreams of others (principally Tirmidhī's wife) about his status as a saint.[97] Another "autobiographical" work is the apologia of 'Ayn al-Quḍāt al-Hamadānī, written to protest his persecution for heresy shortly before his execution in 525/1131.[98] That, like al-Ghazālī's *Deliverance from Error*, is an intellectually programmatic work that defends Sufism from criticism; neither al-Ghazālī nor 'Ayn al-Quḍāt uses an autobiographical format to reveal inner experiences at any length. We do know of a tradition of autobiographical writing in North African Sufism that focuses on visions or dreams of the Prophet Muḥammad. Jonathan Katz has argued that this tradition began in an irregular fashion in the late seventh/thirteenth century, and later became a widespread social phenomenon; visions of the Prophet confirmed the sainthood of the visionaries and certified them as intercessors who could aid their own followers to attain salvation.[99] Rūzbihān's visions are of a different type, however, consisting mostly of visions of God, although the Prophet Muḥammad as well as angels, other prophets, and saints also play notable roles, and the technical density of the vocabulary of the visions restricted them to elite disciples rather than the broad public. We will have to look elsewhere to find literary precedents for Rūzbihān's visions.

I have suggested above that in form *The Unveiling of Secrets* is a combination of a retrospective memoir and an ongoing visionary diary. The significance of the work, judging from the reasons for its composition as stated by Rūzbihān, is to provide a record of his spiritual experiences for the edification of a friend, most likely a disciple. Most of these experiences are so extravagant by modern standards that it may be tempting to relegate them to the status of dream and fantasy. For Rūzbihān and his contemporaries, the waking visions that filled his days and nights were far from fantasy; they were proof of his sainthood. One of Rūzbihān's visions has been the subject of an analysis from the point of view of dream interpretation, comparing one of his initiatic encounters with the dreams of modern Pakistani Sufis. In this study, Katherine P. Ewing has made a good case for the shared cultural "template" that can be found as enduring elements in Rūzbihān's vision and in the dreams of contemporary Pakistanis; she has pointed out striking similarities between Rūzbihān's initiatic vision of the Little Bear (§19–20) and dreams reported by modern Pakistanis connected to Sufi masters.[100] While she relates the Pakistani dreams to conflict situations deriving from postcolonial dilemmas and idiosyncratic components that generate the dream as the center for a new self-representation, she has reserved judgment about Rūzbihān's personal conflicts, noting only that his vision "was clearly significant for Rūzbihān's system of self representations, and, ultimately his public significance" as a saint.[101] That still leaves open the question of whether or not to interpret *The Unveiling of Secrets* as a transcription of idiosyncratic personal life events. If we reconsider briefly the vision of the stars of the Little Bear (above, p. 46), it is important to consider a portion of that sequence omitted from the earlier discussion, the experience that follows upon God's manifestation from the "windows" of the polar constellation:

> I passed with my conscience through the regions of the created, and my spirit ascended to the heavens. I saw in every heaven the angels of God most high, but I passed them by until I reached the presence. I saw his creations, the angels, were greater than his creatures on earth; they were performing prayer, witnessing the nearness of God, with voices thundering his praise. Then I rose up to the world of shining light to ask about it, and I was told that this world is called the throne. I trembled through an atmosphere without space, until [I reached] the doors of eternity. There I saw deserts and oceans; I was being annihilated, bewildered, vanishing, astonished, not knowing from where God appeared, beyond place and direction (§20).

This is a narrative of an ascension, with all the classic elements of passing through the heavens, seeing the angels, and reaching the throne of God. It is, far from being a unique event, part of a long tradition of ascension literature with roots going back to the ancient near east.[102] While there may indeed be idiosyncratic aspects to Rūzbihān's visionary diary, these may bear a marginal significance in comparison with the overriding themes of the ascension to heaven as an attribute of sainthood. It is also necessary to consider the difference between dream and vision, especially if mystical experience requires a different hermeneutic than does the dream.[103] In short, while we may regard *The Unveiling of Secrets* as a self-presentation, its literary interpretation will be greatly aided by coming to an understanding of what kind of text it is.

Having reformulated the question of the autobiographical

status of *The Unveiling of Secrets*, I would like to press further the "autobiographical" aspects of the text in the most general sense, to examine the presentation of self that emerges from these visions. This will involve especially a consideration of passages in which Rūzbihān sees himself as an actor, and visions relating to his family. The "autobiographical" tidbits that can be extracted from these passages will permit some further reflection on the literary genre of *The Unveiling of Secrets*, especially when they are juxtaposed with some reactions to the text by Rūzbihān's contemporaries.

The occasions when Rūzbihān sees himself in visions are common; perhaps a tenth of the sequences in *The Unveiling of Secrets* include the phrase, "I saw myself . . . " Yet in none of these cases is the vision of autobiographical aspects of himself objectified, so that he sees himself acting in an externalized way. The vision of himself often serves as an introduction that locates the vision in an internal landscape or spiritual station, but it quickly shifts into subjectivity, recording his perceptions, actions, and dialogues. Here are some examples:

> I saw myself beneath the earth, in an atmosphere of light, and God appeared to me there. Then I said to him, "My God, I sought you above every above . . . " (§27).
>
> I saw him in the deserts of the Hidden, and I saw myself rolling in the dust before him in these deserts, and I rolled before him from the first desert to the last desert, more than a thousand times (§157).
>
> Then I saw myself in the abode of majesty on the carpet of intimacy with God, and he poured me a wine I cannot describe (§158).
>
> Last night it was as though I saw myself in the desert of China, and God arose in the form of clothing with divinity, in the forms of Turks (§168).
>
> It happened that I saw myself above Mt. Sinai, and I saw God in the gardens of pre-eternity (§204).

In the visions where these sentences occur, the mention of Rūzbihān seeing himself is meant to convey immediacy, not objectification or distance. As many of his visions of the garden of paradise suggest, the model for mystical vision is the vision of God that is granted to the faithful in paradise. Rūzbihān observes in another context, "The existence of the faithful in paradise is all vision, because spirit and body there are a single thing, like the sun and its heat. One sees God with all the limbs."[104]

Yet there is a sense in which Rūzbihān is looking back critically at his earliest experiences of childhood, and in these recollections he speaks as a mature Sufi looking at the experiences of a novice. "I was in my youth, and in the days of my intoxication, extravagance, and effervescence" (§6). Although he had even in childhood tasted certain experiences of a spiritual order, he observed, "I did not know the reality of what happened" (§8). So Rūzbihān interprets these inchoate experiences as similar to the results of the Sufi practices of recollecting God and meditating (§8–9). A few other times (§15, §22, §34) Rūzbihān refers to experiences from his "days of youth," but without any criticism or distancing that would indicate that these were incomplete or misunderstood. Unlike Augustine, who reflects in his *Confessions* on the true motivation and significance of actions that he understood differently at the time, Rūzbihān as a narrator does not stand apart from the protagonist of his narrative.[105] A further distinction between Augustine and Rūzbihān can be seen in the conversion experience. For Augustine this is a pivotal point in the book, which deliberately invokes a literary model, the conversion of St. Anthony. Rūzbihān's conversion, though dramatic, is not modelled on a hagiographical predecessor; an apparitional figure speaking words he hardly understands sends him into a rapture that causes him to jettison his belongings and head to the desert. If there is anything conventional about this conversion narrative, it is that Rūzbihān interprets each vision by the language that he uses, which is densely filled with the technical terms of Sufi mystical psychology. The resulting interpretation is deliberate and self-conscious, as also seen from the constant employment of comparisons beginning with the phrase, "it was as though . . . " The narration of the visions has the effect of imaginatively recreating the vision for the reader without any mediation other than the words of the narrative, but that mediation by mystical analysis sets up a model of mystical experience which the narrative is meant to illustrate.

Another angle from which to examine the autobiographical aspect of *The Unveiling of Secrets* is Rūzbihān's concept of self. Here we face a major difficulty that derives from one of the primary topics of Sufi mysticism, which is the elimination of the self.[106] If elimination of the self is accepted without further qualification as

Rūzbihān's goal, then any intrusion of a self would appear to be problematic, the remnant of a false self. One would suppose that it is above all in the station of annihilation (*fanā'*) that the self or ego is eliminated. A glance at passages where Rūzbihān talks about undergoing annihilation indicates that the matter is not so simple. Annihilation of the self occurs primarily when a powerful manifestation of divine Attributes overwhelms Rūzbihān, but typically the dialogue with God proceeds after annihilation with no interruption. Here are some examples:

> I said, "I want to see you with the quality you had in pre-eternity." He said, "There is no way for you to [know] that." And I implored him and said, "I want that!" And the lights of greatness appeared, and I became vanishing, annihilated. The temporal does not abide after that typhoon of greatness. Then my conscience was addressed . . . (§62)

In other episodes, Rūzbihān announces that he has been annihilated, and that is the end of the account, though it is immediately followed by another.

> He said, "Everything is perishing but his face" (Qur'ān 28:88). That is the station of singleness and annihilation. I remained astonished and was annihilated, and I do not know where I was (§109).
> Then he approached me until he drew near, and drew near, until I was hidden and annihilated. God is beyond every fancy and indication and expression (§111).

In other cases Rūzbihān is nearly annihilated, but returns to normality.

> I saw oceans upon oceans, greatness upon greatness, fields upon fields, and I nearly was annihilated in the accumulated oceans of pre-eternity. When he realized my inability to bear the weight of the calamities of unity, he abandoned me and left. I returned to where I was (§179).

It seems to me that the key element common to these passages is the sense of a dialectic between different movements in the divine being as defining human identity. The tides and surges of divine manifestation pull the human self into eddies or hurl it ashore. The self is not destroyed in any final or absolute sense, but it is completely dependent for its identity on the measured manifestation of the Attributes, while an excess of divine presence overwhelms and scatters the self for the time being. The self that is exhibited in these visions is the self constituted by meditative experiences.

One account in particular claims our interest for the way it shows the protagonist in a most dramatic role, in a passage where Rūzbihān imagines his own funeral. It is an eerie vision that is partly a demonstration of Rūzbihān's sainthood.

> I thought in my heart about my death in the middle of some night. My heart was happy at the light that befell it, and my limbs opened up, and my hair and skin were luminous. I saw the people of the angelic realm turning their beautiful faces to me, wearing the clothes of condolence, in a form more beautiful than I had ever seen. Then I saw Gabriel, Michael, Israfil, and 'Azrā'īl, the bearers of the throne, and all the angels, wearing (?) [*al-K?FY*] on their heads, of a frightening aspect. So also was our Prophet, and all the prophets and saints. I saw God manifest to me in the form of clothing with divinity, and he appeared to me as though he were giving condolences. Then he came to me, and with him were all the prophets, messengers, angels, and saints, and he took me by the hand and brought me to the world of majesty and beauty, in a presence with gardens and happiness. Then the houris removed the veils from their heads, and passed cups around, in which was wine, and the angels sang. God said to me, "This is how your death will be" (§181).

It is a strange combination of a funeral and a party. All the angels, prophets, saints, houris, and God himself are dressed as mourners, and Rūzbihān has a body of light. After the ceremony, all adjourn to a paradisal garden for celestial wine and music. This sequence follows another vision of annihilation, in which the lion of God's wrath has just left Rūzbihān for dead. Death, like annihilation, seems to be the necessary prelude to a season of intimacy with God. The self that dies and is resurrected is the self of visionary experience.

In any writing considered autobiographical, one expects to find a presentation of the author's primary location in society, the family. Here Rūzbihān provides an unexpectedly rich view of his family relations in his visions. For the most part his visions seem to indicate that he enjoyed extremely warm relations with his family. Despite the harsh words he used to describe the relatives among whom he grew up, Rūzbihān evidently had become reconciled to his parents at least, as we see from visions in which they appear transfigured in paradise, alongside his wives.

> Then I saw what I saw of majesty and beauty, which the temporal is unable to hear. I reached a world where 100,000 thrones are smaller than an atom, and I saw nothing there but might and power. When I departed from that, I saw a great house high above, and I saw my family sitting and talking about me, reciting poetry, and it was a happiness like that of the first encounter. I saw all my womenfolk sitting happily, and I saw my children there, and a group of people. Then I saw my mother, and she was a woman who knew and loved God, and she stuck her head in my family's house and said, in Pasawī dialect, "*hī lillāh wāl ū*," meaning, "there is no god but he." And they were recalling their weddings. Then I saw my father riding a red horse, wearing silk brocade and a white turban on his head, with angels alongside, returning from a visit to God. He was an upright man, a lover of God – for God has his saints – and he was inclined to weeping and sensitivity (§69–70).

This charming domestic portrait shows an idyllic setting of a great family house in paradise, where all is harmony, and the grandparents chant sacred phrases and visit God like a neighbor. This appears not to have been an isolated concern, for in another passage Rūzbihān uses a Qur'ānic text to enlarge on the importance of meeting one's family in paradise.

> Then I saw my wife in one of the gardens in the presence of God, and she was leaving him. And I saw the qualities of God in the forms of Turks. Then I saw my family among the *gharf* trees of the garden in the presence of God, and those trees were of red ruby. My family was sitting near God in a row, as though they expected me. Then I heard from the hidden his divine saying, "with the righteous among their parents, and their spouses," (Qur'ān 13:23). So I thought about this message, and returned to

> the beginning of the verse where it says, "Gardens of Eden which they shall enter with the righteous among their parents, and their spouses, and their children" (13:23). And I knew that this was good news for me, and at dawn I sat meditating on the daybreak of eternity (§82).

Coming and going with God in the garden, divine manifestations like Turkish beloveds, a garden transfigured like jewels – this is a fitting environment in which to meditate on the destinies of one's family in the afterlife. Rūzbihān takes the Qur'ānic text as a personal message, permitting him to see his family among the saved.

Not everything was rosy in the family, all the time; like anyone else, Rūzbihān had to face problems of a financial nature, and evidently he came in for some criticism occasionally. A lengthy vision (§174) recounts the aftermath of a family quarrel. Rūzbihān's response initially is to seek solace in meditation, and he grows impatient for a divine response.

> It happened one night that my breast was constricted on account of a quarrel with my family, and their complaint about certain necessities. I awoke after midnight, and I despaired about the openings of the hidden. My conscience settled, my intimacy continued, and my spirit was graced. I awaited the wonders of unveiling of the world of the angelic realm, and I saw God in the form of clothing with divinity, in an assembly. My momentary state was joyful, my conscience was agitated, my longing increased, and my ecstasy multiplied. I was disturbed and shouted.

A powerful series of visions and manifestations ensues, culminating in the revelation of a Qur'ānic verse that promises sustenance, possibly resolving the practical difficulties faced by Rūzbihān's family.

> Then he hid from me, and opened the world of the angelic realm. I saw oceans of fresh pearls, and he took jewels from them and showered them over my head repeatedly. So also did the prophets and the angels, until I reached the world of eternity. God manifested in the form of pre-eternity, and there was the place of annihilation. Then he hid from me and

> I melted in the state of pulverization – "where the fruits of every thing are brought as sustenance from us" (28:57).

The vision does not end on this positive note, though. God then manifests as power and authority, pronouncing frightful consequences if Rūzbihān is further criticized.

> Then he said to me, "Is it not [true] from above the throne to the stable earth, that I am the ruler of creatures, and in my hand are the keys of everything? I administer my kingdom as indicated. Does not the flow of fates issue from my will? Say, they are meddlers and complainers about me; let them silence their complaint and give thanks to me for the equivalence of my bounty – otherwise I will destroy them." I was afraid from this rebuke, for he had demonstrated authority. I awoke in the night after midnight, near dawn, and my sleep had been a sweet sleep.

Rūzbihān was greatly comforted by this reassertion of his own authority.

Difficulties of a more poignant sort are revealed in narratives that show Rūzbihān awake late at night with a sick child. His prayers brought a mysterious angelic visitor who healed the boy and blessed them both.

> It happened one night that I was concerned on account of my son Aḥmad, who was suffering from dysentery. This constricted my breast greatly, and I asked my beloved to make a substitution [for my son's illness].[107] I slept while Aḥmad did, and awoke at his shout; I came to him, though I was between waking and sleeping. I saw a person leaving from the side of my house, saying in Pasawī Persian, "May your night be a safe and blessed night."[108] Then he said [to my son], "Tonight he descends for your sake and for the sake of your father. God, He, is yours." I said to myself, "My breast was constricted at this time, so how will the unveiling be prepared for me?" I pursued the verses of good news from the Qur'ān, which announce the opening of the gates of the Hidden. For that reason, some [divine] speech is from the Actions, and some from inspiration (*ilhām*) (§122).

The significance of this account lies in the angelic encounter, and the announcement that God has descended for their sake. Once the boy has been healed, Rūzbihān is concerned mainly about how his next mystical experience will be brought about.

Some time later, the boy Aḥmad was sick once again, during the plague that affected Shiraz in 585/1189.

> It happened that I sat before midnight with my son Aḥmad, when he had a severe fever. All my heart melted from concern. I saw God suddenly in the form of majesty, and he was kind to me and to him, though he was sleeping. Ecstasy and agitation overwhelmed me, and my soul settled down from disturbance, so that it grew inattentive. That was difficult for me. I said, "My God! Why do you test me, when I am waiting for your help?" He said, "Do not sorrow; I am yours." I said, "My God! Why do you not speak to me as you spoke to Moses?" He said, "Be satisfied that whoever loves you loves me, and whoever sees you sees me." When I heard that, many ecstasies overwhelmed me. I stood, and God called in the wombs of the Hidden and said, "Remedy!" A remedy came to him. The town was filled with the sick, unlike anything we ever saw. But the cure was released to the town, and it spread throughout all of Persia. I was in ecstasy, spiritual states, and crying. He was kind to my son, and gave him to drink (§202).[109]

Again, a miraculous cure comes from divine intervention. What is striking is that Rūzbihān freely complains to God when help is not forthcoming quickly enough, and that he simultaneously asks for both a plague cure and a revelation like that of Moses. God's reply to this request comes close to filling the needs of the hagiographer, promising that those who love and see Rūzbihān love and see God. This pronouncement, which releases the cure of the general plague, puts Rūzbihān remarkably close to the position of the Prophet Muḥammad, who had said, "One who sees me has seen God."[110] In both the incidents just described, Rūzbihān's touching concern for his son is relevant only because of the divine response that it engenders.

Rūzbihān's personal connections can also be examined in situations where he had to cope with the death of a friend. In one case, he sees his friend transfigured in paradise, and God and the angels perform his funeral service.

> One of my companions died. I saw a desert beyond the seven heavens, made of red clay, filled with the dead, lying on their shrouds. I said, "What is this desert?" They said, "This is the place of the martyrs of God and his pure ones." I saw a funeral bier borne on the shoulders of the angels; they brought it and put it down. I saw God praying over it – God Most High was praying over all of them. I asked, "Who is this person?" They said, "Your companion." I wept bitterly, for he was a youth from among us. Then I saw him on a wall of the orchards in paradise, and I said, "Master! What are you doing?" He spread his hands and built a wall from blue emeralds, saying, "I [am preparing] your house and your orchards in paradise" (§38).

This connection remained strong even after death, as Rūzbihān saw his friend working to prepare him an abode in heaven, though it is a spiritual friendship that rests on the status of the companion as one of the chosen ones of God. Rūzbihān also (§195) records a vision of another companion who had died, but evidently one who, though a Sufi, did not achieve the states he had claimed in life. Rūzbihān sees him begging underneath a house filled with light, along with the rest of humanity and their rulers. The focus of both these visions of departed companions is on their spiritual status rather than their personal character as friends.

Rūzbihān shows more emotion when he reveals the depression he felt after the death of a favorite wife. This is recalled on an occasion when he had purchased an orchard in Pasā after her death, but he wondered despondently how he could enjoy it in her absence (§109). On another occasion, Rūzbihān thinks of her again after he received a vision of all of existence reduced to specks on the head of a pin. This left all his faculties stunned.

> Then I thought in my heart of my wife who has died (may God have mercy on her). When I implored him, I said in my thought, "My God! Do you see what you have done to me, when you took her and left me wild?" He spoke to me in Persian and said, "*kar dar ān nā-kardan-ast.*"[111] He meant by that that he nearly unveiled to me the world of the angelic realm and made me dwell there [i.e., he nearly had me die also]. So I understood that. Then after ablutions, God spoke

> to me, saying, "Rejoice in the bargain you have made" (Qur'ān 9:111) (§131).

Here too, as with the death of his friend, Rūzbihān feels free to challenge God for taking his wife and leaving him distraught. The consolation he receives is that God could have kept them joined in death, but has decreed otherwise.

Rūzbihān continued to think of this unnamed favorite wife, and visions of her kept recurring, again in the form of a vision of paradise. This time the vision came at a moment when he was wondering about how to provide for his family after his death.

> I thought in my heart about my livelihood and certain pieces of land, how they would fare after my [death]. The garden was unveiled to me, and I saw its rivers, trees, and castles. I saw my wife wearing the clothing of the people of paradise, and she was in the same form as they were; she was waiting at the door of one of the castles, as though she were expecting my arrival, and my delay in the world was to her but a moment. I saw a group of my wives, sons, daughters, and relatives, and I entered ecstasy, and my heart was happy to see them (§168).

A final vision shows Rūzbihān his wife and family in a paradise filled with sugar, a bit of which she gives to him (§187). As the vision continues, God recites to Rūzbihān a passage from the Qur'ān (68:1–4) that speaks of the character of the Prophet Muḥammad and the rewards promised to him, and then Rūzbihān is elevated to a sublime position next to God. He seems finally reconciled to his wife's death, though she is accompanied in these visions by her entire family, many of whom were presumably still living.

What do these accounts of Rūzbihān's family tell us? The details indicate such personal items as a concern about family finances, and, despite the occasional disagreement, a surprisingly positive evaluation of family life. He sees all of his family residing in paradise in bliss, even the parents who must have been so irreligious according to his earlier account. One ventures to think that even modern psychologists might find Rūzbihān to be remarkably well-adjusted for a mystic. His fondness for his wife, in particular, forms a strong contrast to the behavior of his ultra-ascetic predecessor in Shiraz, Ibn al-Khafīf.[112] But all this information about Rūzbihān's relations with his favorite wife and his concern for his sick boy has been conveyed only in order to illustrate his spiritual unveilings. This is especially clear in the story of his deceased companions, who are described primarily in terms of their spiritual attainments.

The Unveiling of Secrets can only be called autobiographical in the broadest sense of the term, in that it is written in the first person and has some limited references to the life-events of the author. These are, however, meant to reveal a self in a very different sense than what is understood by that term in modern literature, whether autobiographical or psychological. The "self" disclosed by a Sufi like Rūzbihān consists of the ebb and flow of experiences categorized by the technical terms of Sufism – manifestation, annihilation, Essence, Attributes. The personal and family life of Rūzbihān is subsumed into visions of paradise, from which it would be hard to extrapolate much in the way of psychological analysis, for the true subject is the vision itself. Readers and interpreters of *The Unveiling of Secrets* rejected or accepted it in accordance with their own notions of sainthood and their relation with the saint. His descendants in particular tended to reshape the text to conform to their own ideas of sanctity and religious devotion, in the process making Rūzbihān fit the model of a Sufi saint to serve as the focus of a local shrine cult. Reading Rūzbihān's text against the interpretations of his hagiographers allows us to hear his voice a little more distinctly. Like the brief ecstatic sayings that Rūzbihān has explained in his *Commentary on Ecstatic Sayings*, his unveilings are framed by a transcendental rhetoric of hyperbole. His astonishingly powerful visions simply and straightforwardly present him as the recipient of unparalleled divine graces; prophets, angels, and outstanding figures from earlier Islamic tradition appear only as witnesses to acknowledge his transfiguration, or as intermediaries to convey divine blessings. Most of all, his visions tell of his encounters with God, expressing them in distinctively Persian metaphors of intense poetic lushness.

Ecstatic Speech and Ascension Narrative

The autobiographical passages just given from *The Unveiling of Secrets* do add to our picture of Rūzbihān's personality, but the modern autobiographical concerns with historical and biographical information and presentation of the self are not really the subject of this text. One has to read against the grain and sort through a large amount of visionary material to extract a few bits of personal information. If we wish to have a better approximation of the proper literary category to apply to this work, we will have to move outside the modern category of autobiography in its strictest sense. Two categories of literary text, both well-attested in early Sufism, are particularly suitable for understanding *The Unveiling of Secrets*: the genre of ecstatic speech (*shaṭḥ*), which was a special interest of Rūzbihān, and the ascension narrative as associated with Abū Yazīd al-Bisṭāmī.

A quick glance at the references to *The Unveiling of Secrets* in Rūzbihān's hagiographies shows, not surprisingly, that readers understood this to be a book about mystical experiences. As Sharaf al-Dīn Ibrāhīm observes, "The entire book *The Unveiling of Secrets*, which is one of his writings, is the essence of ecstatic speech (*shaṭḥ*)."[113] An alternate title for the book is simply *Unveilings* (*Kashfiyyāt*).[114] This does not mean that everyone simply accepted the contents of this book as valid. Several stories relate examples of people who read Rūzbihān's ecstatic sayings there and decided that he was a deluded heretic.[115] In one case, a certain Shams al-Dīn Ṣafī encountered some of these sayings, and as he put it, "Those words were difficult for me, and I inwardly rejected them (*inkār kardam*)." He tossed Rūzbihān's book away in disgust, but a visit from the Prophet Muḥammad in a dream soon convinced him that he had insulted one of the friends of God, and he went to the Sonqurī mosque to find Rūzbihān and apologize personally.[117] The hagiographers relate that a certain scholar from Iraq doubted these sayings as well, and he went to the extent of mocking Rūzbihān in public; his two sons died as a result.[118] There is also a story of some Sufis from Isfahan who heard Rūzbihān's ecstatic sayings. They resolved, "Let us go and remove his Sufi cloak as a penalty for these words, and extract justice from him."[119] Their misguided zeal ended in their unfortunate deaths. While these responses could not be said to display very sophisticated interpretations of *The Unveiling of Secrets*, the hagiographers classed them as reactions to Rūzbihān's ecstatic sayings. A more nuanced account is attached to the name of one of Rūzbihān's former *ḥadīth* teachers, Fakhr al-Dīn ibn Maryam (d.

565/1169–70).[120] When asked to resolve the status of Rūzbihān's unveilings, he studied the book and found it quite stimulating, until he read a long vision (§162–63) about the status of Rūzbihān. This is the vision in which God feasts with Rūzbihān on a mountaintop while all the great Sufi shaykhs, led by Abū Yazīd al-Bisṭāmī, mill around on horseback in the foothills, wishing they could join the feast; they are finally permitted to go into ecstasy when into their midst falls just one of the many roses that God has showered on Rūzbihān.

> One day a group of deniers of the shaykh who were among my students brought me the *Unveilings* of the shaykh, saying, "He says words such as these; are they right or not?" I said, "Let this book be with me until tonight, so I can see it, and tomorrow I will give an answer." That night I was busy reading it, and from each unveiling I understood a subtle meaning, until I arrived at that unveiling that is here related: "I was on the top of the mountain of greatness, and red roses scattered from my face and tresses. A rose from my face fell among the shaykhs; they all cried out and danced." I wondered and reflected over this unveiling, and I did not approve of it. I put the book down and went to sleep. In a dream I saw the emperor of the shaykhs Abū Yazīd, who said, "That sincere one speaks rightly, and my sense of smell is still perfumed with that rose." The next day I set the matter before the deniers. All of them left the desert of denial for the Ka'ba of acceptance. The beginner was astonished at this unveiling, and the expert received the fortunate key to the door of gnosis.[121]

Although Fakhr al-Dīn ibn Maryam only briefly summarized the gist of the vision, he rightly seized on the issue of Rūzbihān's authority over the early Sufi masters as the key to the vision. His doubts were dispelled, however, when one of the masters from Rūzbihān's vision appeared in his own dream to confirm the power of the rose dropped by Rūzbihān.

What emerges from this review of the interpretation of *The Unveiling of Secrets* is that it belongs to the class of literature that makes a claim to its author's holiness. Granted, readers will differ in what criteria they set for the demonstration, and sometimes this will involve rejecting or redefining the claims of a putative saint.

Unveilings required some kind of response in the Islamicate society of Rūzbihān's day, and that response would be dictated by the reader's relation to the saint. The longest single treatment of *The Unveiling of Secrets* is the summary and translation of Shams al-Dīn 'Abd al-Laṭīf, who in his biographical sketch of Rūzbihān cites over a dozen sections of the text.[122] As shown above, he felt compelled to suppress certain elements that did not fit his portrait of Rūzbihān's sainthood, such as the voice that called Rūzbihān a prophet, and the inexperienced shaykh under whom Rūzbihān achieved his first unveiling. In concluding his review of the text, he enlarged again on its importance as a demonstration of saintly authority, parallel to the authority of prophets: "Beware, lest critics talk at length of spiritual states, profaning the results of gnosis, and so fall into the ocean of destruction. Faith in the unveilings and miracles of the gnostics is required, because one who lacks faith in the unveilings and witnessings of the saints also lacks faith in the signs of the prophets and messengers."[123] In support he quoted Rūzbihān: "The oceans of sainthood and prophethood interpenetrate each other" (§5). Probably the best description of the purpose of *The Unveiling of Secrets* is a passage from the text that records a short speech that Rūzbihān had delivered to his disciples:

> It happened one Thursday night that I discussed with my companions the realities of secrets. I said to them, "One who gets revelation from God must be either an angel, a prophet, or a saint. Revelation comes from him after unveiling and witnessing. The angels have a form that, when apparent, removes suspicion when it is seen. The prophets have evidentiary miracles; when these appear from them, they remove the doubt regarding the truth of their revelation. The saints have charismatic miracles; when these [miracles] appear from them, no doubt remains about their revelation either. I am not in these three categories, for I do not perform charismatic miracles. My purpose in that is to reveal the truths of gnosis and the rare divine sciences that God has chosen me to receive, which take advantage of the appearance of God to teach me by a word of a station beyond the station of charismatic miracles" (§140).

This passage contains a declaration that would be little to the liking of Rūzbihān's hagiographers, a bold statement that he does not perform the charismatic miracles (*karāmāt*) of the saints, though it is an article of faith with him that these do take place with others. The hagiographers have reserved a major portion of their works to record the miracles believed to have occurred through the blessings of Rūzbihān. Yet he told his disciples that his purpose was higher than that: to reveal truths indicative of a station beyond that of miracles. In the end, *The Unveiling of Secrets* is designed to achieve precisely that goal. It is a collection of mystical experiences that demonstrate sainthood for the benefit of the elite disciples whom he guides as a Sufi master. The hagiographies and the miracle stories they contain were intended, to the contrary, for a wider audience of potential devotees and pilgrims.

In its own day, *The Unveiling of Secrets* was a work best viewed as belonging to the category of ecstatic sayings (*shaṭḥiyyāt*), which are the prerogative of the saints. We can, however, enlarge upon that category by a thematic comparison with one of the most powerful images in early Sufism, the ascension of Abū Yazīd al-Bisṭāmī. Abū Yazīd was the first Sufi we know of to re-enact the ascension (*mi'rāj*) of the Prophet Muḥammad in his own mystical experience. The subject of the Prophet's ascension is a vast one, since from its origins in a few enigmatic passages in the Qur'ān it has formed the subject of innumerable elaborations and commentaries, and I will not attempt to recapitulate here its main features and divergent traditions.[124] It is important, however, to recognize the continuity between the Islamic prophetic ascension narrative and the long tradition of ascension literature beginning in the ancient near east and continued in Gnostic, Jewish, and Christian mystical texts. Muḥammad's ascension also made an impact in Christian circles, through the Spanish, Latin, and French translations known as "the Book of the Ladder," which may well have served in turn as a model for the ascension of Dante Alighieri in his *Divine Comedy*.[125] There are many details that show the continuity between the *mi'rāj* and especially the Jewish *hekaloth* texts, which depict the ascension through celestial mansions to the vision of the throne of God.[126] One notes as a typical example the number seventy, especially in the magnified form 70,000, as a cosmological motif (ultimately of Babylonian origin) denoting the creative activity of God in the celestial realm, which recurs constantly in Rūzbihān's visions as well.[127] One must recognize that much of this literature not only contains speculations about the celestial pleroma and the afterlife, but also is linked to visualization practices that made these recitals "lived experience" in Ioan Culianu's phrase.[128] I suggest that in terms of both the visualization technique and the content, much of *The Unveiling of Secrets* can be understood as belonging to the tradition of ascension literature.

Abū Yazīd's ascension is known primarily from texts transmitted by Sarrāj, Hujwīrī, 'Aṭṭār, and Rūzbihān. These versions all show Abū Yazīd ascending through the heavens in the form of a bird seeking God, having astounding visions, but in the end denouncing the visions as a deceit. The first three of these texts have been compared by Zaehner, who pointed out that Hujwīrī and 'Aṭṭār introduced new elements into their versions, toning down the audacious character of the narrative by inserting humble references to the Prophet at the culmination of the ascension. In comparing Rūzbihān's version of this narrative with the others, I was initially puzzled by his ambiguous attitude as preserved in the Persian *Commentary on Ecstatic Sayings*; he seemed to regard the visions themselves as high mystical experiences, but at the same time he approved of Abū Yazīd seeing through them as illusions.[129] When some years later I got access to the Arabic original of Rūzbihān's commentary on the same passage in *The Language of Consciences*, it was striking to see the differences between the earlier Arabic version and the quite independent comments in the Persian translation (see the tabular comparison in Appendix B). It becomes clear, for instance, that in his Persian presentation of the original text Rūzbihān has inserted his own interpretations of the heavenly tree (Appendix B, line 359). Overall, the Arabic version stresses much more the limitations of knowledge and visions, in the context of God's temptation of the mystic with a ruse (*makr*); this is still fairly close to the early interpretations of Junayd, who is quoted here. The Persian commentary, on the other hand, omits some of these standard conclusions and adds instead a dense and highly sophisticated meditation on the problem of visionary experience from the perspective of radical transcendence. As Rūzbihān reiterates throughout *The Unveiling of Secrets*, the embodiment of God in visible form is a necessary feature of revelation, though it is in essence impossible. This contrast suggests the importance of a critical comparison between the full texts of *The Language of Consciences* and *Commentary on Ecstatic Sayings* as a prerequisite for understanding the development of

Rūzbihān's thinking on the nature of mystical symbolism. But in itself this glance at the two commentaries on Abū Yazīd's vision does not tell us more about ascension narratives in general, because of the ambiguity of Rūzbihān's comments and his failure even to describe this as an ascension; nor does this material directly shed light on the structure of *The Unveiling of Secrets* in particular.

It is only when we turn to another early version of Abū Yazīd's ascension that the relevance of this topic to *The Unveiling of Secrets* becomes apparent. This version is contained in an Arabic text called *al-Qaṣd ilā allāh* [*The Search for God*], attributed to Abū al-Qasim al-'Ārif and dated 395/1005.[130] This account is much closer to the main lines of the ascension of the Prophet Muḥammad than the brief vision of Abū Yazīd just described. Here Abū Yazīd in a dream goes through a detailed ascension that stops for a look at each of the seven heavens. The entire vision is a kind of test, for at each stage Abū Yazīd is tempted by an amazing gift or angelic kingdom. He sees innumerable angels surrounded with light and power, but he continues to long for God alone. At the seventh heaven, having passed the test, Abū Yazīd is transformed into a bird, as in the shorter version mentioned above, and he then ascends to the very throne of God. This ascension narrative offers a way to understand some of the principal motifs of *The Unveiling of Secrets*. Like Rūzbihān, Abū Yazīd sees the angels in forms both beautiful and militant. He crosses seas of light, until "all between the empyrean and the lowest depth – the Cherubim and the Bearers of the Throne and all others whom God hath created in heaven and earth – seemed less than a mustard-seed betwixt heaven and earth to the flight of my inmost heart in its quest of Him."[131] The comparison of all creation to a mustard seed, a favorite image for Rūzbihān, is an archaic element found in stories of Muḥammad's ascension preserved in *ḥadīth.* God addresses Abū Yazīd tenderly as his chosen one, echoing the singling out of Muḥammad before the other prophets, but Abū Yazīd's phrasing is remarkably close to Rūzbihān's:

> He said, " ... Thou art My chosen and My beloved and My elect from amongst My creatures." And thereat I was melting as lead melts. Then He gave me a draught from the fountain of grace in the cup of friendship; then He changed me to a

> state which I have no power to describe; then He brought Me nigh unto Him and brought me so nigh that I became nigher to Him than the spirit to the body. Then I was met by the Spirits of all the Prophets, and they saluted me and magnified my case and spoke with me and I spoke with them.[132]

This is not to say that all of *The Unveiling of Secrets* is reducible to the half-dozen pages of Abū Yazīd's vision, but it is undeniable that some of Rūzbihān's key metaphors, figures of speech, and themes occur prominently in Abū Yazīd's ascension (in the example above, one can note particularly the melting from joy, the ineffable states, and the confirmation by the prophets). Most importantly, Abū Yazīd's lengthy dialogues with God as reported by al-Sahlagī (d. 1083), which may be considered as the culminations of his ascension, are the clearest precedents for the daily encounters with God reported in *The Unveiling of Secrets*.[133] Other elements in Rūzbihān's visions, like the heavens of pearl and the celestial oceans, are found in the archaic *ḥadīth* versions of Muḥammad's ascension, though not in Bisṭāmī's. Elements like the vision of paradise as a royal court conducting festivals can also be found in *ḥadīth* texts.[134] Unlike Ibn 'Arabī (whose own ascension is not modelled on Bisṭāmī's), Rūzbihān in his ascension did not make use of the Hellenistic tradition that includes the seven planets in the seven heavens that are traversed.[135] Rūzbihān seems to have seized on the visionary character of the *mi'rāj* that was explicitly recognized in early interpretations of it as a visionary rather than a physical journey. As we have seen in the case of Rūzbihān's visions of angels, their appearance is widely recorded in the miniature paintings illustrating the ascension of the Prophet. J.-P. Guillaume has commented on the paradoxical character of the original *mi'rāj* in its use of vision to suggest the transcendence of space.

> There is something like a third term between the irrepressible and spontaneous need to represent the sacred, and the prohibition against doing so for fear of violating the divine transcendence, by degrading it to the level of sensible reality; the representation of the thing implies at the same time its non-representability. Here, the compromise is not just an accommodation dictated by considerations of pure opportunity; it opens up into the vision of a radically new space,

> splendid and bewildering. On this vision rests one of the most powerfully original esthetic effects of the text.[136]

The same may be said of the visions of Rūzbihān, but in his case the ascension functioned as a resource available at any moment rather than as an unrepeated paradigmatic event. *The Unveiling of Secrets* records on a daily basis the ascents and descents that Rūzbihān experienced in his prayers and meditations, typically during night-time vigil or at dawn. These are modeled on the example of the Prophet Muḥammad but seen in the Bisṭāmian fashion. In his visions Rūzbihān vividly experienced the truth of the Prophetic saying, "ritual prayer is the ascension (*mi'rāj*) of the believer."[137] From this point of view, we may say that *The Unveiling of Secrets* is written as a series of ecstatic sayings that invoke the authoritative model of the visionary journey to the throne of God, the mystical ascension of the soul.

Notes

1. Nwyia, p. 387.
2. Janet Varner Gunn, "Autobiography," *Encyclopedia of Religion*, 2:7–10, notes the rarity of studies of non-Western autobiographies.
3. Marshall G.S. Hodgson, *The Venture of Islam: Conscience and History in a World Civilization*, vol. 2, *The Expansion of Islam in the Middle Periods* (Chicago: The University of Chicago Press, 1974), pp. 180–92.
4. Cf. Farid Jabre, *Essai sur le lexique de Ghazali: Contribution à l'étude de la terminologie de Ghazali dans ses principaux ouvrages à l'exception du* **Tahāfut**, Études Philosophiques et Sociales, 5 (Beirut: l'Université Libanaise, n.d.), pp. 242–47; William Chittick, *The Sufi Path of Knowledge: Ibn al-'Arabi's Metaphysics of Imagination* (Albany: SUNY Press, 1989), index, s.v. "unveiling."
5. L. Gardet, "Kashf," EI^2, IV, 696–97 (1976).
6. *Sharḥ-i shaṭḥiyyāt*, p. 557. The first sentence of Rūzbihān's definition renders into Persian the definition of Sarrāj, who moreover adds two quotations: "Abū Muḥammad al-Jurayrī said, 'One who does not treat his relationship to God with piety and meditation will not reach unveiling and witnessing.' al-Nūrī said, 'The unveilings of the eyes are through vision, but the unveilings of hearts are through union'" (*Luma'*, p. 346).
7. In *Mashrab al-arwāḥ*, nearly fifty of the 1001 states are characterized as visions (*ru'ya*), while no other general category is used even half as frequently.
8. In choosing the term "conscience" rather than "consciousness" (which has an awkward plural in English), I am following the French usage of *conscience* by Corbin and others, which preserves

the archaic sense of "awareness," the noetic faculty called by the Scholastics *synteresis* (from Greek *sunoida*, cf. Latin *conscio*); I do not intend here the later moralistic sense of conscience as a judge of good or evil action. For a review of these terms, see C. S. Lewis, *Studies in Words*, 2nd ed. (Cambridge: Cambridge University Press, 1979), pp. 181–214.

9. *Sharḥ-i shaṭḥiyyāt*, p. 574.
10. One MS is Mashhad IV, 220, no. 931, MS 829, dated Jum. II 1064/ May 1654, containing fifty folios. I would like to thank Prof. James Morris and Dr. Amir Moezzi for making available copies of this MS and Corbin's unpublished partial edition (covering up to §87, approximately one third of the work), which also referred to the MSS of Massignon and Nwyia. The photocopy of the Mashhad MS had been numbered by Corbin up to §122, and the remainder (ending at §210) is numbered according to my own divisions. The other MS is described in Massignon, "La Vie," pp. 451–52. I would like to express my gratitude to Dr. Daniel Massignon for providing me with a copy of this manuscript.
11. Corbin, *En Islam iranien*, III, 45–64.
12. Ibid., p. 45.
13. *Rūḥ al-jinān*, p. 168, where (in Persian translation of §10) Rūzbihān is made to say only that he heard great voices with the ear of his soul.
14. Ravishing (*walah*) and bewilderment (*hayamān*) are the ninth and tenth of the eleven stages of human love as described by al-Daylamī, which was expanded by Rūzbihān to include levels of divine love; cf. "The Stages of Love in Early Persian Sufism."
15. *Mashrab al-arwāḥ*, p. 287.
16. Corbin translates, "il me semblait être dans quelque taverne" (introduction to *'Abhar al-'āshiqīn*, p. 34), but *kharāb* here seems more likely to mean an abandoned ruin rather than a tavern.
17. Reading *min al-idṭarāb* rather than *min al-arḍ ṭarāb*; cf. the Persian translation, *az idṭirāb sākin shudam*, in *Rūḥ al-jinān*, p. 169.
18. *Rūḥ al-jinān*, p. 169.
19. On Ash'arism and Sufism, see Schimmel, *Dimensions*, 88–90; Ritter, *Das Meer der Seele*, 596–97; and the creed of Ibn al-Khafīf, in Daylamī, *Sīrat Ibn Khafīf Shīrazī, pp. 284–308.*
20. Abū al-Qāsim 'Abd al-Karīm al-Qushayrī describes this in his "Complaint of the Sunnīs about the Persecution they have Suffered," in *al-Rasā'il al- Qushayriyya*, ed. and Urdu trans. Muḥammad Ḥassān (Karachi: Nashrat Ma'had al-Markazī lil-Abḥāth al-Islāmiyya, 1384/1964), pp. 1–49 (Arabic text), 1–38 (Urdu trans.).
21. *Maslak al-tawḥīd*, ed. Ballanfat, §3.
22. Ibid., 4.
23. Ibid., 7.
24. Technically *'arsh* is the vaulted canopy suspended over the seat or platform which is the *kursī*, but the terms "throne" and "footstool" have become fairly entrenched, so they are retained here. See W. M. Thackston, Jr., trans., *The Tales of the Prophets of al-Kisa'i*, Library of

Classical Arabic Literature, 2 (Boston: Twayne Publishers, 1978), p. 337, n. 3.
25. Ibid., pp. 6–7.
26. *Mashrab al-arwāḥ*, p. 255.
27. Jabre, pp. 218, 256–57.
28. Rūzbihān defines *ghayb* as "that which the heart sees of the realm of the afterlife," and "the hidden of the hidden" (*ghayb al-ghayb*) as "the degrees of knowledge in the hidden" (*Sharḥ-i shaṭḥiyyāt*, p. 631).
29. *Malakūt* can be derived from *mulk*, "kingdom," so that etymologically it would mean something like "dominion." It can also be derived from *malak*, "angel," however, and I prefer using this sense as a better reflection of the way Rūzbihān refers to his visions of angels and other supernal beings.
30. *Mashrab al-arwāḥ*, p. 210.
31. Jabre, p. 46; L. Gardet, "'Ālam," EI[2].
32. *Mashrab al-arwāḥ*, p. 210.
33. Ibid., pp. 218–19.
34. *Sharḥ-i shaṭḥiyyāt*, p. 626.
35. For an overview of states and stations, see Schimmel, *Dimensions*, pp. 109–30; see also "The Stages of Love" and "Mystical Language" for further details of Rūzbihān's understanding of states and stations.
36. *Sharḥ-i shaṭḥiyyāt*, p. 551.
37. Ibid., p. 548.
38. Ibid.
39. Ibid., p. 549
40. Ibid., p. 553.
41. Ibid.
42. Ibid., p. 556.
43. Ibid., p. 558.
44. Ibid., p. 557.
45. Ibid., p. 569.
46. *Mashrab al-arwāḥ*, p. 223.
47. Ibid., p. 617; cf. Sarrāj, p. 363, line 2.
48. *Sharḥ-i shaṭḥiyyāt*, p. 568. According to Sarrāj (p. 349), this is the highest state of the "sincere ones" (*ṣiddīqūn*).
49. *Sharḥ-i shaṭḥiyyāt*, p. 569. Rūzbihān has altered Sarrāj's definition (p. 349) by substituting "the Graceful Forgiver" (*laṭīf-i ghaffār*) for "the Overpowering King" (*al-malik al-jabbār*), and by adding the phrase about indigence.
50. *Sharḥ-i shaṭḥiyyāt*, pp. 553–54.
51. Ibid., p. 554.
52. *Sharḥ-i shaṭḥiyyāt*, pp. 63, 435. In commenting on Ḥallāj's presentation of Iblīs in the *Ṭāsīn al-azal wal-iltibās* (ibid., pp. 508–9, 513), Rūzbihān uses *iltibās* in the sense of "covering up" or "confusion," alluding to the hypocrisy of Iblīs as he presents himself as the true lover of God.
53. Badī' al-Zamān Furūzānfar, *Aḥādīth-i mathnawī* (Tehran, 1334/1955), p. 115, no. 346 (*khalaqa 'llāhu ādama 'alā ṣūratih*). Chittick

translates this as "God created Adam upon His own form" (*The Sufi Path of Knowledge*, Index of Hadiths and Sayings, p. 437).

54. On this saying see Ritter, *Das Meer der Seele*, pp. 445–46 (*ra'aytu rabbī fī aḥsani ṣūratin*); Schimmel, *Dimensions*, p. 290; Henry Corbin, *Creative Imagination in the Sufism of Ibn 'Arabī*, trans. Ralph Manheim, Bollingen Series 91 (Princeton: Princeton University Press, 1969), pp. 272–81.
55. Chittick, p. 283. This saying, *takhallaqū bi-akhlāq allāh*, contains an untranslatable play on words alluding to *khalq*, "creation," and *khuluq*, "quality, ethos."
56. In this respect I question Corbin's use of the term "amphibolie" to translate *iltibās* (*En islam iranien*, III, 18, 54–58, 75–76, etc.), meaning by that an "intercorrespondance" between this world and the divine realm, in which everything has a "double sense." This seems an excessively abstract overtranslation, and it fails to convey the sense of the root L-B-S as "clothing." I qualify it as "clothing with divinity" when the context makes it clear that *iltibās* means a theophany clothed in visible form.
57. See Corbin, *En Islam iranien*, 3:30–44. Ballanfat, like Corbin, prefers the alternate title *Kitāb al-ighāna*, rendering it as *Le Livre de l'ennuagement du coeur*, "The Book of the Clouding of the Heart."
58. For an example where Abū Yazīd al-Bisṭāmī uses the same image, see *Words of Ecstasy*, p. 27.
59. This term unsatisfactorily renders the phrase *ahl al-nahy*, "the people of negation," which might be translated as "apophatics," in allusion to the practitioners of the negative theology who deny created attributes to God.
60. Cf. *Ghalaṭāt al-sālikīn*, p. 94, where Rūzbihān criticizes those weak and deluded souls who mistake their imaginings and physical visions for unveilings.
61. Cf. *Words of Ecstasy*, p. 76.
62. Hujwīrī, p. 253; cf. trans. Nicholson, p. 288, where "witness" (*shāhid*) is translated as "evidence." Further on majesty and beauty, see Rūmī, *Mathnawī*, ed. Nicholson, I, 393, 498, 759, 1746–48, 2036; Ibn 'Arabī, *Futūḥāt*, II, 133:10–12.
63. *Words of Ecstasy*, p. 39.
64. Schimmel, *Dimensions*, pp. 200–3.
65. The closest constellation to the celestial north pole is the Little Bear (Ursa Minor, *al-dubb al-aṣghar* or *banāt na'sh al-aṣghar*), now called the Little Dipper, which in Arab lore is composed of seven stars (Ptolemy counted eight). It includes the star now called Polaris, used for millenia for navigation, and the two stars called by the Arabs *farqadān*, which are synonymous with the pole. Rūzbihān generally calls it just *banāt na'sh*, which could mean either the Great or the Little Bear, but in one place he refers to it as the Great Bear (*banāt na'sh al-kubrā*, §19); that is probably a copyist's error, as that constellation is farther from the pole and has twenty-seven stars. See Abū al-Ḥusayn 'Abd al-Raḥmān al-Ṣūfī, *Ṣuwar al-kawākib* (Hyderabad: Dā'irat al-Ma'ārif al-'Uthmāniyya, 1373/1954), pp. 27–29; "Ursa Major" and "Ursa

Minor," *Encyclopaedia Britannica* (11th ed., New York, 1911), vol. 27, p. 802. Corbin (*En Islam Iranien*, III, 27) refers to it as the Great Bear, and though he also considers the Little Bear and the Great Bear as a single constellation, the editors of the English translation of *The Man of Light* have correctly placed al-Ṣūfī's illustration of the Little Bear as a frontispiece.

66. Michel Chodkiewicz, *Le Sceau des saints*, p. 59, citing Hoca's edition of *Kashf al-asrār*, p. 103 (this recension differs slightly from that found in the Massignon and Mashhad MSS, and in place of the last two sentences quoted above, it contains lines from the encounter with Khiḍr in §16, in which Rūzbihān drinks an ocean of gnosis).
67. That primordial investiture took on the qualities of sainthood after Adam and Eve left the garden, when they were told (in language echoing Qur'ān 10:62 on "the friends of God"), that "those who follow my guidance have no fear over them, neither do they sorrow" (10:38). Cf. Chodkiewicz, p. 36.
68. Following the reading of Nwyia (*tajrī*) and Hoca (*yajrī*); the MSS read *li-ākhirī*.
69. Cf. *Eternal Garden*, p. 225.
70. The number 70,000 has a traditional cosmic significance, designating for instance the number of angels who daily enter the "house of life" (*al-bayt al-ma'mūr*), in accounts of the Prophet's ascension; cf. Wensinck, II, 398b.
71. Ballanfat, *L'itinéraire*, p. 48, n. 248, citing *'Arā'is al-bayān*, MS Berlin, fol. 420.
72. Further on Khiḍr see Schimmel, *Dimensions*, index, s.n.
73. Corbin (*En Islam iranien*, III, 58) translates the last phrase as "Chacun d'eux est un Ange, et toi tu es un Ange de la Perse," reading *malak*, "angel," rather than *malik*, "king." In view of the strong images of Persian kingship discussed below, I prefer the latter reading.
74. *Adab al-mulūk fī bayān ḥaqā'iq al-taṣawwuf*, ed. Bernd Ratke, Beiruter Texte und Studien, 37 (Beirut/Stuttgart: Franz Steiner Verlag, 1991), p. 7.
75. Schimmel, *Dimensions*, index, s.v. "Light of Muḥammad."
76. The MSS appear to read here *ṣāḥa*, which can mean "a barren plain" (Lane, 1743c), but I emend this to *ṣabāḥa*, "brightness, beauty."
77. G.-C. Anawati and Louis Gardet, *Mystique musulmane: aspects et tendances – expériences et techniques*, Études Musulmanes, 7 (4th ed., Paris: Librairie Philosophique J. Vrin, 1986), pp. 261–71.
78. *Sharḥ-i shaṭḥiyyāt*, pp. 23–27, 30–35; *Words of Ecstasy*, pp. 131–32.
79. *Words of Ecstasy*, pp. 102–110.
80. *Mashrab al-arwāḥ*, p. 290.
81. "The Symbolism of Birds," passim.
82. Corbin (*En Islam iranien*, III, 59) misreads *hay'a*, "shape," as *hayba*, "l'aspect numineux," and somehow renders *taḥruqu*, "consumes," as "embrase," perhaps reading it as *taḥūtu*.
83. Massignon, *Passion*, III, 287, n. 4. Rūzbihān also cites this *ḥadīth* in *'Abhar al-'ashiqīn*, p. 34, no. 77, and *Sharḥ-i shaṭḥiyyāt*, p. 153, no. 265;

cf. Schimmel, *Dimensions*, pp. 222, 298–99. Ritter (*Meer*, p. 456) cites Nallino (*Raccolta*, II, 247 n. 2; II, 297, 302) as suggesting a Neoplatonic origin for this metaphor, as developed by Pseudo-Dionysius, but this seems unnecessary.

84. Joseph van Ess, *The Youthful God: Anthropomorphism in Early Islam*, Ninth Annual University Lecture in Religion (Tempe, AZ: Arizona State University, 1989), pp. 1–20.

85. Annemarie Schimmel, "Turk and Hindu: A Poetical Image and its Application to Historical Fact," in *Islam and Cultural Change in the Middle Ages*, ed. Speros Vryonis, Jr. (Wiesbaden: Otto Harrassowitz, 1975), pp. 107–126; Ehsan Yarshater, "The Theme of Wine-drinking and the Concept of the Beloved in Early Persian Poetry," *Studia Islamica* XIII (1960), pp. 43–54.

86. Mu'īn, Introduction to *'Abhar al-'āshiqīn*, pp. 94–99.

87. The MSS here read *ḥujja*, "proof," but it seems more likely that this is a repetition from the previous line of *ḥajal* (pl. *ḥajāl*), "curtained canopy for a bride."

88. It is difficult to know what to make of Rūzbihān's reference to the shaykh as one "whose appearance was unknown" (*majhūl al-shakl*). Corbin (*En Islam iranien*, III, 56) translates with a gloss, "dont la vraie figure était ignorée du commun des gens." Perhaps the implication is that the shaykh was a recluse whose appearance was only known to his disciples.

89. For a discussion of the different versions of this saying, which later authors attributed to Rūzbihān, see "Rūzbihān Baqlī on Love as 'Essential Desire.'"

90. The verse, which has several untranslatable puns, reads: *a yabdū al-ṣubḥa muḥmarr al-ma'āqi / wa lam tar'uf khayāshīm al-zaqāqi // tadārak ayyuhā al-sāqī nufūsan / taraqqat bil-humūm ilā al-turāqī*. This suggests that if one awakens with bloodshot eyes at dawn, it is silly to maintain that the wineskin did not pour out blood-red wine, so the winebearer should avert the drinkers' fears of imminent death by administering his wares. I am grateful to Prof. Wolfhart Heinrichs of Harvard University for clarifying this verse, in which, as he notes, "the disgusting imagery is certainly intended for its comical effect" (personal communication).

91. Following Massignon's MS, *tadhākartu* rather than Mashhad's *tadāraktu*.

92. Ḥallāğ, *Kitāb al-ṭawāsīn*, ed. Paul Nwyia, Mélanges de l'Université Saint-Joseph, 47 (Beirut: Imprimerie Catholique, 1972), II.8; cf. also III.1, III.3, IV.1.

93. Shihâboddîn Yahyâ Sohravardî Shaykh al-Ishrâq, *L'Archange empourpré, Quinze traités et récits mystiques*, trans. Henry Corbin (Paris: Fayard, 1976), p. 215, n. 7, and index, s.v. "désert."

94. Marie-Rose Séguy, *The Miraculous Journey of Mahomet: Mirâj Nâmeh*, trans. Richard Pevear (New York: George Braziller, 1977), p. 25. I am indebted to Scott Kugle of Duke University for pointing out the significance of the ascension miniatures for Rūzbihān's angelology.

95. William C. Spengemann, *The Forms of Autobiography: Episodes in the*

History of a Literary Genre (New Haven: Yale University Press, 1980), pp. 175–89.

96. A survey and anthology of autobiographical types of writing in Islamic culture is forthcoming from a group of scholars including Michael Cooperson of Harvard University, who has discussed some literary and psychological aspects of biography and autobiography in Arabic (with a bow to Freud) in "al-Khiṭāb niyāba ʻan al-ākhir [Discourse Representing the Other]," *al-Qāhira* (March 1993), pp. 58-65.
97. I am indebted to Michael Cooperson for sharing with me his unpublished translation, "Al-Ḥakīm al-Tirmidhī: How it All Began."
98. ʻAbū al-Maʻālī ʻAbd Allāh ibn Muḥammad ibn ʻAlī ibn al-Ḥasan ibn ʻAlī al-Miyānajī al-Hamadānī "ʻAyn al-Quḍāt," *Risālat shakwā al-gharīb*, ed. ʻAfīf ʻUsayrān, Intishārāt-i Dānishgāh-i Tihrān, 695 (Tehran: Dānishgāh, 1962); trans. A. J. Arberry, *A Sufi Martyr, The Apologia of ʻAin al-Quḍāt al-Hamadhānī* (London: George Allen & Unwin, 1969).
99. Jonathan G. Katz, "The Worldly Pursuits of a Would-be Walī: Muḥammad al-Zawāwī al-Bijāʼī (d. 882/1477)," *Al-Qanṭara* XII (1991), pp. 497–520; id., "Visionary Experience, Autobiography, and Sainthood in North African Islam," *Princeton Papers in Near Eastern Studies* 1 (1992), pp. 85–118.
100. Katherine P. Ewing, "The Dream of Spiritual Initiation and the Organization of Self Representation among Pakistani Sufis," *American Ethnologist* (1990), pp. 56–74, esp. pp. 61–63, citing Corbin, "The Visionary Dream," pp. 390–91. Common elements in Rūzbihān's vision and the modern dream include the appearance of two impressive figures robed in white, and the presentation of food; the modern dream also has features of the present day such as a telephone booth.
101. Ibid., p. 64.
102. Ioan Petru Culianu, "Ascension," *Encyclopedia of Religion*, I, 435–41.
103. Rūzbihān only refers to dreams on a couple of occasions in *Kashf al-asrār* (§50–51, 151); in one case thinking about dreams leads him into a waking vision of the Prophet, and in the other an experience began with a dream, but he awoke and it turned into an unveiling. On dream interpretation in Sufism, an important tool in guiding novices, see Richard Gramlich, *Die Schiitischen Derwischorden Persiens*, vol. 2, *Glaube und Lehre*, Abhandlungen für die Kunde des Morgenlandes, 36/2–4 (Wiesbaden: Franz Steiner, 1976), 213–17.
104. Rūzbihān, *Sayr al-arwāḥ*, ed. Ballanfat, §37.
105. Spengemann, pp. 6–16.
106. See *Words of Ecstasy*, pp. 25–28.
107. The text may be corrupt here, but appears to read *wa-ḍāqa ṣadrī jiddan fīmā* [=*fīhā*?] *wa-ʻuḍtu ḥabībī*. For this interpretation, see Lane's Lexicon, s.v. ʻWḌ, 8th form.
108. The Persian *ḥubb-ast wa shab-i nīkū* seems rather to mean, "It is love, and good night."

109. This passage is also given, with some improved readings, in *Rūḥ al-jinān*, p. 350.
110. Furūzānfar, no. 163, p. 63 (from both Bukhārī and Muslim).
111. Roughly, "Doing that is not to be done" (?). Nwyia (no. 23) reads, *kar dar ān bā-kardan-ast,* and translates it as "Would that you did to yourself as was done to you."
112. Abū al-Ḥasan Daylamī, *Sīrat-i shaykh-i kabīr Abū 'Abd Allāh ibn Khafīf Shīrāzī*, Persian trans. Rukn al-Dīn Yaḥyā ibn Junayd Shīrazī, ed. Annemarie Schimmel (Ankara, 1955; reprint ed., Tehran: Intishārāt-i Bābak, 1363/1984), pp. 224–25; cf. Schimmel, *Dimensions*, p. 36, on the anti-family attitudes of certain ascetics.
113. *Tuḥfat ahl al-'irfān*, p. 105.
114. *Tuḥfat ahl al-'irfā*n, p. 33; *Rūḥ al-jinān*, p. 232.
115. It might be supposed that these stories relate to reactions to Rūzbihān's *Commentary on Ecstatic Sayings*, but that work consists of his commentary on the ecstatic sayings of others. While we know of another writing of Rūzbihān that provoked controversy (*Salwat al-'āshiqīn*, of which only one quotation survives, in *Rūḥ al-jinān*, pp. 195–96), it seems likely that whenever "unveilings" or "ecstatic sayings" of Rūzbihān are mentioned without further qualification, *The Unveiling of Secrets* is intended.
116. *Tuḥfat ahl al-'irfān*, p. 38.
117. *Rūḥ al-jinān*, p. 214, where a fuller version of the story is given.
118. *Rūḥ al-jinān*, p. 218 (the offensive speech: "We have spoken plenty of rational (*'aqlī*) and traditional (*naqlī*) words, now we want to hear the words of Baqlī").
119. *Rūḥ al-jinān*, p. 217.
120. His death date has been reported to be anywhere from 565 to after 600, but the earlier date seems more likely; cf. *Hazār mazār*, p. 430, n. 154. This would place Fakhr al-Dīn's death before the composition of *Kashf al-asrār*, but the significance of the story is not in its facticity.
121. *Rūḥ al-jinān*, pp. 232–33. This account is followed by a quotation of the Arabic text of *Kashf al-asrār*, §162–63, with only minor divergences from the MSS.
122. *Ruḥ al-jinān*, pp. 167–74, citing *Kashf al-asrār*, §8–14, 19, 20, 31, 28, 30, 32, 35, 49, 57, 39.
123. *Ruḥ al-jinān*, p. 174.
124. B. Schrieke et al., "Mi'rādj," EI^2, VII, 97–105 (1991), which unfortunately lacks a discussion of Persian literature on this topic; G. Böwering, "Mi'rāj," *Encyclopedia of Religion*, IX, 552–56 (1987).
125. The classic work on this subject is Miguel Asín Palacios, *La Escatología musulmana en la Divine Comedia, seguida de la historia y crítica de una polémica* (3rd ed., Madrid: Instituto Hispano Arabe de Cultura, 1961). See most recently Gisèle Besson and Michèle Brossard-Dandré, ed. and trans., *Le livre de l'échelle de Mahomet: Liber Scale Machometi*, Lettres Gothiques (Paris: Le Livre de Poche, 1991).
126. Ioan P. Couliano [sic], *Expériences de l'extase: extase, ascension et récit*

visionnaire de l'hellénisme au moyen âge (Paris: Payot, 1984), p. 171; see also pp. 153–72 for a good analysis of the *mi'rāj* in general.

127. Ibid., p. 159.
128. Ibid., p. 14.
129. *Words of Ecstasy*, Appendix, pp. 168–69.
130. Reynold A. Nicholson, "An Early Arabic Version of the *Mi'rāj* of Abū Yazīd al-Bisṭāmī," *Islamica* II (1926), pp. 402–15, edited from two Indian MSS.
131. Ibid., p. 413, trans. Nicholson.
132. Ibid., p. 414, trans. Nicholson.
133. See 'Abd al-Rahmān, *Shaṭaḥāt al-Ṣūfiyya*, Part One, *Abū Yazīd al-Bisṭāmī*, Darāsāt Islāmiyya 9 (Cairo: Maktaba al-Nahḍa al-Miṣriyya, 1949), esp. pp. 86, 89, 116, for short versions of the "bird" ascension vision; trans. Abdelwahab Meddeb, *Les Dits de Bistami: Shatahât*, L'espace interieur 38 (Paris: Fayard, 1989), p. 74, no. 131; p. 80, no. 140; p. 125, no. 291.
134. Asín, pp. 308–12.
135. Asín, pp. 76–84 and passim; James Winston Morris, "The Spiritual Ascension: Ibn 'Arabī and the Mi'rāj," *Journal of the American Oriental Society* 107 (1987), pp. 629–52; 108 (1988), pp. 63–77.
136. J.-P. Guillaume, "Le texte sous le texte: les sources du *Livre de l'Échelle* et le thème du *mi'rāj* dans l'imaginaire islamique," in *Le Livre de l'Échelle*, p. 48.
137. Schimmel, *Dimensions*, pp. 148, 218.

III

Institutionalizing a Sufi Order

A. The Biographies of Rūzbihān Baqlī

One of the most prominent aspects of the history of Sufism is the process of institutionalization that took place beginning from the eleventh century, when teaching lineages and hospices began to form around outstanding Sufi masters. The general outlines of this process have been frequently sketched, as for instance in the case of Abū Sa'īd-i Abū al-Khayr.[1] Through his charismatic teaching he gained a large following and set up a communal hospice or khānqāh; after his death his tomb became a place of pilgrimage under the direction of his heirs, and his life was memorialized by them in the form of hagiography. His good relations with political figures, as portrayed in hagiography, reinforced the patronage of the shrine as an important function of government. Abū Sa'īd did not become the focus of a Sufi tariqa or "order," however. Sufi lineages began to take concrete form as distinct spiritual genealogies only in the twelfth and especially the thirteenth centuries, when we see the emergence of distinct groups such as the Qādiriyya, the Suhrawardiyya, and so forth. Various reasons have been advanced to explain the ramification of Sufism in this fashion. As a popularization of what had earlier been a more private form of piety, the Sufi orders became a public form of Sunnī Islam that attracted the support of rulers like the Seljuks and the Ayyūbids. These rulers probably viewed Sufism as a source of Islamic legitimation, as an ally in resisting the attraction of Shī'ism, and as a direct conduit to divine grace. The Caliph al-Nāṣir sponsored both Sufi orders and *futuwwa* guild associations as spiritual organizations for revivifying Islam under his leadership.

Islamic society was severely strained, however, by the Mongol onslaught of the thirteenth century. Not only did the Mongols overthrow the Caliphate and destroy many cities of the Islamic east, but also they overwhelmed the networks of patronage and support of religion by pulling many local Muslim rulers into submission to pagan overlords. This catastrophe did not, however, retard the public development of Sufism. Perhaps it was in response to the spiritual vacuum created by the end of the Caliphate that Sufi orders accelerated their penetration of the social arena at this time. Whatever the cause, the outcome was that under the new Mongol overlords of Iran, the Il-Khans (1256–1335), the Sufi orders became more prominent than ever under Mongol patronage.[2] Standard histories of this era refer to a few well-known figures such as 'Alā' al-Dawla Simnānī who had close contact with the Mongol court, but these accounts are cursory; there were many places where Sufi orders took hold about which we still know very little in terms of their social and political development.[3]

It is in this context that the religious and social legacy of Rūzbihān Baqlī needs to be understood. The biographies of Rūzbihān written by his descendants are the main sources of information about the institutionalization of the Rūzbihāniyya Sufi order. Although the Rūzbihāniyya was limited to four generations of the founder's descendants, the way in which it developed illustrates some important themes that are worth considering in any overall interpretation of the rise of the Sufi orders during the thirteenth century. An examination of hagiographies written by Rūzbihān's descendants documents the process of "the routinization of charisma" in detail. Rūzbihān was an ecstatic mystic and prolific author who fulfilled the role of the "educator shaykh" for a number of elite disciples, though he also had a public role for many ordinary residents of Shiraz. His pious descendants were in contrast committed to publicizing the cult of his shrine, which they pursued through establishing close relations with first the Salghurid Atābegs of Fārs and later the Mongol governors of the region. Yet somehow the Rūzbihāniyya did not survive, while other Sufi groups in the region flourished for centuries; it lacked both the highly developed training courses of the Kubrawiyya and the far-flung patronage networks of the Kāzarūniyya. Although Rūzbihān was an experienced Sufi teacher who wrote a number of treatises to guide the meditation of novices, his descendants in the Rūzbihāniyya did not sustain this aspect of Sufi practice. The attempts of the hagiographers to furnish Rūzbihān with a repertoire of saintly miracles met with a limited success in attracting followers. Nonetheless, the form of the hagiographical narrative that portrays the deeds of Rūzbihān and his descendants testifies to the changing religious situation of the post-Mongol period. Even the example of such a short-lived institution shows how urgent was the need to establish local centers where divine grace could be made publicly available through the agency of the saint's tomb.

The two biographies of Rūzbihān written by his two great-grandsons illustrate the authority of Rūzbihān and the importance of his tomb as a focus of pilgrimage. Sharaf al-Dīn Ibrāhīm and Shams al-Dīn 'Abd al-Laṭīf were both sons of Rūzbihān's grandson Ṣadr al-Dīn Rūzbihān II (d. 685/1286). Sharaf al-Dīn Ibrāhīm wrote the first of these hagiographies under the title *Tuhfat ahl al-'irfān* [*The Gift of the People of Gnosis*] in 700/1300, while his brother Shams al-Dīn compiled *Rūḥ al-jinān* [*The Spirit of the Gardens*] five years later in 705/1305. Both biographies have been published in Iran some years ago.[4]

Sharaf al-Dīn Ibrāhīm relates as follows the circumstances surrounding his composition of the earlier biography:

> The story of his [Rūzbihān's] miracles and mysticism is famous and well known throughout the world. He has written many books on Qur'ānic exegesis, commentaries on *ḥadīth*, and the principles of jurisprudence. But the miracles and wonders of his blessed states have not reached from speech to writing, and his noble biography relating his great states has not come to the pen. Some ninety-four years after his blessed passing away [i.e., in 700/1300], a group of notables (*akābir*) of Shiraz requested this helpless one, the author of this book, the least of his children and grandchildren, [Sharaf al-Dīn] Ibrāhīm ibn Rūzbihān [II], to put together a biography of the master. A collection of disciples and a group of sincere lovers of the revered great master were desirous of this outcome....
>
> This helpless one was not capable of this task, for how should an explanation of the state of the royal threshold come about from a helpless slave? What does the hornet's buzzing have to do with the chanting of psalms? Finally certain masters of the heart, who believed in the author of this book, and whose rank is such that they have found abiding pleasure and a complete portion in God's path, pleaded for this result. After seeking omen and help, resolve appeared from the

> sacred spirit of the master (may God freshen his spirit), and I collected this blessed book as a gift for the masters of the heart, naming it *The Gift [of the People] of Gnosis, in Memory of the Chief Axis of the World Rūzbihān.*[5]

The outline of Sharaf al-Dīn's hagiography is as follows:

I. On the Birth and Origin of the Shaykh.
II. On the Great Saints who were his Contemporaries.
III. Stories and Miracles.
IV. Comments of the Shaykh on Scriptural Exegesis and *Ḥadīth* from a Mystical Perspective, and Commentary on Ten Sayings of the Shaykh.
V. Diverse Sayings [a bibliography of his writings, with excerpts].
VI. On his Children and Grandchildren, and Notes on Ṣadr al-Dīn Rūzbihān II.
VII. The Death of the Shaykh and Miracles at his Shrine.
Conclusion.

The primary motivation for this biography appears to have been the interest of devotees in having a record of the master's miracles and spiritual states. As he explains, "The author has compiled these blessed and fortunate words so that those who read this blessed biography (*sīrat nāma*) may obtain a full portion of the blessing of his fortunate words."[6]

The second biography by Shams al-Dīn has a different appearance, due to its highly florid Arabicized style and its dedication to a political figure. The author relates that after much travel to distant lands he had encountered many great and famous people, who desired to hear an account of his grandfather's life. Having told these stories, he conceived the idea of writing them down. His overexposure to courtly styles of expression can be seen from the following:

> Friends who were extremely reliable and pure asked this weak one to write a book on the life of the sultan of the gnostics of the world, Shaykh Rūzbihān (peace be upon him), in which the pearls of useful morals should be joined together, and on the field of which the wondrous banners of his gnosis were displayed, on which the steed of expression and eloquence should charge over the plains of rhetoric and

> skill, with an example of each of the famous writings of the master, as a memento for the wayfarers of the spiritual path and reality. But I made the pretense of 'maybe' and 'perhaps' [to wait and see] what would emerge flawlessly from behind the hidden veil [of the future].[7]

It was only when he went to attend upon the throne of the Atābeg of Luristan, Nuṣrat al-Dīn Ahmad (r. 696-733/1296-1333), that Shams al-Dīn conceived of writing the book and presenting it to that ruler, clothing his dedication in a fulsome prose that I will refrain from translating. The contents are as follows:

Introduction on Sainthood

I. On his Birth, Certain of his Spiritual States and Unveilings, his Teachers, his Masters, with Reference to the Source of the Affiliation and its Reality, and the Initiatic Genealogy of his Cloak.

II. On Certain Stories regarding his Miracles and Spiritual States [containing forty stories].

III. On his Writings, with Extracts from his Sayings

IV. On his Sons, with Certain Virtues of his Virtuous Grandson Ṣadr al-Dīn Rūzbihān II.

Advice to the Patron Nuṣrat al-Dīn, and Conclusion

It is noteworthy that, while Shams al-Dīn does express the confidence that the book will be useful to travelers of the spiritual path, he then in a sense separates himself and the dedicatee from that endeavor. After referring to the seekers of God, Shams al-Dīn remarks that he hopes they will remember that emperor and himself with their their saving prayers.[8]

Both biographies are scholarly and preserve significant portions of Rūzbihān's writings, including some works otherwise not available, but their audience is more devotional than contemplative. If we wish to contrast the emphases of the two books, we could say that Sharaf al-Dīn's *The Gift of the People of Gnosis* carries with it more of the intimacy of the close circle of the religious classes of Shiraz, who after nearly a century still regard the shaykh as a central figure in their religious life. Shams al-Dīn, on the other hand, conveys in *The Spirit of the Gardens* the situation of the courtier who regards religion as an important aspect of life, but who regards Sufis (even his own grandfather) as important primarily for the benefits they bring to society and above all its leaders. The texts overlap to a considerable degree, so that, for instance, half of the miracle stories told by Shams al-Dīn can also be found in Sharaf al-Dīn's collection. Both texts represent stages in the institutionalization of Rūzbihān's Sufism.

I would like to trace out the details of that institutionalizing process by examining three topics that the biographies treat: first, their portrayal of Rūzbihān through stories of his miracles and spiritual status; second, the picture that emerges of Rūzbihān's descendants (with some supplementary information from other biographical sources); and third, the relation of the Rūzbihāniyya with political power.

B. Stories of Rūzbihān in the Early Hagiographical Narratives

Most of the stories about Rūzbihān in his hagiographies focus on the spiritual experiences of his disciples. Rūzbihān's disciples tell about receiving visions from him that solve spiritual problems, or just his advice that explains events occurring during their meditation. Many of his disciples relied on his guidance in undertaking retreats and forty-day seclusions.[9] Rūzbihān himself often took refuge in his own private retreat room.[10] Disciples describe him receiving visits from Khiḍr[11] or levitating in the air from joy when some street musicians passed by his *ribāṭ*.[12] One disciple went into a trance the moment he began to think about Rūzbihān's status.[13] Those who disobeyed Rūzbihān's instructions suffered intensely, especially if they revealed their experiences without permission.[14] Several relate experiences of seeing Rūzbihān in his old age borne through an immense crowd in his palanquin and wishing they could speak to him, upon which he stopped and summoned them for an intimate contact.[15] A number of disciples on pilgrimage to Mecca were saved from the perils of the desert, such as lions and thirst.[16] Rūzbihān also intervened in the lives of ordinary people, sending gifts to ward off starvation or fix up a ruined house.[17] These miracle stories are relatively modest, demonstrating the master's spiritual and physical care for the welfare of disciples, combining teaching with authority. Other stories recount the refutation of doubters, whose verbal or mental incredulity was shattered by demonstrations of the divine power given to the saint.[18] Although the content of these miracle stories is pretty much what one would expect to happen in the atmosphere of a charismatic saint like Rūzbihān, the function of the stories in terms of hagiography is only intelligible as part of the cult of the saint. The primary audience for these tales was the circle of disciples and potential disciples, for whom the stories function as validation of saintly authority. Frequently the stories conclude with the remark that "many of those present became disciples," clearly an encouragement for wavering listeners to do the same. Several stories are aimed specifically at the doubting friends of Rūzbihān's disciples; initially reluctant to accept him, they were persuaded by dreams or by his ability to resolve a spiritual difficulty.[19] Even people from remote regions became his followers through dreams.[20]

A secondary subject of the stories about Rūzbihān is his impact on ordinary Islamic religious scholars. On one occasion, Rūzbihān was awakened from a siesta by the Prophet in order to greet a jurist who came to meet him.[21] Imams and religious scholars observed him perform miracles such as producing water for a crowd to perform ablutions with, or sending a messenger with a comb in the night in response to an unspoken wish.[22] We see a qāḍī becoming enchanted with Rūzbihān after hearing him perform dhikr, and in the same way an imam was so impressed by seeing Rūzbihān in ecstasy that he became a disciple.[23] One jurist even told of how Rūzbihān miraculously resolved a domestic dispute between his parents.[24] This class of stories portrays Rūzbihān as an ecstatic saint, no doubt, but one who closely observes the sharīʻa and has warm relations with the ʻulamā'.

A smaller number of stories relate testimonies about Rūzbihān from famous Sufis and scholars from other parts of the Islamic world. While these are not numerous, they are given unusual prominence by being placed at the beginning of the chapters describing Rūzbihān's miracles. These testimonies sometimes take the form of "floating" narratives, in which the principal figures and structure of the story remain the same in different versions of the tale, but significant details have been altered. Comparison between the different versions of these "floating" stories reveals the differing hagiographical agendas of Rūzbihān's biographers, so the divergences are worth exploring in some detail. For instance, in *The Gift of the People of Gnosis* a Sufi of Shiraz named Najīb al-Dīn

Buzghush (d. 678/1280) tells how one day he was in Baghdad with the great Sufi master Shihāb al-Dīn Suhrawardī (632/1234), "the axis of the age," when the subject of Rūzbihān came up and someone began to read one of his books aloud. Initially Suhrawardī doubted the worth of Rūzbihān's writings, calling them "strange and extraordinary," but the next day he asked for Rūzbihān's book and took great delight in it. When asked about his change of heart, he replied that in the night he was convinced of Rūzbihān's lofty status by a dream of the assembly of the saints; in this dream Bāyazīd Bisṭāmī was named as the one who is united with God, Rūzbihān was proclaimed as the lover of God, and Suhrawardī was hailed as the knower of God. Suhrawardī explained that anyone so honored by God and the saints was worth reading.[25] This version elevates the status of Rūzbihān by having it announced in the assembly of saints and attested by the single authoritative figure of Suhrawardī.

The Spirit of the Gardens gives a much expanded version of this story as narrated by a Syrian shaykh named Aḥmad Ṣūfī. His account specifies that he was the one who read out from one of the writings of Rūzbihān, from a book called *Salwat al-qulūb* (*Hearts' Consolation*), and the passage in question contained Rūzbihān's boast that he had surpassed the stations of Bāyazīd and Ḥallāj.[26] When questioned about this claim, Suhrawardī replied, "It is the talk of the intoxicated; cast it aside, and attend to the talk of the sober." When Aḥmad protested that he found Rūzbihān's writings to be valuable, Suhrawardī bluntly told him, "If you do not abandon the words of Rūzbihān, you will abandon our company!" The scene was then switched to the dream of Suhrawardī, where he saw all humanity assembled at the resurrection. A crier summoned several great saints, identifying them by their characteristic: Bāyazīd, the one who is united with God; Junayd, the one who describes God; Abū Isḥāq Kāzarūnī, the one who has realized God; Rūzbihān Baqlī, the lover of God; and finally, Suhrawardī, the knower of God. Suhrawardī related that of these five saints, all were on the ground except Rūzbihān, who was dancing in the air, proclaiming to Suhrawardī his ability to transcend time and space. The next day Suhrawardī summoned Aḥmad Ṣūfī and requested him to read from the book.[27] This version has several additional features not found in the first version: the Shirazi transmitter is dropped and the narrative switches to a participant in the story, the text that disturbed Suhrawardī is quoted in full, and the issue is stated in terms of the opposition between intoxication and sobriety, a common Sufi theme though often oversimplified.[28] Furthermore, the scene is not simply the assembly of the saints but the final resurrection of all humanity, and Rūzbihān is depicted in a triumphal ecstasy beyond all other saints. The author of *The Spirit of the Gardens* finds confirmation of Rūzbihān's status in some of his verses:

When I found his beauty from the attraction of his
majesty, I die pursuing union, beauty, and glory.
When I sigh in union from seeing the pre-eternal
unveiling, I blow bubbles with a hundred thrones on
the pre-eternal carpet.

This is a form of textual proof that Sharaf al-Dīn also resorts to when he quotes the following verses:

In this age I am the upholder of the path of God
from the farthest east to the threshold of the ultimate.
How will the wayfarers of gnosis see me,
when my station lies beyond the beyond?[29]

This was considered memorable enough for it to be repeated by the later hagiographers Ibn Junayd and Jāmī.[30]

There is a third account of homage to Rūzbihān from Suhrawardī found in *Hazār mazār* (*A Thousand Tombs*), a local hagiography composed around 791/1389 and intended to be a guide for pilgrims visiting the saints' tombs of Shiraz. There we see a much less impressive dream related by one Ibn Qannād in which Buzghush, Suhrawardī, and several saints of Shiraz, along with the seven hidden saints known as the abdāl, all appear as visitors paying homage to the tomb of Rūzbihān.[31] This version retains the element of testimony by various saints, including Suhrawardī, but it remains on the level of the dream of an ordinary person, and it is concerned with the cult of the saint's tomb rather than the value of his writings. All three versions of this floating story pertain to the question of the saint's status after death as debated and confirmed by Sufi authorities not directly connected with his shrine. There are a number of similar stories involving confirmation of Rūzbihān's sainthood by other well-known Sufi figures.[32] One can compare this floating narrative to other hagiographies, such as the biography of the Egyptian mystical poet Ibn al-Fāriḍ; in what is beginning to look like a standard appeal to authority, here too the name of

Suhrawardī is invoked in an incident testifying to the sainthood of the subject of the hagiography. As in the case of Rūzbihān, Ibn al-Fāriḍ's biography also portrays him as the founder of a Sufi order.[33]

The floating narratives seem to have a purely hagiographical purpose of glorifying the saint. This hagiographic function is especially evident in stories that exist independently in versions that have nothing to do with the saint in question. As an example we may consider two versions of a story of the mysterious figures from the spiritual hierarchy known popularly as "the seven" (*haft-tanān*).[34] *The Gift of the People of Gnosis* relates a story told by a corpse-washer named Shams al-Dīn Muḥammad, who was summoned by Rūzbihān to prepare a corpse for burial in a graveyard outside Shiraz. Under awe-inspiring circumstances, the man observed Rūzbihān and five impressive persons perform prayers over the dead man. Shams al-Dīn kept vigil at a tomb prepared on a mountain, and in the morning Rūzbihān informed him that the dead man was one of "the seven," at the same time swearing him to secrecy during the shaykh's lifetime.[35] The obvious implication of the story is the Rūzbihān was also one of the seven. This appears to be a reworking of a popular story told in *A Thousand Tombs*, in which an anonymous saintly corpse-washer tells of being summoned by a beautiful youth to prepare a corpse for burial. The corpse-washer followed the youth through a locked city gate to a house where he suddenly found his guide was the dead person. Then with the aid of six other youths he performed his task, and they departed with the corpse. The corpse-washer found himself alone in the desert, prayed and fell asleep, and then awoke to find a new tomb beside him. One by one, six more tombs gradually appeared in the same spot. "They say that they were the sevenfold 'pegs' (*awtād*), who love each other, for whom the rain comes, whose prayer is answered, and by whose blessings affliction is removed from the people (God's mercy upon them)."[36] This archaic and anonymous story, which reflects popular beliefs about the invisible hierarchy of saints, has here proved adaptable to the hagiographical purpose of demonstrating Rūzbihān's position as a saint.

The hagiographers occasionally use *The Unveiling of Secrets* as a source to pad out their outline of Rūzbihān's career, but this biographical reading twists the visionary recital out of context and turns his internal encounters to versions of standard miracles. Such is the case with the extraordinary vision of §146, in which Rūzbihān weeps over the fate of the Sufi martyrs, and his tears become the wine of God, the drink with which the angels break their fast. In the midst of this vision, which is part of the sequence of Ramaḍān visions, Rūzbihān receives an intimate initiation, as the Prophet Muḥammad and all the other prophets and angels and saints suck his tongue. As reported by Shams al-Dīn ʻAbd al-Laṭīf in Persian translation, this vision has become altered into an event taking place during Rūzbihān's pilgrimage to Mecca, after his brief sojourn with Abū Ṣafā' in Wasit. The Persian "translation" greatly alters the whole encounter. It substitutes a devotional rhetoric aimed at the Prophet Muḥammad alone in the place of the emotional intensity of the Arabic passage with its striking depiction of the spiritual hierarchy and its erotic overtones. Where the Arabic original shows the Prophet in an epiphany of beauty, dressed in the enticing garb of a warrior Turk, the Persian makes the items of clothing into gifts of investiture, miraculously deposited by the hand of the Prophet into the lap of Rūzbihān as he stands in the shrine of Medina. Here is a tabular comparison of the two versions:

The Unveiling of Secrets, §146	*The Spirit of the Gardens*, pp. 177–78
Then I saw the prophet coming toward me from Medina, with the fearsomeness of a Turkman, wearing a robe (*qabā*) and a hat (*qalansuwa*), with his right hand sticking out from his robe, and he had a bow and some arrows in his left hand. He opened his mouth and took my tongue and sucked my tongue gently. Then I saw Adam, Noah, Abraham, Moses, Jesus, and all the prophets and messengers coming toward me, and they sucked my tongue. Then I saw Gabriel and Michael, Israfil, Azra'il and all	On a certain night I saw the night traveler of "Praise be to him who brought his servant by night" (Qur'an 17:1), the rising sun of "by the dawn" (Qur'an 93:1)[37] (peace and blessings be upon him), extend his blessed hand out from the holy shrine. He clothed me in a cloak (*darāʻa*), and placed a hat (*tāj*) upon my head, and gave me a mantle (*ṭaylasān*) and a flag (*ʻalam*). Then he put his tongue in my mouth, and I sucked it with a long suck. He brought his hand down on my face, and a light appeared in

the angels, and they sucked my tongue. So [did] all the saints and sincere ones. Ecstasies overwhelmed me, and cries and sighs.

my eyes, by which light I saw the face of that leader of creatures and that happiness of the breast of Adam and his children, so that a fragment of the rays of the light of his face made the light of the sun like an insignificant atom.

Rūzbihān's original vision revealed him absorbing the blessings of all the spiritual hierarchy as they each gave him an intense kiss. His descendant turned this into a conventionalized account of a visit to the Prophet's tomb to receive the regalia of a Sufi shaykh, retaining only the unforgettable kiss, though now it is Rūzbihān who does the kissing. It must be admitted that this particular vision poses problems for the interpreter. I know of no other example of a Sufi claiming this kind of physical intimacy with the prophets, angels, and saints in a vision. For Rūzbihān, it seems to be understood primarily as a form of initiation into esoteric knowledge. He mentions it in an early vision (§29), in which the Prophet Muḥammad feeds Rūzbihān dates, places his tongue in Rūzbihān's mouth, and then puts a turban on his head. Both the feeding and the presentation of the turban are standard images for initiation, and so the kiss is framed in this way. Still, this erotically-tinged encounter with the Prophet Muḥammad might well be viewed as offensive lese-majesté by some.

Rūzbihān's visions could also be reinterpreted in terms of other kinds of devotionalism, like the popular forms of devotion to 'Alī and the Shī'ī imams that were encouraged by the later Salghurid Atābegs of Shiraz.[38] This 'Alid loyalism, as Hodgson called it, took root among Rūzbihān's descendants, so that his two great-great-grandsons Ṣadr al-Dīn Rūzbihān III and 'Izz al-Dīn Mas'ūd were both known for their public preaching at the 'Āshūrā ceremonies commemorating the martyrdom of Ḥusayn.[39] It should be remarked in passing that devotion to 'Ali is not synonymous with Shī'ism, despite Corbin's tendency to see signs of Shī'ism everywhere. In any case, it is striking to see the transformation that has occurred in one of Rūzbihān's visions in which 'Alī plays a part, when it is refracted through the prism of 'Alid devotion. Here are the parallel passages:

The Unveiling of Secrets, §17	*The Gift of the People of Gnosis,* p. 33
One day I also saw as though I were on the mountain of the east, and I saw a group of angels, and an ocean that seemed to go from east to west. And they said to me, "Enter this sea, and swim in it to the west." So I entered the sea, and swam in it. And when I reached the place of the sun at evening time, I saw the mountains of the east and west like little hills. I saw a group of angels on the mountain of the west, and they were glowing with the light of the sun. They shouted and said, "Whoever you are, swim and don't be afraid." So when I reached the mountain they said, "No one has crossed this ocean except ʻAlī ibn Abī Ṭālib (God ennoble his countenance), and you after him."	In the world of unveiling I saw a mighty ocean, and I wanted to swim in that ocean. The battling armies of waves would not let me go. I saw someone swimming in that ocean who crossed the ocean. I followed behind him, and by the blessing of his passing I found the path and crossed the ocean. I went on this path to meaning for years. When I reached the shore, I saw the Commander of the Faithful ʻAlī (may God ennoble his countenance). I fell at his blessed feet, and he caressed me and said, "Rūzbihān! I have crossed this ocean, and you by the blessing of following me have crossed it. Let this be good news, that your offspring shall never be cut off!" And God knows best.

Here we find an even greater difference between the Arabic original and the Persian "translation." In Rūzbihān's vision, ʻAlī appears at the very end, only to provide a standard of comparison to measure the status and spiritual greatness of Rūzbihān. The version of Sharaf al-Dīn Ibrāhīm truncates the intricate vision into a single image, in which Rūzbihān's greatness derives solely from his devotion to ʻAlī. The point of the anecdote is now that the future of Rūzbihān's family is secure, thanks to the grace of ʻAlī.

There are instances where a brief encounter in *The Unveiling of Secrets* seems to have served for the inspiration for a much more grandiose scenario in the hagiographies. This occurs in a vision that begins with Rūzbihān addressing God by one of the divine names, "the Giver" (*wahhāb*):

> I was wakeful one night at midnight, and was between sleep and waking. I said in my heart: "Giver!" And God appeared with the quality of majesty and beauty, manifest and adorned with jewels of light, from which he scattered on me a great abundance. That largesse that was scattered was from his eternal face. He said, "Since you called out, 'Giver,' take this from the Giver, for I am the generous Giver" (§23).

This appears to be a typical manifestation of divine qualities based on a divine name, revealed in visions of celestial jewels. A roughly comparable dialogue takes place in the hagiographies as an addition to a story about Rūzbihān getting lost in the desert, where he asks God to save him from dying there; God tells him not to worry, because this particular spot was destined to be touched by his feet. The two hagiographers differ on the question of why Rūzbihān asked to be spared from death; Sharaf al-Dīn maintains that it was because Rūzbihān wanted his funeral to be carried out in accordance with the Prophetic norm (*sunna*), while Shams al-Dīn suggests that Rūzbihān realized that his death would remove the only person alive who truly fulfilled Islamic law. The two hagiographers then relate the boons that God proceeds to heap on Rūzbihān, only now instead of being visions of celestial jewels, the gift that God gives Rūzbihān is the power of intercession at the resurrection for his descendants and all pilgrims to the tomb of Rūzbihān. As usual, *The Spirit of the Gardens* offers a somewhat more extravagant version.

The Gift of the People of Gnosis, p. 114

[God said,] "We have made this land your goal at this time, and have bestowed sainthood upon you, and have given you gifts; now we give you your children and grandchildren on the morning of the resurrection." I said, "My God, give more than this, for you are the Giver (*bakhshānīda*)." The reply came, "Whoever comes to you with sincerity I give to you on the

The Spirit of the Gardens, pp. 235–36

[God said,] " . . . we have brought you to this land at this time." He [Rūzbihān] said, when this reply came, the experience became overwhelming and my momentary state sweeter. I said, "Lord! Does Rūzbihān have this nearness and degree in your presence?" The reply came, "Yes." I said, "Lord, I see that the carpet of your mercy is unfurled, and morning of the resurrection." I said, "My God, give more than this, for you are the Giver (*bakhshānīda*)." Then the reply came, "Whoever enters into the net of your *ribāṭ* and with sincerity performs pilgrimage to you I give to you on the morning of the resurrection."

the limitless treasury of your grace is open; give me more than this!" The reply came, "I gave this to you, and I dressed you in the garment of honor." Again I said, "Lord! I want more than this." The reply came, "I give you your children." Again I said, "Lord! I want more than this." The reply came, "Whoever comes to your tomb after your death and performs pilgrimage I give to you." Again I said, "Lord! I want more than this." The reply came, "Whoever hears your name and loves you I give to you." I asked up to seventy times, and all requests were granted, falling into the place of acceptance.

The Arabic text of *The Unveiling of Secrets* is followed more closely in *The Gift of the People of Gnosis*, at least in the verbal echo of addressing God as the Giver. The shift from vision to hagiography radically changes the contents of this dialogue, transforming it from a purely internal event to divine certification of pilgrimage to Rūzbihān's tomb.

Another distinctive aspect of the two hagiographies is that they provide for the first time full-fledged spiritual genealogies for the saint (see Chart 2). *The Gift of the People of Gnosis* describes Rūzbihān as the representative of a Sufi chain of transmission through the Kāzarūnī order. It goes back via Abū Isḥāq al-Kāzarūnī to the great Shirazi master Ibn Khafīf, and then proceeds by either of two branches (one in Khurasan, one in Baghdad) to the Prophet. *The Spirit of the Gardens* presents roughly the same picture of the genealogy, though both the Khurasan and Baghdad branches differ in certain names. A significant addition has occurred as sub-branch II, consisting of the first eight Shīʿī imams (minus Ḥasan ibn ʿAlī, the second imam). This insertion reflects the ʿAlid piety of the later Rūzbihāniyya, as does the fact that each line is taken only as far as 'Alī rather than to the Prophet Muḥammad. *The Spirit of the Gardens* also provides another, somewhat more obscure genealogy with two branches, which rests upon Rūzbihān's association with Abū al-Ṣafā' al-Wāsiṭī, the only contemporary Sufi whom he names in *The Unveiling of Secrets*. As noted above, Rūzbihān himself showed no interest in demonstrating his position in a lineage. Of the masters in the Kāzarūnī order, he only mentioned one in *The Unveiling of Secrets* (§161), the founder of the order Abū Isḥāq Shahryār al-Kāzarūnī (d. 426/1035).[40] His biographies date from the period in which the possession of a suitable genealogy became indispensable for a saint. Ṣadr al-Dīn Rūzbihān II was also supplied with an additional genealogy, which provided an alternate connection to 'Alī al-Fārmadhī, a figure in one of Rūzbihān's extra genealogies (Chart 2, Genealogy B, Path II, Branch II). Some later texts give Rūzbihān's genealogy from Ibn Khafīf with slightly different lines.[41] Why would the genealogies be of little importance to Rūzbihān and so significant to his hagiographers? Although the initiatic genealogy may have the appearance of a historical document, its primary significance is ritualistic. Copying out one's initiatic genealogy all the way back to the Prophet had the effect of certifying one's spiritual connection by an unbroken transmission with the surest source of authority. The transmission was conceived along the lines of oral transmission of *ḥadīth*, but it was concretized as the physical ritual of the bestowal of the Sufi cloak (*khirqa*). When late reconstructions of the early transmission of Sufism took place, based on the assumption that regular master-disciple relations were necessary, scholars of *ḥadīth* became suspicious of the historical accuracy of these genealogies, pointing out that in a number of cases transmission was chronologically impossible.[42] The question of the factual historicity of these genealogies appears to me relatively unimportant compared to their ritual and religious significance. In the case of Rūzbihān, having or claiming an initiatic genealogy would have been of decidedly secondary importance, especially when compared with his assertion that he was in direct contact with God every day. His references to early Sufi masters in *The Unveiling of Secrets* invoke them primarily to indicate how far he has gone beyond their station.

For the hagiographers, however, the spirituality of their ancestor was inexplicable without reference to the unbroken transmission of a Sufi lineage. Yet to demonstrate this point, they had to appeal to outside sources written after the time of Rūzbihān, when the concretization of the Sufi orders had become more advanced. This is particularly evident in the remarks of Shams al-Dīn 'Abd al-Laṭīf in *The Spirit of the Gardens* when introducing the lineage of Rūzbihān. He prefaces it by quoting passages on the transmission of the Sufi cloak from *The Gifts of Gnosis* (*'Awārif al-ma'ārif*) of Shihāb al-Dīn al-Suhrawardī.[43] Shams al-Dīn also claims that Rūzbihān had many Sufi lineages, though he contents himself with describing two. The primary lineage (given in both hagiographies) is a branch of the Kāzarūnī order, which was probably the most widespread and powerful Sufi order in Fars. The Kāzarūnī genealogy, which also includes the other great saint of Fars, Ibn Khafīf, is given similar prominence in the principal hagiography dedicated to the eponymous founder of the order, Abū Isḥāq al-Kāzarūnī (d. 426/1035). This text, *The Paradise of Guidance* (*Firdaws al-murshidiyya*) by Khaṭīb Imām Abū Bakr (written in Arabic ca. 502/1108–9), is only available in the Persian translation of Maḥmūd ibn 'Uthmān (728/1327, roughly the same time as Rūzbihān's hagiographies); it is impossible, though, to tell precisely when the genealogies of Abū Isḥāq al-Kāzarūnī became firmly established. What is certain is that Rūzbihān's biographers regarded al-Kāzarūnī with great respect, and they present Rūzbihān as the inheritor of his mantle via his lineage.[45]

Although Rūzbihān appears to have had contact with people in areas remote from Shiraz, the hagiographies tend to exaggerate this contact and portray it as a full-fledged international network of mystical authority. This global status is deduced from his status as a saint. As *A Thousand Tombs* puts it, "The shaykh has certain lovers in [different] regions of the world who recognize the excellence of his way (*ṭarīqa*) and know the ocean of his reality, for God most high has clothed him with these dominions (*wilāyāt*), so that the people may have intercession (*mutawassil*) through him."[46]

Rūzbihān's hagiographers used his own writings as proof-texts to demonstrate his authority, as may be seen from their description of a treatise he wrote for Sufi novices, the *Risālat al-quds* or *The Treatise on Holiness*. According to the hagiographical tradition, this work was composed for the benefit of a mystic in Turkestan who had internal contact with Rūzbihān despite never having met him. A merchant named Abū al-Faraj, who was also a follower of

Rūzbihān, had just returned to Shiraz carrying greetings from that mysterious saint in Turkestan. The merchant told Rūzbihān, "The shaykhs of that region, whether of Khurasan or Turkestan, are all longing for you and desire to hear your words." The shaykh then composed this treatise and sent it back with the merchant. Although the hagiographer quotes the passage from *The Treatise on Holiness* containing Rūzbihān's greetings to the saints of Khurasan, Turkestan, and Transoxiana, he also makes it appear that Rūzbihān is in the position of a master greeting his disciples.[47] The hagiographer leaves out the closing paragraphs of the introduction to *The Treatise on Holiness*, in which Rūzbihān humbly addresses his readers as follows:

> Our purpose in revealing these words is that those happy ones should remember us, for whoever they remember belongs to the eternally living ones, while whoever they forget belongs to the company of the annihilated dead. My longing for their beautiful faces cannot be expressed.... I have not written these words capriciously, nor do I need to be remembered by you, but my brother Abū al-Faraj (may God grant him the generosity of the gnostics) made such a spontaneous suggestion ... requesting that I write two or three sections from the station of the masters of love, as a guidance for disciples and as a reminder for masters.[48]

When viewed as a whole, the treatise does not appear to be part of an authoritative teaching addressed to disciples, contrary to the impression given by Rūzbihān's biographer in *The Gift of the People of Gnosis*. It conveys rather the impression of a generous gesture from one colleague to another, in an informal atmosphere predating the more rigid construction of the Sufi order as a closed authoritarian society. The story of the enigmatic saint of Turkestan has the appearance of a hagiographic addition used to flesh out Rūzbihān's sketchy references to the shaykhs of that region.

Rūzbihān's biographers also demonstrated his spiritual authority by making use of passages in his writings concerning the hierarchy of saints. For instance, in his Persian *Sharḥ-i shaṭḥiyyāt* or *Commentary on Ecstatic Sayings*, Rūzbihān gives a lengthy description of the different saints through whom God governs the world. He salutes the 12,000 saints of India, Turkestan, Zanzibar, and Ethiopia, the 400 elite in Rūm and Khurasan and Iran, the 400 on the seacoast, the 300 in zāwiyas on the coasts of Egypt and the Maghrib, the 70 in Yemen, Ta'if, the Hejaz and the Baṭā'iḥ, the 40 in Iraq and Syria, the ten in Mecca, Medina, and the Ka'ba, the seven who travel the world, the three of whom one is in Fars, one in Rūm, and one among the Arabs, and the *ghawth* or *quṭb* who is the "pole" or world-axis.[49] Both of Rūzbihān's biographies follow this quotation with a list of the saints of different regions, culminating in the names of the three great "poles" of Fars, Ibn Khafīf, Abū Isḥāq Kāzarūnī, and Rūzbihān.[50] When his descendants translated his general description of the spiritual hierarchy into an identification of historical individuals, the mystical concept was turned into a local social and political order, in which Rūzbihān was posthumously assigned the leading role.

On a more concrete level, the hagiographies contain frequent references to the hospice (*ribāṭ*) that Rūzbihān constructed in Shiraz, and from that we can form an idea of the nature of this establishment before it became the center of a tomb cult. The *ribāṭ* was clearly of great importance, and the story is told that Rūzbihān miraculously enlarged a beam or ridge-pole that made possible the construction of the roof; relics of the beam were later used to cure the sick.[51] A number of disciples who were stone masons assisted in the digging and construction work, and protracted ecstatic sessions of music followed upon its completion.[52] According to an Arabic inscription placed on the door of the *ribāṭ*, Rūzbihān intended this building as a perpetual trust for the use of "the friends of God among the Sufis," so it probably functioned as a guest-house for traveling Sufis and disciples as well as a mosque and residence for the shaykh.[53] One story refers to Rūzbihān's disciples planting flowers in the *ribāṭ*, suggesting that it was intended to be a pleasant place.[54] Frequently Rūzbihān is portrayed sitting in the miḥrāb of the *ribāṭ*, either meditating in solitude or receiving visitors.[55] At times he would preach from the minbar inside the *ribāṭ*.[56] Occasionally we see him on the roof of the *ribāṭ*, absorbed in ecstasy; it was there that his son Fakhr al-Dīn Ahmad saw him during a winter rainstorm, miraculously dry.[57] Some of his disciples performed their devotions on the front porch.[58] Like many hospices, Rūzbihān's maintained a kitchen, and distribution of food to residents and visitors was an important activity. One account relates that normally there were forty disciples in continuous attendance on the shaykh, and when it fell to the turn of one to supply food for the establishment, he would strive to supply the finest ingredients.[59] After residing and teaching in the *ribāṭ* for forty-six years, Rūzbihān was buried in a tomb constructed inside it. He at first requested to be buried in the south portion of the *ribāṭ*, but then changed his mind. The spot where his grave lies was the site of a tall room without a roof, where he had many times seen visions of the Prophet.[60] Members of his family report that on his deathbed, Rūzbihān said he would protect them from harrassment, and he instructed them to have anyone seeking his aid approach his tomb and speak their wish to him, so that he could convey it directly to God. He also advised them to use water from the well in the *ribāṭ* for ablutions before performing two cycles of prayer at his tomb to seek his intercession, promising that all sincere seekers would be rewarded. After his death, several people heard him speak from his tomb. Stories are related of visitors from afar being drawn to his tomb by its spiritual power without knowing whose it was, and dust from his tomb was used as collyrium to cure eye disease.[61] Although the *ribāṭ* began as a place for meditation and instruction during Rūzbihān's lifetime, it inevitably was transformed into a place of pilgrimage after his death.

C. The Descendants of Rūzbihān

When we turn to Rūzbihān's descendants, we have a full picture of them as a close-knit and highly religious family. Rūzbihān is quoted as saying that he received a divine command to get married and have children.[62] He had two sons and three daughters who are not named. Rūzbihān's affection for his family is apparent in a number of his visions, such as the occasions he watched over his feverish son Aḥmad (above, Chapter II.G).[63] His elder son was Shihāb al-Dīn Muḥammad, a pious mystic who frequently kept silence. He evidently taught the religious sciences and preached publicly for twenty years, also devoting his efforts to Qur'ānic recitation and meditation. Although he traveled in Persia and Iraq, he died in Shiraz during the lifetime of the shaykh.[64] The younger son, Fakhr al-Dīn Aḥmad, was a pious and learned man and an extremely good preacher. He is known for having memorized vast numbers of Prophetic *ḥadīth* and for having written a versification of Ghazālī's *Wajīz* on law, plus poetry in Persian and Arabic.[65] In the next generation, Shihāb al-Dīn Muḥammad had a son named Abū Bakr who was known for his absorption in ecstasy and his habit of fasting and keeping night vigil. One informant states that Shihāb al-Dīn Suhrawardī had sent an initiatic Sufi cloak to Abū Bakr. He is said to have died either in 640/1242 or 641/1243.[66] He was not nearly so well known as his cousin Ṣadr al-Dīn Rūzbihān II (b. 615/1218 or 603/1206, d. 685/1286), who can probably take credit for contributing most to the establishment of Rūzbihān's shrine.[67]

Although Rūzbihān's children were apparently quite religious and even absorbed in meditative practices, unlike their father they did not leave much impact in terms of literary production or creative formulation of spiritual techniques. Instead they attempted to reduplicate Rūzbihān's spirituality in an imitative fashion. Rūzbihān is quoted as saying that he was veiled in his son Fakhr al-Dīn Aḥmad, and Fakhr al-Dīn Aḥmad likewise said that he was veiled in his child Ṣadr al-Dīn Rūzbihān II.[68] We even hear of a grandson of Ṣadr al-Dīn known as Ṣadr al-Dīn ibn Sharaf al-Dīn Ibrāhīm Rūzbihān III; by his names he reincarnated his grandfather and his great-great-grandfather, but he was a derivative figure known primarily for giving speeches at public occasions such as funerals.[69] This imitative mode of spirituality necessarily focused on the cult of Rūzbihān as saint.

Rūzbihān's grandson Ṣadr al-Dīn Rūzbihān II was by no means a negligible person, however. For many years he was one of the principal leaders of Shiraz, viewed by his descendants as a Sufi master with many disciples and as a preacher; other authorities saw him primarily as a public speaker.[70] A few miracle stories are narrated about him, concerning his successful prayer for rain during a drought, and his ability to divine the thoughts of others. As we shall see, he had close relations with the political figures of his day, but his stature derived from his role as representative of his grandfather. We are told that Ṣadr al-Dīn spent most of his time at Rūzbihān's tomb, especially all day every Tuesday, praying in the *ribāṭ*, particularly in between the daytime prayers.[71] He is the principal reporter transmitting accounts of visions and ecstasies that took place at the site of his father's tomb, and he encouraged pilgrims who sought help with their problems to perform ablutions and prayers at the tomb in order to secure the assistance of

Rūzbihān.[72] Ṣadr al-Dīn's own tomb, located next to his father's, later became sought out by pilgrims as a results of visions that occurred there.[73]

It was left then for Ṣadr al-Dīn's two sons Sharaf al-Dīn and Shams al-Dīn to take up the task of memorializing their ancestor by composing their two biographies. Sharaf al-Dīn's *The Gift of the People of Gnosis* is the primary document, and Shams al-Dīn's *The Spirit of the Gardens* shows close dependency on the earlier work in its overall structure and in many details, though it frequently expands on the earlier text. Sharaf al-Dīn was known, like his father, as a preacher, and he also wrote some texts on religious subjects.[74] Shams al-Dīn is not listed or mentioned among the saints and Sufis of Shiraz described in *Hazār mazār*. As we have seen, he had a primarily political career, and he evidently reactivated his family's spiritual connection as a result of interest among his associates at the court in Luristan. The two biographers had another brother, Jalāl al-Dīn Yaḥyā ibn Ṣadr al-Dīn Rūzbihān II, but he is known only from his tombstone, which is found in the family plot.[75] After the brief reference to Sharaf al-Dīn's son Rūzbihān III, the order apparently disappeared. This family Sufi order existed on the impetus of the saint who was regarded as its founder, but in the absence of any fresh infusion of energy it dwindled into a completely retrospective mode, and the Rūzbihāniyya was extinguished after the fifth generation.

D. Political Connections of the Rūzbihāniyya

During Rūzbihān's own lifetime, his relations with the ruling Salghurid Atābegs were fairly cordial initially. When Rūzbihān first came to Shiraz as a Sufi, as we have seen, his extraordinary preaching caused certain dry ascetics and externalists to urge the Atābeg Sonqur (r. 543/1148–556/1161) to banish him for the sake of public order. When the Atābeg sent word to Rūzbihān to depart, the shaykh astounded him with his ability to read thoughts, so that he repented and requested that Rūzbihān undertake to preach twice weekly, in the great 'Atīq mosque and in his own private mosque. Rūzbihān did this for a time, and then departed Shiraz, but when he returned and founded his *ribāṭ*, Rūzbihān continued the custom of preaching publicly twice a week up to the end of his life.[76] There are no accounts of any royal patronage of

Rūzbihān's *ribāṭ* aside from occasional donations. The endowment and construction of this edifice was apparently undertaken by Rūzbihān and his disciples without political sponsorship.

Friendly relations between Rūzbihān and the Salghurids are further illustrated by a story in which rebels against the authority of the Atābeg Sa'īd Taklā (Degele) Zangī (r. 570/1175–590/1194) threatened to attack the *ribāṭ* of Rūzbihān. The rebels apparently regarded Taklā as a follower of Rūzbihān. One of Rūzbihān's disciples, the same Ẓahīr al-Dīn Kirmānī who had once been punished and banished for revealing Rūzbihān's teachings, warned the rebels not to attack. After their defeat by the Atābeg, their heads were exhibited at the *ribāṭ*, allegedly with the shaykh's approval.[77] This story presumes a close relationship between Rūzbihān and the Salghurid Atābeg, at least in the eyes of the rebels, but the relationship is muted by the prediction of rebel defeat being put in the mouth of a lesser disciple instead of being credited to Rūzbihān himself. The story betrays an intrusion of royal historiography into the realm of the hagiography, as what is ostensibly a tale about the destruction of opponents of the saint carries a subtext presuming that the saint guarantees the legitimacy of the ruling power. Another story depicts Rūzbihān blessing Taklā and promising him victory over an invading army.[78] Again, Taklā is the subject of a story in which envious people slandered Rūzbihān and accused him of immoral conduct with a young man (this is the story romanticized in the *Book of Lovers* attributed to 'Irāqī, where the Atābeg Sa'd replaces Taklā), but the plotters were refuted and failed to sway the Atābeg against him. It is difficult to conclude from these hagiographic accounts how Rūzbihān and Taklā viewed their relationship. The hagiographies make no explicit mention of Taklā's cousin and successor Toghrïl, who assumed the throne in 590/1194 but fought a vicious civil war with his younger brother Sa'd for years, until the latter finally triumphed.[80]

Accounts of the Atābeg Sa'd ibn Zangī (r. 601/1203–628/1231, the patron of the poet Sa'dī's father) seem to indicate a tension between the ruler and the shaykh, despite the statement that there was supposed to be mutual affection between them. At least one of Rūzbihān's disciples was a minister in attendance on the Atābeg.[81] Rūzbihān, unlike the other scholars of the city, refused to visit the Atābeg Sa'd on his return from Iraq.[82] Envious people tried to turn the Atābeg against Rūzbihān, so that he threatened to persecute the shaykh. A group of stone carvers who were Rūzbihān's disciples proposed to stand guard at the *ribāṭ* during the night, in case of any attempt on the shaykh's life. In the night the Atābeg saw Rūzbihān appear to him in a warning dream, descending through the air and grabbing him by the ears, saying, "Turk! You will not sit in authority without getting your punishment!" So the following day the Atābeg announced that he had become a disciple and personally brought a donation of a thousand dinars to the shaykh. This incident, which probably occurred during the last five years of Rūzbihān's life, was viewed as a defeat for Rūzbihān's opponents and a victory for his adherents.[83] Another story indicates that the Atābeg sent people to break up the funeral of Rūzbihān, during which time some disciples were beaten with sticks and only with difficulty conveyed the shaykh's body to the tomb.[84] Rūzbihān's biographers evidently reconciled themselves to the rule of the Atābeg, however; in a typical gesture in support of royal authority, they relate that he had met Rūzbihān as a child, and when his hat fell off, it was replaced on his head by the saint. This is said to be the cause of his thirty years' rule in Shiraz.[85]

The ups and downs of the Salghurid period finally gave way to the onslaught of Mongol power, and it was after the beginning of Mongol rule in 668/1270 that the Rūzbihāniyya became fully institutionalized and symbiotically related with the government. Rūzbihān's sons apparently had little to do with the Atābegs, but his grandson Ṣadr al-Dīn Rūzbihān II played as prominent a role in cementing relations with rulers as he did in formalizing the rituals at the shrine of his grandfather. His political role first becomes evident in a minor way in the pre-Mongol period. Although he is referred to as "shaykh al-islām," it is difficult to tell whether this is merely an honorific title or an official position in the bureaucracy. In any case, we are told that an office seeker named Niẓām al-Dīn Riḍwān had been assigned by the Atābeg Abū Bakr Qutlugh Khān (r. 628/1231–658/1260) to a minor post in the debt collection department, though he hoped for something higher. He accordingly went for advice to Ṣadr al-Dīn, who advised him to pray at the tomb of Rūzbihān. After the Atābeg appointed him as chief accountant, Niẓām al-Dīn became a regular devotee of Ṣadr al-Dīn.[86] Although this story does not indicate that Ṣadr al-Dīn had direct influence at the Atābeg's court, it does show the shrine as the resort in need for the upwardly mobile.

Ṣadr al-Dīn tried to stick to the role of the independent Sufi who stays away from court, but he met with as much difficulty as some of the dervishes who are ironically portrayed in Saʿdī's *Gulistān*. One story relates how an official (*amīr*) in Shiraz named Jalāl al-Dīn Abū Bakr ibn Khwāja invited Ṣadr al-Dīn to his house, and several eminent people interceded to persuade him to accept. At last the shaykh agreed. The official, as was customary, prepared a reception, including singers. The shaykh with all his disciples and children arrived. It was a fine occasion. After the meal, the official told a story about his having heard Ṣadr al-Dīn preach in the Badr al-Dīn mosque, with such effect that his preaching responded uncannily to the official's unspoken thoughts. When the shaykh had urged people to change their ways and perform the good, the official also had decided to do something good. A second time he had thought that the shaykh is a saint, perhaps I should invite him and clothe him in a robe. At once the shaykh had turned in his direction and said, we too eat and wear clothes. The official had been thrilled, and at once resolved to present a gift. Now that the shaykh had come, he asked permission to present to the shaykh an official court robe (*khilʿat*) that he himself had received, presumably at the caliphal court. The companions urged the shaykh to accept it. The official then brought out a finely woven woolen cloak (*ṣūf*) and a fine linen turban and gave them to the shaykh. The shaykh put them on. The official asked the shaykh to forgive him for the sake of God for this ill-mannered act; this incident was strictly due to the miracles of the shaykh which he had witnessed, not what he had heard from another. The shaykh prayed for him and returned to the hospice, where he gave the turban and cloak to his children.[87] There are several ironic touches in this tale. Ṣadr al-Dīn unwittingly became the recipient of the governor's charity, receiving a gift that put him into an inferior position in two ways. First, it was a robe of honor from the caliphal court, so it placed Ṣadr al-Dīn into the role of a political subordinate. Second, it was a woolen cloak that at least conceptually paralleled the cloak of Sufi initiation, but here it was forcibly bestowed on the Sufi representative by the political ruler. It must have been quite galling for Ṣadr al-Dīn to submit to this kind of generosity.

Ṣadr al-Dīn's somewhat helpless position in the shrine institution is especially evident in his encounter with the Mongol governor of Shiraz Amīr Bulughān, who was a pagan. One day while hunting, Bulughān had expressed to a friend an interest in meeting Ṣadr al-Dīn Rūzbihān. When some asked why, he related having dreamt for three nights about a Sufi master (*pīr*) who invited him to convert to Islam, at first by advice and then by threatening his destruction. He guessed that this master was Ṣadr al-Dīn. Now the governor wanted to meet him and become a Muslim. The administrators and religious officials of the city pleaded with Ṣadr al-Dīn to forego the Sufi custom of avoiding the court, for this visit would be for the purpose of assisting conversion to Islam. Under such pressure, the shaykh once again reluctantly yielded, and with a group of disciples and companions in attendance went to the Mongol's house. The governor recognized the shaykh from afar as the master who had invited him to convert in the dream. The scene that follows is an ironic demonstration of institutional power overtaking the limited charisma of an epigone. When Ṣadr al-Dīn began to tell him a story, the governor objected, saying, "You should [first] bring Islam and tell me the creed, and after that tell a story." So the shaykh obediently taught him the creed, and the governor became a Muslim. After that he brought much largesse and freed many slaves at the feet of the shaykh. The next day Bulughān came to the hospice with a translator, saying that by the grace of the shaykh, he was already receiving divine guidance through confirmatory dreams in which Ṣadr al-Dīn appeared to him. Then he said that everyone should follow this path. The shaykh prayed, and seventy more Mongols became Muslims. Afterward Bulughān settled several shops on the shaykh and his sons and grandsons as a charitable endowment (*waqf*).[88] This incident probably took place in 680/1281 or 681/1282, when Bulughān was acting as chief Mongol representative (*bāshqāq*) in Shiraz, though his refusal to remit taxes to central Mongol authorities brought about his downfall and flight when Möngke brought an army to Shiraz to correct accounts.[89]

Judging from the hagiographies alone, it is difficult to trace with confidence the emerging patterns of patronage of Sufi institutions by the rulers of Shiraz, but it is probably safe to assume a gradual increase in sponsorship of Sufism. Biographical notices of Sonqur and Saʿd ibn Zangī in *Hazār mazār* praise them for their public works and piety, particularly as evidenced in the construction of mosques. Although Sa'd ibn Zangī is noted as being a friend of dervishes, it is only in the biography of his son Abū Bakr ibn Sa'd that there is any mention of construction of *ribāṭs* along with mosques and madrasas; both father and son, however, contributed charitable trusts for the construction and upkeep of the tomb of the Sufi saint Ibn Khafīf.[90] Sa'd is credited with elevating the support of Sufism to state policy, saying, "Our army consists of the pious and the dervishes."[91] Nonetheless, support was not uniformly forthcoming, for as we have seen, Sa'd ibn Zangī had strained relations with Rūzbihān, and Rūzbihān's hagiographers rarely mention Abū Bakr. Since they also fail to mention any direct financial subsidy from the government until the Mongol period, it seems likely that the later thirteenth century was the period when a more extensive patronage of Sufi institutions became normal government practice under Mongol auspices.

Notes

1. See most recently Hamid Dabashi, "Historical Conditions of Persian Sufism during the Seljuk Period," in *Classical Persian Sufism: from its Origins to Rumi*, ed. Leonard Lewisohn (London: Khaniqahi Nimatullahi, 1994), pp. 137–74.
2. Lawrence Potter has provided an excellent overview of the growth of Sufi orders in "Sufis and Sultans in Post-Mongol Iran," paper presented at the Middle East Studies Association conference, November 1993.
3. Jamal Elias' forthcoming study of 'Alā' al-Dawla Simnānī will provide the first detailed portrait of his teaching methods and his relation to the Mongol court.
4. Muḥammad Taqī Dānish-Puzhūh, *Rūzbihān nāma*, pp. 1–150 (*Tuḥfat ahl al-'irfān*), 151–370 (*Rūḥ al-jinān*); the *Tuḥfat ahl al-'irfān* has also been edited by Javād Nūrbakhsh (Tehran, 1349/1970). All quotations from these texts are from Dānish-Puzhūh's edition.
5. *Tuḥfat ahl al-'irfān*, pp. 10–11.
6. Ibid., p. 22.
7. *Rūḥ al-jinān*, p. 163.
8. Ibid., p. 164.
9. On retreats, see *Tuḥfat ahl al-'irfān*, p. 42; on forty-day seclusions, see *Tuḥfat ahl al-'irfān*, p. 38; *Rūḥ al-jinān*, pp. 211, 234.
10. *Tuḥfat ahl al-'irfān*, pp. 33, 64; *Rūḥ al-jinān*, pp. 201, 321.
11. *Tuḥfat ahl al-'irfān*, pp. 36, 61.
12. Ibid., p. 43.
13. Ibid., p. 39.
14. Ibid., pp. 41, 60.

15. Ibid., p. 49.
16. Ibid., pp. 37, 50, 60, 62.
17. Ibid., pp. 51, 57.
18. Ibid., p. 38, 44, 46, 48, 59.
19. Ibid., p. 55.
20. Ibid., pp. 25, 63.
21. Ibid., p. 33.
22. Ibid., pp. 41, 54.
23. Ibid., pp. 34, 47.
24. Ibid., p. 47.
25. Ibid., pp. 23–24.
26. The title of this book is listed elsewhere, but no copies are known to exist aside from this quotation. Cf. *Rūḥ al-jinān*, p. 341, no. 6.
27. *Rūḥ al-jinān*, pp. 195–96.
28. *Words of Ecstasy*, pp. 49–50.
29. *Tuḥfat ahl al-ʿirfān*, p. 39.
30. *Hazār mazār*, p. 292; *Nafaḥāt*, p. 256, with slight variations.
31. ʿĪsā ibn Junayd al-Shīrazī, *Hazār mazār*, Persian trans. from the Arabic *Shadd al-izār*, ed. Nūrānī Wiṣāl (Shiraz: Kitābkhāna-i Aḥmadī, 1364/1985), p. 350. On Buzghush see *Hazār mazār*, pp. 27, 102, 116, 125, 188, 199, 350–52, 372–6, 412, 451, also Jāmī, *Nafaḥāt*, p. 473.
32. These figures include Najīb al-Dīn Suhrawardī (*Rūḥ al-jinan*, pp. 197–98), Raḍī al-Dīn ʿAlī Lālā' (*Tuḥfat ahl al-ʿirfān*, p. 24, and *Rūḥ al-jinān*, pp. 199–200), Fakhr al-Dīn Rāzī (*Tuḥfat ahl al-ʿirfān*, p. 31).
33. Th. Emil Homerin, *From Arab Poet to Muslim Saint: Ibn al-Fāriḍ, his Verse, and his Shrine*, Studies in Comparative Religion (Columbia: University of South Carolina Press, 1994), chapter 2.
34. "The seven" also appear as spiritual entities among the Kurdish esotericism of the Ahl-i Ḥaqq; cf. Jean During, "The Sacred Music of the Ahl-i Haqq as a Means of Mystical Transmission," in *Manifestations of Sainthood in Islam*, ed. Grace Martin Smith and Carl W. Ernst (Istanbul: Éditions Isis, 1994).
35. *Tuḥfat ahl al-ʿirfān*, pp. 55–56.
36. *Hazār mazār*, pp. 433–34.
37. Both these Qur'ānic passages are associated with the Prophet Muḥammad, the first referring to the "night journey" that preceded his ascension to heaven, and the second as an indication of the "light of Muḥammad" as the pre-existing reality from which God created the universe.
38. Ḥamd Allāh Mustawfī (p. 507) mentions the stipends given by Abū Bakr ibn Saʿd (r. 628/1231–658/1260) to descendants of the family of ʿAlī, even sending donations outside of Fārs.
39. *Hazār mazār*, pp. 297–98.
40. This reference puts Abū Isḥāq al-Kāzarūnī in the company of the famous Sufis who are astounded by the rose that falls from Rūzbihān's encounter with God. In a vague and brief notice of the later Kāzarūni saint Sirāj al-Dīn Mahmūd Khalīfa (d. 562/1166–7) of Shiraz, *Hazār mazār* (p. 343) observes that "he had famous writings on Sufism and

other subjects, and famous men were wrapped in the cloak by his hand," but of these "famous" disciples it only mentions Ruzbihan Baqlī by name. It is possible that this information is simply a speculative extrapolation of the genealogy found in *Tuḥfat ahl al-ʿirfān* and *Rūḥ al-jinān.*

41. According to Qazwīnī (*Hazār mazār*, p. 343, n. 46), Faṣīḥ al-Khwāfī in his *Mujmal* (completed 845/1441–2) gives under the year 606 the following lineage for Rūzbihān: 1. Ibn Khafīf; 2. Ḥusayn Akkār; 3. Abū Isḥāq Kāzarūnī; 4. Khaṭīb Abū al-Qāsim Maḥmūd ibn Aḥmad al-Kāzarūnī; 5. Aḥmad ibn ʿAbd al-Karīm; 6. Sirāj al-Dīn Maḥmūd ibn Khalīfa; 7. Rūzbihān Baqlī. Fritz Meier, Introduction (Persian trans. Kāʾūs Jahāndārī) to Maḥmūd ibn ʿUthmān, *Firdaws al-murshidiyya fī asrār al-ṣamadiyya*, ed. Īraj Afshār, Intishārāt-i Anjuman-i Āthār-i Millī, 148 (3rd ed., Tehran: Anjuman-i Āthār-i Millī, 1358/1980), p. xxv, cites Zayn al-ʿĀbidīn Shīrwānī's *Riyāḍ al-siyāḥa*, completed in 1242/1827 (Isfahan, 1329), p. 144, as giving the following lineage for the order of Rūzbihān, differing significantly from that found in *Tuḥfat ahl al-ʿirfān*: 1. Ibn Khafīf; 2. Ḥusayn Akkār; 3. Abū Isḥāq Kāzarūnī; 4. Abū al-Qāsim Khaṭīb; 5. Abū Nāṣir Muḥammad ibn Khaṭīb; 6. Abū Bakr Muḥammad ibn Khaṭīb; 7. Maḥmūd ibn Khalīfa-i Bayḍāʾī; 8. Rūzbihān Baqlī.
42. Massignon, *Lexique*, pp. 128–30.
43. As pointed out by Dānish-Puzhūh, *Rūḥ al-jinān* (p. 182) contains quotations from chapters 12 and 25 of Suhrawardi's *ʿAwārif.*
44. *Firdaws al-murshidiyya*, p. 24; also given in the same author's abridgement entitled *Anwār al-murshidiyya fī asrār al-ṣamadiyya*, ibid., p. 489, though the author notices there a second manuscript tradition containing the names of Ibrāhīm ibn Adham and Shaybān Rāʿī instead of Salmān Fārsī and Mūsā ibn Zayd. As the editor points out (preface to 2nd edition, p. x; Fritz Meier's introduction, p. viii), anecdotes and poems have been added to the Arabic original by the Persian translator and by later scribes.
45. *Tuḥfat ahl al-ʿirfān*, p. 137 (a dream of the tomb of al-Kāzarūnī leads to initiation by Rūzbihān); *Rūh al-jinān*, pp. 160 (homage to Ibn Khafīf and Kāzarūnī), 205 (insolence at the tomb of Ibn Khafīf is punished by Rūzbihān).
46. *Hazār mazār*, p. 291.
47. *Tuḥfat ahl al-ʿirfān*, in *Rūzbihān nāma*, pp. 19–21.
48. *Risālat al-quds*, pp. 9–10.
49. *Sharḥ-i shaṭḥiyyāt*, p. 10.
50. *Tuḥfat ahl al-ʿirfān*, p. 3; *Rūḥ al-jinān*, pp. 159–60.
51. *Tuḥfat ahl al-ʿirfān*, p. 14; *Rūḥ al-jinān*, p. 217.
52. *Rūḥ al-jinān*, pp. 209–12.
53. Ibid., p. 178.
54. *Tuḥfat ahl al-ʿirfān*, p. 37.
55. Ibid., pp. 21, 35, 36.
56. Ibid., p. 47.
57. Ibid., p. 43, 46 (rainstorm), 62; *Rūḥ al-jinān*, p. 231 (rainstorm).

58. *Tuḥfat ahl al-ʿirfān*, p. 63.
59. Ibid., p. 58.
60. Ibid., p. 142.
61. Ibid., pp. 141–44.
62. *Rūḥ al-jinān*, p. 349, quoting from the lost work *Manhaj al-sālikīn*, which also contains a brief visionary account of Aḥmad's spiritual status.
63. *Rūḥ al-jinān*, p. 349, citing *Kashf al-asrār*, §202.
64. *Tuḥfat ahl al-ʿirfān*, p. 133; *Hazār mazār*, pp. 285–86. The author of *Rūḥ al-jinān*, p. 349, states that he died during the lifetime of the shaykh in Rajab 650/September 1252 (obviously an error) and is buried at Bāgh-i Naw.
65. *Tuḥfat ahl al-ʿirfān*, p. 133; *Rūḥ al-jinān*, p. 349, where he is said to have died Sunday 29 Dhī al-Ḥijja 620/[Tuesday] 23 January 1224. Cf. also *Hazār mazār*, pp. 293–94, where the Persian translator describes visions that he and another person had relating to the tomb of Fakhr al-Dīn Aḥmad.
66. *Hazār mazār*, p. 286.
67. According to *Tuḥfat ahl al-ʿirfān*, p. 140, Ṣadr al-Dīn lived to be seventy, and died 27 Ramaḍān 685/16 November 1286, which would put his birth in 615/1218; it also states (p. 133) that his public religious career lasted sixty years.
68. *Tuḥfat ahl al-ʿirfān*, p. 133; *Rūḥ al-jinān*, p. 349.
69. *Hazār mazār*, p. 297.
70. Ibid., pp. 294–95.
71. *Tuḥfat ahl al-ʿirfān*, p. 148.
72. Ibid., p. 143–44.
73. Ibid., p. 149.
74. *Hazār mazār*, pp. 295–96.
75. Dānish-Puzhūh, *Rūzbihān nāma*, Introduction, p. 72.
76. *Rūḥ al-jinān*, pp. 224–26.
77. *Tuḥfat ahl al-ʿirfān*, p. 63.
78. Ibid., p. 65.
79. *Rūḥ al-jinān*, pp. 221–22. For ʿIrāqī's version, which makes the Atābeg to be Saʿd ibn Zangī, see Arberry, *Shiraz*, pp. 86–87.
80. Arberry, *Shiraz*, p. 45.
81. *Tuḥfat ahl al-ʿirfān*, p. 16, calls this disciple Khwāja Muntajib al-Dīn, a wazīr, while *Rūḥ al-jinān*, pp. 179–81, describes him as a Turk named Mengelī; in both stories, the minister accomplishes his duties at court while fasting and praying most of the night, much to the amazement of a doubter who is made to accompany him for three days. Another disciple, Bahāʾ al-Dīn Yazdī, became an adviser to the caliph al-Nāṣir (r. 575/1180-622/1225), and he visited Shiraz as an ambassador after the death of Rūzbihān (*Tuḥfat ahl al-ʿirfān*, pp. 28–31).
82. Ibid., p. 64.
83. *Tuḥfat ahl al-ʿirfān*, p. 42, also *Rūḥ al-jinān*, pp. 223–24 (with variations).
84. *Tuḥfat ahl al-ʿirfān*, p. 142.

85. Ibid., p. 53.
86. Ibid., p. 146.
87. Ibid., pp. 138–39.
88. *Rūḥ al-jinān*, pp. 135–36.
89. A. K. S. Lambton, "Mongol Fiscal Administration in Persia," *Studia Islamica* LXV (1987), p. 106. In this account I follow Lambton's spelling of the Mongol name Bulughān, though the Persian text of *Rūḥ al-jinān* reads Būlghān.
90. Daylamī, *Sīrat*, p. 309. Cf. also *The Ta'ríkh-i-Guzída*, I, 505, which mentions in addition a *ribāṭ* constructed by Sonqur attached to the great mosque.
91. *Hazār mazār*, pp. 263–68, 301–4.

IV

Conclusion

In the opening lines of *The Unveiling of Secrets*, Rūzbihān presents an extended meditation on the different spiritual vocations. The knowledge and grace made available by God to the different ranks of prophets, saints, and angels differ in degree but not in kind. Rūzbihān portrays this as an unfoldment of divine love, which culminates in the highest type of mystic who passes through intoxication and sobriety to act as a guide to humanity.

> God taught the messengers, the prophets, the angels, and the saints about himself by the special qualities of his signs (*āyāt*), from the throne to the earth; he taught them the signs in the beginnings, and they loved him because of blessings and favor. Then he was unsatisfied with what he had given them, for it was the cause of the conditions of servanthood. So he displayed to them the lights of his presence, anointed their eyes with the collyrium of might, and showed them the sunbeams of the world of his angelic realm. Now they loved him with the special love, but this love in reality is the love of the beginning of the end. Then he unveiled to them the sublimities of his beauty and his majesty, with the quality of manifesting his Essence and Attributes. They knew him and loved him with the great true love that does not alter with the changing of temporality, nor by the descent of afflictions and testing. They witnessed him with the witnessing of reality without a veil. Then he addressed them and spoke to them with rare sciences and wisdom. He instructed them in the incantations of his names, and he taught them the graces of his qualities and characteristics. He made them inhale the perfumed breezes of the rose of near encounters and the herbs of proximities and unions. Then he was expansive to them with his generous intimate conversations, and he unveiled his secrets and was intimate with them with his beauty. He made them lovers with his majesty in these

> degrees, and they bore what they could of the weights of ascetic practices and strivings. They becames the brides of his presence and the men of his kingdom and his angelic realm. Some of them are the people of discipleship, and some are the people of sainthood; some are the people of signs, and some are the people of speeches, counsels, and intimate conversations; some are the people of unveilings, and some are the people of witnessings and conceptions; some are the people of gnosis and grace, and some are the people of divine knowledge and wisdom; some are the people of unity, singleness, and isolation, and some are the people of qualification. Some are the people of unification; if they reach [their goal] and cross the ocean of pre-eternities and eternities, they become raving drunkards. If they remain settled and stand firm in the surging of the disasters of the hidden, from unveilings and ecstasies, they become the sober ones. If they reach the position of standing firm after being ravished, God most high makes them the lamps of the age, the signs of gnosis, the stages of reality, and the guidepost of the religious law–may God place us and you among the people of these states and stations (§3).

Rūzbihān evidently thinks of himself as a member of this most elite rank of sainthood.

In *The Unveiling of Secrets*, Rūzbihān relates many initiatic visions that testify to his status as a saint. He is the pole or axis (*quṭb*) of the world, the vicegerent (*khalīfa*) of God on earth, and the beloved of God. His encounters with the prophets, particularly Muḥammad, confirm him as the heir to their knowledge, and he reduplicates many of their experiences in his visions. The Sufi saints of the past salute Rūzbihān and with their authority certify him as the greatest saint of the age; they wish that they could attain his state of nearness to God. These initiatic visions are complemented by other visions that use the symbolism of Persian kingship to announce Rūzbihān as the spiritual king. The traditional elements upon which Rūzbihān draws to make these assertions are not surprising, and indeed would be familiar to any of his readers. What is remarkable is the cosmic scope and the dramatic power of the visions.

Modern readers are instinctively suspicious of claims like those made by Rūzbihān. The modern climate of opinion still draws on Hume's skepticism about fictive theologies and clerical power, and on Kant's derision for the excesses of "theosophy." The insane asylum is considered to be the best location for those with delusions of divine authority. On the level of cultural style, our society respects the hypocritical virtue of modesty; though it is legitimate to accept praise from others, one should do so with seeming reluctance, never stepping forward to assert one's own preeminence. As my grandmother used to say, "It's not polite to toot your own horn." So the lack of hesitation with which Rūzbihān unblushingly announces his saintly status initially causes some resistance in the contemporary reader, who interprets it as a claim demanding either acceptance or rejection. If we wish to move beyond these options for a more sophisticated reading of the text, let us return to the contrast between the picture of sainthood in *The Unveiling of Secrets* and the way that Rūzbihān's sainthood was portrayed by his hagiographers. This contrast will permit a more refined evaluation of the precise characteristics of the concept and rhetoric of sainthood in both kinds of sources.

The most noticeable difference between *The Unveiling of Secrets* and the hagiographies is that the hagiographies omit the most extraordinary visions of Rūzbihān's authority. *The Spirit of the Gardens* does include some notable visions, such as the Little Bear (§19–20), the ocean of wine (§30), the eating of the scriptures (§32), and the naming of Rūzbihān as vicegerent of God (§49). All in all, however, the two hagiographers cite only a small fraction of the initiatic visions of *The Unveiling of Secrets*, and sometimes with drastic omissions or transformations that radically alter the sense of the text. As we have seen, the hagiographers were also at pains to secure Rūzbihān's reputation as a saint by insisting on his membership in an accepted lineage, and so they supplied him with several spiritual genealogies. Why did the hagiographers lay more stress on Rūzbihān's genealogy than on his visions?

The answer, I think, lies in the logic of mystical experience as it played out in the cultural environment of early Sufism. The experiences of unveiling and clothing with divinity constituted the fundamental mode of mystical experience for Rūzbihān. The tension between the two experiences created a dialectic between vision and transcendence. This tension existed primarily in the "vertical" dimension of ascension, which Rūzbihān re-enacted in his daily meditations. Traditions of prior spiritual authority, which are normally seen as exerting force through a "horizontal" dimension of history, are re-evaluated in the ascension experience and in its literary re-workings. The most complex example of such re-evaluation of tradition through an ascension narrative is probably Dante's *Divine Comedy*, with its many judgments on the spiritual and political leadership of Christian Europe. So attractive was the ascension as providing an Archimedean point from which to judge society that the Arab poet al-Ma'arrī employed it in parody form in his *Epistle of Forgiveness*. The intimacy of direct encounter with God at the apex of the ascension relegates past prophets and saints to a secondary role as witnesses to the ascension of the mystic. History and tradition, which remain normative in the legal and "kerygmatic" orientation of Islamic law, are thus relegated to a secondary position by the mystical experience. What is distinctive about the Sufi rhetoric of sainthood is that unabashed boasting is permitted and even encouraged as a means of indicating one's direct contact with God. Ecstatic utterances partook of the ancient Arabic rhetoric of the boasting contest (*mufākhara*), a point which is explicitly recognized in early Sufi manuals of conduct. The spiritual oneupmanship that is recorded in the conversations of many early Baghdadian and Khurasanian Sufis is typical of this rhetoric of boasting.

When the rhetoric of boasting is combined with the re-evaluation of tradition in the ascension experience, the prophets, angels, and legal scholars are turned into adjuncts of the mystic's ascent, and in particular the experiences of the boldest of the Sufi saints are now reduced to a secondary status. So it is that the great saints of Fars appear primarily as witnesses hailing the status of Rūzbihān, while the ecstatic Abū Yazīd al-Bisṭāmī ineffectually challenges Rūzbihān, only to bow to his supremacy in the end. Abū Yazīd's role as the first Sufi to articulate an ascension and the first to specialize in outrageous ecstatic sayings ensured that later Sufis would use him as the standard to exceed in outrageousness. It is not accidental that Wāsiṭī and Shiblī felt compelled to belittle Abū Yazīd in their own ecstatic sayings.[1] Ibn 'Arabī cites and refers to Abū Yazīd probably more than any other early Sufi, but he also makes oblique critical remarks about him, dismissing the claims of ecstatic speech on the part of others while disingenuously claiming that his own claims are simply God's commands.[2] This transcendental rhetoric of hyperbole contains within itself the unforeseen result that successive generations of Sufis will engage in the devaluation of tradition and the inflation of their own claims to a sometimes astonishing degree. This is particularly evident in the later Naqshbandiyya, as when Aḥmad Sirhindī announced that he had transcended the positions of Ibn 'Arabī and, inevitably, Abū Yazīd al-Bisṭāmī. Neologism ran rampant as succeeding shaykhs had to coin new terms to indicate how their own attainments transcended those of previous masters. One imagines that there was a palpably uncomfortable atmosphere in situations like eighteenth-century Delhi, when different Naqshbandī masters such as Mīr Dard, Shāh Walī Allāh, and Mīrzā Maẓhar Jān-i Jānān all claimed remarkable positions of spiritual status simultaneously.

Rūzbihān's followers found that his claim to have gone beyond the states of Abū Yazīd and Ḥallāj was the most controversial aspect of his experiences. The hagiographers must have felt that stressing this aspect of Rūzbihān's writings would be a mistake when it came to building his image as a saint. Although from Rūzbihān's perspective it is perhaps implicit within the logic of sainthood that his ascension should take him beyond Abū Yazīd, the logic of hagiography sought a safer course. Instead of having him receive sainthood directly from God in the vertical dimension of ascension, the hagiographers found it better to derive his sainthood through the horizontal and historical dimension of the genealogy, through more sober Sufi masters such as Junayd. On one level, this appeal to tradition agrees with the appearance of the Sufis of Fars in Rūzbihān's visions, blessing him and confirming him in his position. But Rūzbihān himself felt no need to insist on an unbroken master-disciple chain linking him to Ibn Khafīf and Abū Isḥāq Kāzarūnī; he saw them periodically in the course of his visions, so he had no need of a genealogical connection. One suspects that one reason for the extinction of the Rūzbihāniyya order after a few generations was that Rūzbihān's descendants redefined his sainthood in terms that better fit the conventions of the emerging popularization of the Sufi orders. The circulation of *The Unveiling of Secrets* in a drastically abridged manuscript edition (discovered by both Nwyia and Hoca), less than one-fifth of the original, indicates that some readers found the complete account of Rūzbihān's vision to be simply too much. Hagiographers (*A Thousand Tombs*, Jāmī) repeated the remark that "he [Rūzbihān] has sayings that have poured forth from him in the state of overpowering and ecstasy, which not everyone can understand."[3] This respectful observation about his incomprehensibility permitted Rūzbihān to be bracketed and ignored by readers lacking the patience to absorb his difficult style. In the later hagiographic tradition Rūzbihān has been reduced to a primarily esthetic figure, one of a series of shaykhs who are enraptured by the love of beautiful young men.

In order to recover as fully as possible the mystical life of a figure such as Rūzbihān, it is essential to examine the structure of experience that underlies the multiple visions of *The Unveiling of Secrets*. This study has undertaken an initial mapping of this remarkable text, though much remains to be done. The effort has been facilitated by some comparisons with other texts by Rūzbihān, which have permitted us to unfold in detail the unveilings and clothings with divinity, the theophanies of majesty, and the theophanies of beauty that filled the meditations of Rūzbihān. It has also been important to use the evidence of the hagiographies, partly to chart better the course of Rūzbihān's historical legacy, and partly to extricate Rūzbihān from the image of sainthood in which his descendants tried to fix his spirituality. Their limited capacity probably made the transmission of his insights impossible within the institutional framework of an organized Sufi order. It was always possible for individuals in the Sufi tradition to encounter the legacy of Rūzbihān in the form of one text or another, and the manuscripts of his writings have been preserved and transmitted in Iran, India, Central Asia, North Africa, Egypt, and Southeastern Europe. It is ironic that only in the late twentieth century has it become possible to reassemble the work of Sufis such as Rūzbihān, in the context of humanistic inquiry in the university rather than in the meditative atmosphere of the Sufi hospice, although a few modern Sufi leaders preserve a keen interest in the writings of Rūzbihān.

The emphasis of this study has been upon the recovery of the mystical life of Rūzbihān, particularly his visionary experience, which is one of the most extraordinary cases of its kind in mystical literature. But perhaps it would be fitting to close with a nod to the hagiographic tradition, acknowledging that Muslim saints achieve their status not only by mystical experience but also through the devotion of their followers. So it is that Rūzbihān's great-grandson Sharaf al-Dīn eulogizes his ancestor in a Persian lyric:

> The peace of God be upon the soul of Rūzbihān for the
> treasury of the soul's mysteries is Rūzbihān.
> Love's perfume comes from the dust of his shrine – go,
> and with eyelashes sweep the threshold of Rūzbihān.
> Know for certain that they give you freedom from the
> world if they give you leftovers from the table of
> Rūzbihān.
> The hidden things that are veiled from the sight of men
> are open, by God's grace, to the vision of Rūzbihān.
> The knowers of reality are firmly aware that the key to
> the treasure of realities is the tongue of Rūzbihān.
> The secret meaning of "I am the Truth" and the
> mystery of "Glory be to me" is not unveiled except
> when explained by Rūzbihān.
> Sharaf, though a child of his by descent, is also the very
> least of the slaves of Rūzbihān.[4]

This tribute can be accepted as a legitimate, if limited, perspective on the saint. Yet if we do not approach Rūzbihān as disciples or devotees, what response is appropriate? From a humanistic perspective, Rūzbihān should be regarded like any provocative and original religious thinker or mystic, like Hildegard of Bingen, Lao Tzu, or Kabīr; for all our efforts there is something that escapes us, but we can imaginatively recreate the world of meaning that is evoked in the literary work of the mystic. This will permit us at the very least to characterize what is distinctive and fundamental to the message that the mystic has tried to convey. With this in mind, we can give the last word to Rūzbihān, quoting this Arabic epigram found written on the outside of one of his books, exemplifying in brief his lyrical imagery, his ecstasy, and his density of expression: "At the daybreak of pre-eternity I heard the realities of knowledge, and I became a divinely learned master, one who speaks ecstatically in self-glorification, and an eternal gnostic."[5]

Notes

1. *Words of Ecstasy*, p. 38.
2. Cf. my "The Man without Attributes: Ibn 'Arabī's Interpretation of Abū Yazīd al-Bisṭāmī," *Journal of the Muhyiddin Ibn 'Arabi Society* XIII (1993), pp. 1–19.

3. *Nafaḥāt*, p. 255.
4. *Tuhfat ahl al-ʿirfān*, p. 22.
5. *Rūḥ al-jinān*, p. 236.

Appendix A

The Writings of Rūzbihān Baqlī: A Checklist

The first bibliographical efforts to describe the writings of Rūzbihān are found in the biographies written by his two great-grandsons Sharaf al-Dīn Ibrāhīm and Shams al-Dīn ʿAbd al-Laṭīf. Sharaf al-Dīn observes in the first chapter of *Tuḥfat ahl al-ʿirfān* that some sixty-odd books were written by the shaykh, but that many of them were dispersed after his death.[1] He himself enumerates twenty-two titles in the first chapter of his biography, dividing them into the customary genres of Qur'ānic commentary, *ḥadīth*, Islamic law, jurisprudence, and Sufism.[2] In the fifth chapter of the same work, Sharaf al-Dīn attempts a more comprehensive approach to the shaykh's writings, dividing them into three classes according to their audiences: 1) the most difficult and lofty writings, which most people cannot understand; 2) those intended for Sufi masters; 3) those meant for the religious scholars. He does not, however, attempt to classify Rūzbihān's writings by these categories. The other biographer, Shams al-Dīn in *Rūḥ al-jinān,* likewise puts the total of Rūzbihān's writings at sixty-odd, giving substantial extracts from sixteen, but he lists forty titles.[3] Ibn Junayd Shīrāzī lists twenty-nine titles.[4] There is also a list of twenty-seven titles inscribed in a plaque on a wall of the restored tomb of Rūzbihān in Shiraz.[5] My collation of these sources yields a total of forty-five titles that can be reliably assigned to Rūzbihān; of these, eighteen no longer survive, leaving twenty-seven texts (nineteen in Arabic, eight in Persian) wholly or partially preserved in manuscript. The titles below are cited according to their numbering in the lists of Sharaf al-Dīn and Shams al-Dīn (as published by Dānish-Puzhūh in *Rūzbihān nāma*), with current information about the language of extant works, extracts, known manuscripts, and editions. Also listed are details of the two biographies and several works dubiously attributed to Rūzbihān. Titles are alphabetized within each category without reference to the definite article *al-* or the terms *kitāb* ("book") or *risāla* ("treatise"). Published works are described in full in the bibliography.

Abbreviations:

T *Tuḥfat ahl al-ʿirfān* by Sharaf al-Dīn Ibrāhīm
R *Rūḥ al-jinān* by Shams al-Dīn ʿAbd al-Laṭīf

Qur'ānic Exegesis

1. *ʿArā'is al-bayān fī ḥaqā'iq al-qur'ān/The Brides of Explanation on the Realities of the Qur'ān* (Arabic: T no. 2, R no. 2).
   Extracts: T 66–81; R 242–58
   For full information about lithographed editions, over fifty known MSS, and a partial critical edition and translation, see the forthcoming work of Alan Godlas.
2. *Laṭā'if al-bayān min tafsīr al-qur'ān/The Graces of Explanation Commenting on the Qur'ān* (Arabic: T no. 1, R no. 1).
   Fragments discovered by Godlas will be described in a forthcoming study.

Ḥadīth

3. *al-Mafātīḥ fī sharḥ al-maṣābīḥ/The Keys to the Commentary on the Maṣābīḥ* (Arabic: T no. 4; R no. 21).
   Not extant.
4. *Sharḥ maknūn al-ḥadīth/The Commentary on the Hidden Contents of Ḥadīth* (Arabic: T no. 3; R no. 3).
   Extracts: T 81–92, R 258–64
   MS: Marʿashī, Qum, dated 895/1490

Islamic law

5. *ʿIlm al-farā'iḍ/The Science of Duties* (R no. 29).
   Not extant.
6. *al-Muwashshaḥ/The Adornment* (Arabic: T no. 5; R no. 19).
   Extracts: R 317–18

Theology

7. *al-Ḥaqā'iq fil-'aqā'id/The Realities in the Creeds* (Arabic: R no. 15). Extracts: R 280
8. *al-Intiqād fil-i'tiqād/The Value of Belief* (R no. 32)] Not extant.
9. *Masālik al-tawḥīd/The Paths of Unity* or *Maslak al-tawḥīd/The Path of Unity* (Arabic: T no. 36; R no. 23).
   MS: Ahmet Salis 1460/35b–56a, Topkapı Museum Library, Istanbul
   Edition: P. Ballanfat, forthcoming.

Principles of jurisprudence

10. *al-Irshād/The Guidance* (T no. 6; R no. 22). Not extant.
11. *al-Miftāḥ/The Key* (R no. 24). Not extant.

Language and Grammar

12. *al-Hidāya fī 'ilm al-naḥw/Guidance in Syntax* (R no. 39). Not extant.
13. *al-Mirṣād fil-aḍdād/The Path to Contraries* (R no. 33). Not extant.
14. *Taṣrīf, Kitāb fil-/The Book on Conjugation* (R no. 40). Not extant.

Sufism

15. *'Abhar al-'āshiqīn/The Jasmine of the Lovers* (Persian: T no. 32; R no. 26).
   MSS:
   - Ayasofia 1959
   - Dr. Khāverī, Shiraz, 12th c.
   - Konya İzzet Koyunoğlu Müzesi, Kütüphâne kismi, fols. 121b–222b
   - Majlis, 2871/3, dated 1208/1794
   - Malik 3971/4, dated 1286/1868
   - Ni'matullāhī library, Tehran, 2 MSS

Tehran University 4097, dated 1243/1827
Editions:
H. Corbin and M. Mu'īn (Tehran, 1958).
J. Nūrbakhsh (Tehran, 1349/1971).
Translation: H. Corbin (French), ch. 1 only (Tehran, 1958), pp. 112–26.

16. *Dīvan-i ma'ārif/Mystical Poems* (Persian: T no. 41; R no. 20).
Extracts: T 15, 39, 122–31; R 161–61, 175, 196, 237–40, 324–41, 343–45
MSS:
Konya İzzet Koyunoğlu Müzesi, Kütüphâne kismi, fols. 66b–73b
Excerpts on margins of *Dīvan-i Qāsim-i Dīvāna*, (d. after 1135/1723–24), Ethé 1693/84a, India Office Library, London
Excerpts in *Ash'ār-i mutafarriqa*, Ethé 1747/68b, India Office Library, London
Excerpts in another anthology, Ethé 1766/30a, India Office Library, London
Editions:
N. Hoca, *Rūzbihān al-Baḳlī* (Istanbul, 1971), pp. 121–38.
M. T. Mīr (Shiraz, 1354/1975), pp. 52–88.
G. Āryā (Tehran, 1363/1984), pp. 78–122.

17. *Ghalaṭāt al-sālikīn/The Errors of the Wayfarers* (Persian: R no. 18).
Extracts: R 315–17
MS: Ni'matullahi library, Tehran, dated 822/1419
Edition: J. Nūrbakhsh, *Risālat al-quds wa ghalaṭāt al-sālikīn* (Tehran, 1351/1972), pp. 81–102.

Hazār u yik maqām. See *Mashrab al-arwāḥ*.

18. *Hidāyat al-ṭālibīn/Guidance for Seekers* (R no. 27).
Not extant.

al-Ighāna. See *Sharh al-ḥujub wal-astār fī maqāmāt ahl al-anwār wal asrār*.

19. *al-'Irfān fī khalq al-insān/Gnosis on the Creation of Humanity* (Arabic: R no. 10).
Extracts: R 269–71
A MS discovered by Godlas will be described in a forthcoming study.

20. *Kanz al-futūḥ/The Treasury of Victories* (R no. 38).
Not extant.

21. *Kashf al-asrār/The Unveiling of Secrets* (Arabic: T no. 35; R no. 4).

Extracts: T 13, 33; R 167–74, 232–33, 350
MSS:
Mashhad 829 (catalog IV, 220, no. 931), dated 1064/1654
Massignon, Paris, dated 665/1266
Editions:
P. Ballanfat, forthcoming.
N. Hoca, *Rūzbihān al-Baḳlī* (Istanbul, 1971), pp. 103–18 (abridged version), from MS in Konya İzzet Koyunoğlu Müzesi, Kütüphâne kismi, 59a–66a.
P. Nwyia, in *al-Mashriq* LXIV/4–5 (1970), pp. 385–406 (abridged version). Based on MS from Baghdad copied by Darwīsh Ḥasan ibn ʿAlī al-Khilwatī in 1126/1714; also bears name of Shaykh Shaʿbān Qasṭamūnī.
Translations:
P. Ballanfat (French), forthcoming.
C. Ernst, *The Unveiling of Secrets* (Chapel Hill NC: Parvardigar Press, forthcoming).

22. *Laʾālī al-ḥikma/Pearls of Wisdom* (R no. 36).
Not extant.

23. *Lawāmiʿ al-tawḥīd/Flashes of Unity* (Arabic: T no. 9; R no. 8).
Extracts: R 264–66
MS: Ahmet Salis 1460/1–35a, Topkapı Museum Library, Istanbul
Edition: P. Ballanfat, forthcoming.

24. *Manṭiq al-asrār/The Language of Consciences* (Arabic: T no. 7; R no. 25).
MSS:
Mashhad 156 ḥikmat u kalām (catalogue I, 48), dated 1145/1732–3
Mashhad 871 (catalogue IV, 199), dated 1064/1654
Massignon, Paris, dated 665/1266
Tashkent (entitled *Tafsīr al-shaṭḥiyyāt bi-lisān al-ṣūfiyya*, anonymous)
Edition: P. Ballanfat and C. Ernst, forthcoming.

25. *Maqāʾīs al-samāʿ/The Measures of Listening to Music* (T no. 40; R no. 28).
Not extant.

26. *Mashrab al-arwāḥ/The Spirits' Font*, also known by the Persian title *Hazār u yik maqām/1001 Stations* (Arabic: R no. 11).
Extracts: R 271–75

MS: Diyaribakir Genel Kütüphânesi 1529B, copied in 812/1409.
Edition: N. Hoca (Istanbul, 1974).

27. *Minhāj al-murīdīn/The Path of the Disciples* (R no. 31).
Not extant.

28. *Minhāj al-sālikīn* or *Manhaj al-sālikīn/The Path of the Wayfarers* (Arabic: T no. 39; R no. 12).
Extracts: R 222, 275–76

29. *Nukāt al-mutaṣawwifa al-rūzbihāniyya, Risālat/Sufistic Points of Rūzbihān* (Persian: the lexicon from *Sharḥ-i shaṭḥiyyāt*, circulated separately).
MS: Supplement Persane 1851/148b–166b, Paris, dated 897/1491–2 (Blochet IV, 200, no. 2250)

30. *Quds, Risālat al-* or *Risālat al-qudsiyya/The Treatise on Holiness* (Persian: T no. 42; R no. 7).
Extracts: T 19–21; R 227–30
MSS:
Istanbul University 144/5, dated 980/1572–3
Konya İzzet Koyunoğlu Müzesi, Kütüphâne kismi, fols. 74a–94a
Khāverī collection, Shiraz, dated 1065/1655
Majlis 621/21, Tehran
Malik 4020/1, Tehran, dated 1015/1606
Manisa Genel Kitaplik 1489
Mashhad (catalogue IV, 314)
Nafīsī 373/516–606, Tehran, dated 1024/1615
Ni'matullahi library, Tehran, 3 MSS, one dated 822/1419, one dated 831/1427–8, one undated
Supplement Persane 1356/160b–195b, Paris (Blochet, I, 122, no. 159), dated 877/1472–3
Edition:
Najīb al-Dīn Riḍā-yi Tabrīzī, *Sab' al-mathānī* (Shiraz, 1342/1923–4), pp. 344–392, on margins.
J. Nurbakhsh (Tehran, 1351/1972).

31. *Rūḥ al-rūḥ/The Spirit of the Spirit* (R no. 5).
Not extant.

32. *Ṣafwat mashārib al-'ishq/The Quintessence of the Fonts of Love* (T no. 37; R no. 37).
Not extant.

33. *Salwat al-'āshiqīn/The Lovers' Consolation* (T no. 38; R no. 30).

Not extant.

34. *Salwat al-qulūb/The Hearts' Consolation* (Arabic: R no. 6).
Extracts: R 195

35. *Sayr al-arwāḥ/The Way of the Spirits* (Arabic: T no. 31; R no. 9).
Extracts: R 266–69
MSS:
'Ashīr Efendī II, 432/1–6, Süleimaniya, Istanbul (fragments).
Ayasofya 2160/244-284, Süleimaniya, Istanbul
Fatih 2650/1–37b, Süleimaniya, Istanbul
Konya İzzet Koyunoğlu Müzesi, Kütüphâne kismi, fols. 109b–116b
Malik 4044/27–30, Tehran (fragments).
Mashhad
Topkapı
Veliuddin 1819/110–113, Süleimaniya, Istanbul, 9th/15th cent. (fragments)
Edition: P. Ballanfat, forthcoming, with French translation.

36. *Sharḥ al-ḥujub wal-astār fī maqāmāt ahl al-anwār wal-asrār/The Commentary on Veils and Curtains on the Stations of the People of Lights and Secrets* or *al-Ighāna/The Clouding* (Arabic: T no. 33; R no. 16).
Extracts: T 84–87; R 280–89
MSS:
Mashhad 661 ḥikmat (catalogue IV, 131), dated 1050/1640–1
Ayasofya 2160/285–315, Suleimaniya, Istanbul
India Office Library 1252 Arabic, London
Editions:
M. al-Husaynī (Hyderabad, 1333/1914–5).
P. Ballanfat, forthcoming.

37. *Sharḥ-i shaṭḥiyyāt/The Commentary on Ecstatic Sayings* (Persian: R no. 17), Rūzbihān's own translation and expansion of *Manṭiq al-asrār*.
Extracts: T 3, 92–104; R 289–315
MSS:
Şehit Ali 1342/267–399b, Suleimaniya, Istanbul, dated 889/1484
Qāḍī'askar 1271 (1290 in catalogue), Süleimaniya, Istanbul, dated after 900/1494
Edition: H. Corbin (Tehran, 1966).

38. *Sharḥ al-ṭawāsīn/The Commentary on the Ṭawāsīn* (Arabic: T no. 8; R no. 14).
    Part of *Manṭiq al-asrār*, circulated separately; not extant in this form.
39. *Tuḥfat al-ʿirfān/The Gift of the Gnostics* (Persian: mathnawī verse).
    MS: Istanbul University 538/18, dated 826/1423
    Editions:
    M. T. Dānish-Puzhūh, *Rūzbihān nāma*, pp. 375–86.
    G. Āryā, *Shaykh-i shaṭṭāḥ* (Tehran, 1363/1984), pp. 123–33.
40. *Ṭuḥfat al-muḥibbīn/The Gift of the Lovers* (Arabic: T no. 34; R no. 13).
    Extracts: R 276
41. *al-Uns fī rūḥ al-quds/Intimacy in the Spirit of Holiness* (T no. 30; R no. 34).
    Not extant (possibly the same as *Risālat al-quds*).
42. *ʿUqūd al-laʾālī/Strings of Pearls* (R no. 35).
    Not extant.
43. *al-Yawāsīn, Kitāb/The Book of YS* (Arabic), inspired by the *Kitāb al-ṭawāsīn* of Ḥallāj.
    Extracts: R 276–79
44. Prayers (Arabic).
    Extracts: R 318–19
45. Letters (Persian).
    Extracts: T 117–21, R 319–24

Biographies

1. *Tuhfat ahl al-ʿirfān fī dhikr sayyid al-aqṭāb Rūzbihān/The Gift of the People of Gnosis, in Memory of the Chief Axis of the World Rūzbihān*, by Sharaf al-Dīn Ibrāhīm ibn Ṣadr al-Dīn Rūzbihān II (Persian).
   MSS:
   Malik 4020, Tehran, dated 1015/1606
   Niʿmatullahi library, Tehran, dated 1361/1942
   Shiraz, acquired by Ivanow, ninth/fifteenth cent. (fragmentary).
   Editions:
   M. T. Dānish-Puzhūh, *Rūzbihān nāma* (Tehran, 1347/1969), pp. 1–149.
   J. Nūrbakhsh (Tehran, 1349/1970).
2. *Rūḥ al-jinān fī sīrat al-shaykh Rūzbihān/The Spirit of the Gardens, on the Life of the Master Rūzbihān*, by Shams al-Dīn ʿAbd al-Laṭīf

ibn Ṣadr al-Dīn Rūzbihān II (Persian).
MS: Akademia Nauk D456, Leningrad[6]
Edition: M. T. Danish-Puzhuh, *Rūzbihān nāma* (Tehran, 1347/1969), pp. 152–370.

Works dubiously attributed to Rūzbihān

1. *al-Aḥadiyya, Risālat/The Treatise on Singleness* (Arabic).
   MS: Šehit Ali Paša 1390/78–108, Suleimaniya, Istanbul[7]
2. *al-Anwār fī kashf al-asrār/The Lights unveiling the Secrets* (Arabic).
   MS: Tashkent 2578/2, dated Muharram 789/1387.[8] This entry and its title are mistaken conjectures of the cataloguer. Ballanfat has concluded that this is part of another treatise.
3. *Bayān al-maqāmāt/The Explanation of Stations* (Arabic: a treatise on one hundred spiritual states).
   MS: Tashkent 2578/4, dated Muḥarram 789/1387.[9] Ballanfat has examined this and found it to be erroneously catalogued; it is instead the *Tabyīn al-maqāmāt* of 'Alā' al-Dawla Simnānī.
4. *Sharḥ sirr al-waḥdat/The Commentary on the Secret of Oneness*, text by Rūzbihān and commentary by Ṣadr al-Dīn Qunawī (Arabic).
   MS: Istanbul University, Arabça Yazma 3524.[10]

Notes

1. *Tuḥfat ahl al-'irfān*, p. 18.
2. Ibid., pp. 18–19.
3. *Rūḥ al-jinān*, p. 241–340 (extracts), 341–45 (titles).
4. *Hazār mazār*, pp. 290–91; Massignon, "La Vie," pp. 457–58, gives a working list of manuscripts of nine texts.
5. Mīr, *Sharḥ-i ḥāl*, second photograph after p. 20 (one title, *Sayr al-arwāḥ*, is listed twice, as no. 13 and again as no. 18).
6. N. D. Miklukho-Maklai, *Opesanie Tadzhikskikh i Persidskikh Rukopisei Instituta Narodov Azii* (Moscow: Izdatel'stbo Vostochnoi Literaturi, 1961), II, 93–99.
7. Osman Yahia, *Histoire et classification de l'œuvre d'Ibn 'Arabī* (2 vols., Damascus: Institut Français de Damas, 1964), I, 146, calling the work "inachevée."
8. A. A. Semenova, *Sobranie Vostochnikh Rukopisei Akademii Nauk Uzbekskoi SSR* (Tashkent: Izdatel'stvo Akademii Nauk Uz.S.S.R., 1965), III, 176, no. 2188.
9. Ibid., III, 177, no. 2189.
10. Corbin, Introduction to *'Abhar al-'āshiqīn*, pp. 90–91.

Appendix B

Rūzbihān's Two Commentaries on the "Ascension" of Abū Yazīd al-Bisṭāmī

Below is given a tabular comparison of Rūzbihān's two commentaries on the vision of Abū Yazīd often called his "ascension" (*mi'rāj*). The Arabic original is found in the *Manṭiq al-asrār* (MS Massignon, fol. 67b–68a) and its Persian translation is given in the *Sharḥ-i shaṭḥiyyāt* (no. 36, pp. 81–82), although the two texts only partially correspond. These are arranged in the numerical order of the lines as given by R. C. Zaehner's analysis of the ascension narrative (*Hindu and Muslim Mysticism*, Appendix B.I, pp. 198–218), with some changes to my previously published translation of the Persian (*Words of Ecstasy in Sufism*, Appendix, pp. 168–69).

Line	Persian translation	Arabic original
342	Abū Yazīd said,	Abū Yazīd also said,
343	"In unicity	"At first I went to unicity
351	I became a bird	and became a bird
352	(with) body of oneness	whose body was of oneness
353	and wings of everlastingness.	and whose wings were of everlastingness.
354	I was flying in an atmosphere without (sic) quality for some years	I kept flying in the atmosphere of quality for ten years
355	until I entered an atmosphere. After that atmosphere (in) which I was,	until I went to an atmosphere like that
356	I flew a hundred million times in that atmosphere,	a hundred million times. I kept flying
357	until I entered the plains of pre-eternity.	until I went to the plains of pre-eternity.
358	I saw the tree of oneness.	In it I saw the tree of oneness."

359	It had its root in the earth of eternity and its branch in the atmosphere of post-eternity. The fruits of that tree were Majesty and Beauty. I ate the fruits of that tree.	Then he described its earth, its root, its branch, its limbs, and its fruits.
361	When I looked well, I saw that all was trick upon trick." [Commentary:] This state is higher than the first state, because there gnosis came with the nature of unity; that is,	He said, "I looked, and I knew that this was all deceit." [Commentary:] This saying is similar to the first saying; their meaning is one, but here his conscience went up and his heart came back with the nature of unity.
343		But his saying, "First I entered unicity," means, "The first thing I scented was the fragrance of unity."
351		"And I became a bird," that is, "My spirit and conscience became like a bird
352	"My soul became the body of gnosis by the soul of gnosis."	whose body is singleness." That means humanity was exchanged for the Attribute of oneness. "The authority of power conquered me and annihilated me, so that I was annihilated in it. Oneness subsisted and humanity was annihilated." This is also part of the station of unification.
353	"I flew with the wings of the light of unity and isolation in pre- and post-eternity. After I became isolated from self and existence, God clothed me with the garment of everlastingness and pre-	"Whose wings were of everlastingness" means, "God manifested to my conscience with the light of eternity and the light of subsistence. He gave me eternity as a vast body," that is, as a principle from oneness; "and he gave

	eternality. He gave me a body of eternity. He caused the wings of oneness to grow Attributes from him."	me everlastingness as two wings from the Attribute of selfhood."
354	The bird of eternity flew in the eternity of eternities. It sought union with reality.	"I was flying by the light of eternity and subsistence in the mysteries of the depth of eternity, seeking union with the reality of eternity." And that is the meaning of his saying, "I kept flying in the atmosphere of quality and of no quality." "Of no quality" is considered foolish, but I will show you how to reach the limits in gnosis of the known; in this is a way that cannot be blocked, and a sight that cannot be missed. His saying, "for ten years,
355		until I reached an atmosphere" is an expression of his lingering in his beginning stage, in contemplating oneness. But this is not the expression of those who are firmly settled, for among them it is considered foolish to conceive in terms of time and space.
356		His saying, "a hundred million times" is an obstacle to intellects, not to realities; the intellect is ignorant of the comprehension of pre-eternities, so it abides in [external] traces, the habit of existence, and the states of flesh. These descriptions are likenesses

which he sees in the unveilings of magnificence, greatness, majesty, beauty, splendor, glory, oneness, and permanence. They have no foundation in unity; they are only an expression from the height of intoxication and expansiveness.

357 "After I sought reality in the depths of the deserts of quality, he burned my wings with the fire of greatness. I was consumed in the light of the candle of pre-eternity. He cast the seeing eye into pure primordiality. He cast me in the endless ocean, in the sources of the Attributes. I became subsistent through the Attributes."

358 "I received the fruits of subsistence from the tree of eternity. My astonishment increased in astonishment. Subsistence took my hand from annihilation. I put on the garment of knowledge. I fell into gnosis with knowledge. I saw the deserts of unknowings with the eyes of gnosis."

361 His saying, "I looked, and I knew that this was all deception," is true. He only comprehended that which he did not comprehend from the eye of eternity: less than a mustard seed in existence. God aston-

ishes the people of gnosis with the plunderings of eternity. The appearance of unicity in the station of clothing with divinity is a ruse to the people of unity, because of their jealousy about God's oneness. God said, "None is safe from God's ruse" (7:99). What Abū Yazīd found in this station was the level of his beginning stages. Junayd (God have mercy on him) said, "What Abū Yazīd described in this station was only part of the path."

369 "I knew that everything I saw, all was I. It was not God. It was the deception of manifestation in [apparent] declaration of God's sanctity. Transcendence in an Action was a ruse. Intimate mystical states were [carnal] thoughts. Thoughts were infidelities. God was God. I was not."

That which he said in describing the bird and the tree was all a likeness. The meaning of "quality" was "to seek the depths of eternity." "Air" and "space" are greatness upon greatness, "year" and "month" are timeless time, for illuminated consciences. Otherwise, what sort of story is it? Existence is not worth an atom in the beak of the western phoenix of eternity. Temporal forms and bodies are not a [divine] ruse. He did not display that which he did not give. He did not give that which he did not make known. When the gnostic fell in the ocean of pre-eternity, he became a green drop in the sea of pre-eternity. He becomes that ocean. A drop from that ocean takes on the color of the ocean, so that it is consumed in the billow of substantiality. The soul that is eloquent without a tongue, the familiar hearing that is deaf, the First Intellect that is confused, the life that is lifeless, the soul that is soulless, see nothing but the wrath of one of the crashing waves of the luminous oceans of pre-eternity. When that ocean casts the foam of temporality on the temporal, that drop thinks that it has encompassed the ocean, although it is more dry than wet. Otherwise, there are a hundred thousand deserts of waterless mirage on the coast of pre-eternity. That which he mentioned concerns the eclipse of the Attributes; if

not, it concerns [the
eclipse] of the Essence–
alas!

SELECT BIBLIOGRAPHY

PRIMARY ARABIC AND PERSIAN TEXTS BY AND ABOUT RUZBIHAN

Muḥammad Taqī Dānish-puzhūh, ed. *Rūzbihān nāma*. Silsila-i Intishārāt-i Anjuman-i Āthār-i Millī, 60. Tehran: Anjuman-i Āthār-i Milli, 1347/1969 (Persian).

Rūzbihān Baqlī Shīrāzī. *'Abhar al-'āshiqīn*. Ed. Javād Nūrbakhsh. Tehran, 1349/1971 (Persian).

— *'Arā'is al-bayān fī ḥaqā'iq al-qur'ān*. Cawnpore, 1285/1868–9; Calcutta, 1300/1883; Lucknow, 1310/1892–3 (Arabic lithographs).

— *Commentaire sur les paradoxes des Soufis (Sharh-e Shathîyât)*. Ed. Henry Corbin. Bibliothèque Iranienne, no. 12. Tehran: Departement d'Iranologie de l'Institut Franco-Iranien, 1966 (Persian).

— *Le Jasmin des Fidèles d'amour, Kitâb-e 'Abhar al-'âshiqîn*. Ed. Henry Corbin and Muḥammad Mu'īn. Bibliothèque Iranienne, 8. Tehran: Institut Français d'Iranologie de Téhéran, 1958; reprint ed., Tehran: Intishārāt-i Manūchihrī, 1365/1981. (Persian).

— *Kashf al-asrār*. MS Louis Massignon collection, Paris (Arabic MS). Abridged version: "Waqā'i' al-Shaykh Rūzbihān al-Baqlī al-Shīrāzī muqtaṭafāt min kitāb *Kashf al-asrār wa mukāshafat al-anwār*." Ed. Paul Nwyia. *al-Mashriq* LXIV/4–5 (1970), pp. 385–406 (Arabic); Ed. Nazif Hoca. *Rūzbihān al-Baklī ve Kitāb Kaşf al-asrār'ı ile Farsça bāzi Şiirleri*. Istanbul Üniversitesi Edebiyat Fakültesi Yayinları No. 1678. Istanbul: Edebiyat Fakültesi Matbaası, 1971 (Arabic and Persian).

— *Manṭiq al-asrār*. MS Louis Massignon collection, Paris (Arabic MS).

— *Maşrab al-arvāḥ, Kitāb*. Ed. Nazif M. Hoca. İstanbul Üniversitesi Edebiyat Fakültesi Yayinları, no. 1876. Istanbul: Edebiyat Fakültesi Matbaası, 1974 (Arabic).

— *Risālat al-quds wa risāla-i ghalaṭāt al-sālikīn*. Ed. Javād Nūrbakhsh. Intishārāt-i Khāniqāh-i Ni'mat Allāhī, 48. Tehran: Chāp-khāna-yi Firdawsī, 1351/1972 (Persian).

— *Sharḥ al-ḥujub wal-astār fī maqāmāt ahl al-anwār wal-asrār*. Ed. Muḥammad Makhdūm al-Ḥusaynī al-Qādirī al-Niẓāmī. Silsila-i Ishā'at al-'Ulūm, Hyderabad-Deccan, no. 41. Hyderabad: Dā'irat al-Ma'ārif al-Niẓāmiyya, 1333/1914–5.

Sharaf al-Dīn Ibrāhīm ibn Ṣadr al-Dīn Rūzbihān Thānī. *Tuhfat ahl al-'irfān*. Ed. Javād Nūrbakhsh. Tehran, 1349/1970 (Persian).

MODERN SECONDARY STUDIES ON RUZBIHAN

Arberry, Arthur J. *Shiraz, Persian City of Saints and Poets*. Norman: University of Oklahoma Press, 1960.

Āriyā, Ghulam 'Alī. *Sharḥ-i aḥwāl wa āthār wa majmū'a-i ash'ār ba-dast āmada-i Shaykh-i Shaṭṭāḥ Rūzbihān Baqlī*. Tehran: Rūzbihān, 1363/1984.

Ballanfat, Paul. "Aspects de la pensée de Rûzbehân Baqlî, soufi à Shîrâz au XIIème siècle." Ph.D. diss., Sorbonne, 1994.

Corbin, Henry. "'Abhar al-'Āšeqīn." *Encyclopaedia Iranica*, II, 214–15.

— *En Islam iranien: Aspects spirituels et philosophiques*, vol. 3, *Les Fidèles d'amour, Shî'isme et soufisme*. Bibliothèque des Idées. Paris: Gallimard, 1972.

— *L'homme de lumière dans le soufisme iranien*. Collection "Le Soleil dans le Cour." Paris: Éditions Présence, 1971. English edition: *The Man of Light in Iranian Sufism*. Trans. Nancy Pearson. Boulder: Shambala, 1978.

— "Rûzbehân Baqlî de Shîrâz." In *Henry Corbin*, ed. Christian Jambet, Les Cahiers de l'Herne (Paris: Éditions de l'Herne, 1983), pp. 150–67.

— "The Visionary Dream in Islamic Spirituality." In *The Dream and Human Societies*, ed. G. E. von Grunebaum and Roger Caillois (Berkeley: University of California Press, 1966), pp. 381–408.

During, Jean. *Musique et extase: L'audition mystique dans la tradition soufie*. Spiritualités vivantes. Paris: Albin Michel, 1988. Annexe I, "Le samâ' et le dhikr de Rûzbehân Baqlî Shirâzi," pp. 207–16.

Ernst, Carl W. "Mystical Language and the Teaching Context in the Early Sufi Lexicons." In *Mysticism and Language*, ed. Steven T. Katz (Oxford: Oxford University Press, 1992), pp. 181–201.

— "Rūzbihān Baqlī on Love as 'Essential Desire.'" In *Gott is schön und Er liebt die Schönheit/God is Beautiful and Loves Beauty: Festschrift für Annemarie Schimmel*, ed. Alma Giese and J. Christoph Bürgel (Bern: Peter Lang, 1994), pp. 181–89.

— "The Stages of Love in Early Persian Sufism from Rābi'a to Rūzbihān." In *Classical Persian Sufism from its Origins to Rumi*, ed. Leonard Lewisohn (London: Khaniqahi Nimatullahi, 1994), pp. 435–55; also in *Sufi* 14 (1992), pp. 16–23; Persian translation by Mojde-i Bayat as "Marāḥil-i 'ishq dar nakhustīn advār-i taṣavvuf-i Īrān, az Rābi'a ta Rūzbihān." *Ṣūfī* 16 (1371/1992), pp. 6–17.

— "The Symbolism of Birds and Flight in the Writings of Rūzbihān Baqlī." In *The Legacy of Medival Persian Sufism*, ed. Leonard Lewisohn (London: Khaniqahi Nimatullahi, 1992), pp. 353–66; also in *Sufi* 11 (Autumn, 1991), pp. 5–12.

— *Words of Ecstasy in Sufism*. SUNY Series in Islam. Albany: State University of New York Press, 1985.

Ewing, Katherine P. "The Dream of Spiritual Initiation and the

Organization of Self Representation among Pakistani Sufis." *American Ethnologist* (1990), pp. 56–74.

Godlas, Alan. "The *'Arā'is al-bayān,* the Mystical Qur'anic Exegesis of Ruzbihan al-Baqli." Ph.D. diss., University of California at Berkeley, 1991.

Hoca, Nazif. "Das arabische Werk *Kitāb mašrab al-arwāḥ.*" In *Akten des VII. Kongresses für Arabistik und Islamwissenschaft, Göttingen, 15. bis 22. August 1974,* ed. Albert Dietrich, Abhandlungen der Akademie der Wissenschaften in Göttingen, Philologisch-historische Klasse, Dritte Folge, no. 98 (Göttingen: Vandenhoeck & Ruprecht, 1976), pp. 208–11.

Ivanow, W. "A Biography of Ruzbihan al-Baqli." *Journal and Proceedings of the Asiatic Society of Bengal* N.S. XXIV (1928), pp. 353–61.

— "More on Biography of Ruzbihan al-Baqli." *Journal of the Bombay Branch of the Royal Asiatic Society* VII (1931), p. 1–7.

Maḥallātī, Ṣadr al-Dīn. *Majalla-i Dānishkada-i Adabiyyat-i Shīrāz* I/1 (1345/1967–8), pp. 22–43.

Massignon, Louis. *La Passion de Husayn Ibn Mansûr Hallâj, martyr mystique de l'Islam exécuté à Bagdad le 26 mars 922, Étude d'histoire religieuse.* 2nd ed., 4 vols., Paris: Gallimard, 1975. English edition: *The Passion of al-Hallāj, Mystic and Martyr of Islam.* Trans. Herbert Mason. Bollingen Series XCVIII. 4 vols., Princeton: Princeton University Press, 1982.

— "La Vie et les œuvres de Ruzbehan Baqli." In *Studia orientalia Joanni Pedersen septuagenario ... a collegis discipulis amicis dicata* (Copenhagen: E. Munksgaard, 1953), pp. 275–88; reprinted in Louis Massignon, *Opera Minora,* ed. Y. Moubarac (Beirut: Dār al-Ma'ārif, 1963), II, 451–65.

Mīr, Muḥammad Taqī. *Sharḥ-i ḥāl wa āthār wa ash'ār-i Shaykh Rūzbihān Baqlī.* Tehran: Dānishgāh-i Pahlavī, 1354/1975.

Muginov, A. M. "Leningradskaya Rukopis' 'Zhizneopisaniya Sheĭha Rūzbihāna.'" *Sovetskoe Vostokovedenie* 1957, no. 5, pp. 114–116.

Nadīmī, Ghulāmḥusayn. *Rūzbihān, yā shaṭṭāḥ-i Fārs.* Shiraz: Kitābkhāna-i Aḥmadī, 1345/1966.

Nasr, Seyyed Hossein. "Islam and Music: The Views of Rūzbahān Baqlī, the Patron Saint of Shiraz." *Studies in Comparative Religion* 10 (1976), pp. 37–45.

Rehder, R. M. "*Le Jasmin des fidèles d'amour*: Review Article." *Muslim World* 53 (1963), pp. 314–23.

Index of Names

Najīb al-Dīn Buzghush, 117, 119
Nakīr, 79
Naqshbandīs, 9, 10, 11, 147
Nāṣir, al- (caliph), 111, 140 n. 81
Neoplatonists, 32
Ni'matullahis, 11
Niẓam al-Dīn Awliyā', 11
Niẓam al-Dīn Riḍwān, 134
Noah, 56, 121
North Africa, 81
Nūr al-Dīn Abū al-Futūḥ Aḥmad
  Ṭāwūsī, 8, 14 n. 42
Nuṣrat al-Dīn Aḥmad, 115

Pakistanis, 81
Pasā, 2, 3, 4, 5, 28, 44, 47, 54, 76, 91
Persia, 130
Punjab, 11

Qādirīs, 11, 111
Qaf, Mt., 65
Qur'ān, 27, 30
  2:30, 48
  2:109, 42
  2:285, 26
  3:73, 21
  7:73, 54
  9:111, 92
  10:62, 47
  12:31, 70
  12:100, 68
  13:23, 87
  16:28, 56
  17:79, 59
  19:17, 73
  20:39, 52
  28:57, 89
  28:88, 85
  30:27, 37, 69, 70
  37:1-3, 78
  37:3, 77
  41:53, 69
  42:11, 36, 37, 69, 70
  50:22, 17
  53:14, 51
  68:1-4, 52, 92
  74:50-51, 23
  97:4, 79
  107:11, 48
  commentaries on, 10, 11, 18, 71, 113
  recitation of, 77
Qushayrī, 17, 29
Quṭb al-Dīn Muḥammad Nahrawālī,
  9, 14 n. 42

Rāja 'Alī Khān Fārūqī, 11
Ramaḍān, 20, 78, 79, 121
Riḍwān, 78, 79
Rūm, 128, 129
Rūmī, Jalāl al-Dīn, 5
Ruwaym, 55
Rūzbihān Baqlī Shīrāzī, passim
  biographies of
    Gift to the People of Gnosis, 7, 113-15, 117, 120, 123-25, 128, 132
    Spirit of the Gardens, 7, 28, 113-15, 118, 119, 121, 124-27, 132
  funeral of, 134
  life, 1-6, 20-28, 84
  name, 22, 108 n. 118
  family of, 86-93
  tomb of, 6, 8
  relations with 'ulamā', 117
  writings
    Brides of Explanation, 10, 11, 71
    Commentary on Ecstatic Sayings, 5, 11, 34, 35, 64, 93, 98, 128
    Hearts' Consolation, 118
    Jasmine of the Lovers, 4, 9, 10, 71
    Paths of Unity, 30
    Spirits' Font, 5, 13 n. 26, 13 n. 27, 25, 34, 65
    Unveiling of Secrets, 5, 11 n. 2, 17-101 passim, 108 n. 115
Rūzbihān Miṣrī, 3
Rūzbihānīs, 6-11

Sa'dī, 7, 133, 135
Sa'd ibn Zangī, 133, 136
Ṣadr al-Dīn ibn Sharaf al-Dīn
  Ibrāhīm Rūzbihān III, 8, 122, 131
Ṣadr al-Dīn Rūzbihān II, 8, 9, 113, 126, 131, 134, 135, 136, 140 n. 67
Safavids, 7
Sahlagī, 100
Salghurids, 1, 58, 112, 122, 133, 134
Samarra, 2
Sarī al-Saqatī, 59

Glossary and Index of Terms and Subjects

Note: Terms marked with asterisk (*) have a separate index entry. Italicized words are Arabic unless otherwise noted.